Key Concepts in
The Philosophy of Social Research

Recent volumes include:

Key Concepts in Urban Studies 2e
Mark Gottdiener, Leslie Budd and Panu Lehtovuori

Key Concepts in Race and Ethnicity
Nasar Meer

Key Concepts in Migration
David Bartram, Maritsa V Poros and Pierre Monforte

Key Concepts in Social Research
Geoff Payne and Judy Payne

Key Concepts in Medical Sociology 2e
Jonathan Gabe and Lee Monaghan

The SAGE Key Concepts series provides students with accessible and authoritative knowledge of the essential topics in a variety of disciplines. Cross-referenced throughout, the format encourages critical evaluation through understanding. Written by experienced and respected academics, the books are indispensable study aids and guides to comprehension.

Key Concepts in The Philosophy of Social Research

MALCOLM WILLIAMS

Los Angeles | London | New Delhi
Singapore | Washington DC | Melbourne

Los Angeles | London | New Delhi
Singapore | Washington DC | Melbourne

SAGE Publications Ltd
1 Oliver's Yard
55 City Road
London EC1Y 1SP

SAGE Publications Inc.
2455 Teller Road
Thousand Oaks, California 91320

SAGE Publications India Pvt Ltd
B 1/I 1 Mohan Cooperative Industrial Area
Mathura Road
New Delhi 110 044

SAGE Publications Asia-Pacific Pte Ltd
3 Church Street
#10-04 Samsung Hub
Singapore 049483

Editor: Chris Rojek
Assistant editor: Delayna Spencer
Production editor: Katherine Haw
Copyeditor: Solveig Gardner Servian
Proofreader: Bryan Crampbell
Marketing manager: Sally Ransom
Cover design: Wendy Scott
Typeset by: C&M Digitals (P) Ltd, Chennai, India
Printed in India at Replika Press Pvt Ltd

First published 2016

Library of Congress Control Number: 2016933344

British Library Cataloguing in Publication data

A catalogue record for this book is available from the British Library

ISBN 978-0-85702-741-2
ISBN 978-0-85702-742-9 (pbk)

For JJ who began it all

Contents

About the Author

Malcolm Williams is Professor and Director of the Cardiff Q-Step Centre at Cardiff University. Prior to joining Cardiff in 2010, as Director of the School of Social Sciences, he was Professor of Social Research Methodology and Head of the School of Psychosocial Sciences at the University of Plymouth where he taught for 16 years.

Williams has designed and taught modules in the philosophy of social research for 18 years at both undergraduate and postgraduate level. In these he has introduced a number of innovative pedagogic techniques, such as 'Problem-Based Learning' and 'Concept Speed Dating', in which students take a key idea and move from table to table attempting to build conceptual links between ideas.

Additionally he has taught many modules/short courses in social theory, research design, questionnaire design, scaling, sampling, scientific method and history of science.

Williams has an extensive publishing record in philosophy of social research: with Tim May *Introduction to Philosophy of Social Research* (1996), also with Tim May edited *Knowing the Social World*, with essays by Rom Harré, William Outhwaite, David-Hillel Ruben, John Scott etc. *Science and Social Science* (2000) received wide critical acclaim. In 2006 he edited the Sage 4-volume set *Philosophical Foundations of Social Research* and more recently, jointly written with Gayle Letherby and John Scott, *Objectivity and Subjectivity in Social Research* (Sage 2013).

Introduction

This book is not a book for philosophers! Rather, it is a book for social researchers, or those thinking of doing social research, who would like to understand better the philosophical issues that lurk behind our surveys, our interviews, our observations and our data analyses. Every single entry here has been, or could be, a book in its own right and it may still only deal with the subject fairly superficially.

Yet if by beginning with a hand-waving understanding of a concept leads to deeper insights, then I will have done my job in taking the reader to the next level. Even if those deeper insights are not to be had, for reasons of taste or time, but instead some understanding of these key concepts alleviates anxiety, then the money you, or your library, paid for the book was well spent!

In this introduction I want to make the case for why any of this matters and to contextualise some of the debates in the practice of social research. I will conclude with a few clarifications, pointers to reading the book and one or two excuses.

SOCIAL RESEARCH AND PHILOSOPHY

I do not want to draw the boundaries too tightly on how we define social research, partly because its assumptions, ambition and methods are ever changing, but also to define is often to implicitly suggest what is good or authentic. Yet for most of us it is captured by methods of enquiry (e.g. surveys, secondary analysis, observations, experiments, interviews and more recently, online methods) and disciplines (e.g. social policy, politics, sociology, criminology and education). Some people will use the term 'social science research' in order to emphasise its scientific credentials, but what makes social research different is that it is not just influenced by science, but by art and the humanities. The term 'social research' then captures both scientific and humanistic approaches. Social science, as a description, on the face of it, would seem to suggest a scientific orientation, but what counts as science in this case is contested (more of this below). Also social science, unlike social research, is not wholly concerned with empirical investigation and a great deal of it consists of theorisation that may only tangentially refer to social research. There is more about this in the section on theory.

Social science has its own branch of philosophy, called the 'Philosophy of the Social Sciences' (and is represented by a very good journal of the same name). There is an inevitable overlap between 'philosophy of the social sciences' and that of 'philosophy of social research'; the latter can be seen as a sub set of the former, but is especially concerned with the philosophical issues raised by social research (and vice versa, the philosophical issues that impact upon the practice of social research). The philosophy of the social sciences has broader concerns that transcend the empirical and may be more concerned with what we might call the metaphysics of social life. I'll say a bit more about metaphysics below. Also, philosophy of the social sciences often draws on (frequently idealised) economic exemplars to make arguments and illustrate. Though I have used a few simple examples from economics, the disciplines of economics and social research are somewhat separate activities. However, having said these things, it is also true to say that the line between the philosophies of social science and social research is rather blurred, and one which I have undoubtedly crossed several times in this book.

Often, when students are confronted with the need to learn some philosophy alongside research methods, they will ask 'why?'. Their concerns are often very specific and concerned with social problems, social practices or identities. It seems rather like asking a plumber to study hydrology! But let us take three examples of why some knowledge of the philosophical issues underlying social research are important:

- *Statistics*: Most students studying social research will have to get to grips with basic statistical concepts, such as measures of central tendency, descriptive statistics, inferential statistics, hypotheses and so on. These can appear bewildering and complex and for all of us, as social researchers, some knowledge of these concepts are a rite of passage and often a painful one at that. Yet, at the risk of over simplifying, it is true to say that at the heart of statistics lie some relatively simple principles of probability. Though mathematical in expression, these are philosophical issues, and an understanding of these makes us better critical consumers and users of statistics. For example, what is called the 'law of large numbers' sets the limits and possibilities of probability sampling. And as we learn a little more about probability and statistics, despite these apparently natural mathematical limits, we find that many of our conventions are 'socially constructed', that is they were developed often as a result of historical practices, practical needs and the epistemological views of the statisticians.

- *Objectivity*: To read many social research text books one would think objectivity was either a state of grace to aim for, completely impossible or something that one tries to have more of, like loyalty points! That it is so contested actually suggests that it is a deeply philosophical issue, grounded in views about what humans are like, our long developed scientific practice and mostly whether social research is about the 'is' of describing and explaining, or the 'ought' of moral, or political action. If you do social research, whether you intend it or not, you must take a position on objectivity.
- *Quantity or Quality*: If you are already engaged in research you will be using methods that can be described as 'qualitative' or 'quantitative'. They may sometimes appear hybrid, but their component parts, with very few exceptions, can be so described. You may also be aware that the world contains researchers who favour one approach over the other (sometimes quite passionately) or are pluralists about method. They may present their choices as pragmatic, that some things are better known through observation or interview and some through surveys or experiments. Some will go further and say, for example, that social life cannot be known through the measurement instruments of surveys and experiments, because of the infinite variability of human interpretation, action and interaction. Their opposites may claim that unstructured observation and depth interviews are not rigorous or replicable and tell us more about the researcher, than the researched.

This antinomy, albeit put somewhat starkly here, is a reflection of a deep debate about what humans are like and whether we can use the nomothetic methods of science to describe and explain social life, or the idiographic methods of the arts to interpret human understandings and actions. It has led to the question of whether a science of the social is indeed possible and is therefore a deeply philosophical question about our humanity. It is fair to say that most researchers, in their day-to-day work, do not trouble themselves unduly with these deep issues and matters of 'quantity' or 'quality' will be practical ones, but the decision to use one or the other and to subsequently make claims about the social world on the basis of the findings is ultimately to make claims that have a philosophical provenance.

These three examples are somewhat general, but hopefully illustrate that philosophical issues are ever present. The late Cathie Marsh, one of the greatest British survey researchers, often used to say that it was important that researchers were detectives, not lawyers. She was writing at a time in British social research when there were indeed too many of the latter and not enough of the former. I agree very much with her, we should be detectives, but good detectives should also know a little of the law, lest they find themselves in trouble with it!

PHILOSOPHY AND SOCIAL RESEARCH

For those who are not philosophers, philosophy seems like a rather abstract activity, maybe even an indulgence. It can be both of these and it can certainly be obfuscating and difficult. Anyone who says it is not the latter is possibly very clever, but probably not – you decide. But like cookery and playing the piano, you can do it at different levels and still obtain satisfaction. The thing about philosophy is that there are only a very few big philosophical problems, but there are thousands and thousands of approaches and answers to these. Some of the problems are unanswerable, so we just have to shrug and move on.

Existence

How do you know you exist? And if you do, what is that exists? In the 18th century a cleric called George Berkeley believed that you could not show there was anything in the world beyond your own perceptions of it. The world was what you perceived. This view became known as 'solipsism' and ultimately it is irrefutable – you can deny, but you can't refute it! A modern version of this is depicted in the film *The Matrix*, in which reality as perceived by most people is in fact a simulation.[1]

The French philosopher René Descartes thought he had resolved the existence problem, and his solution is summed up in the motto 'I think, therefore I am' (you can refer to it airily as 'The Cogito'). His argument was that suppose an evil demon had tricked him into believing he

[1] See: http://www.simulation-argument.com/simulation.html

existed, it was nevertheless undeniable that something existed to have such thoughts of existence and the fact that he was aware of existing through thinking these things, proved that he existed.

What has any of this got to do with social research? It is the case that through our investigations we claim to know other minds. This is especially true when we use methods of interpretation, where we aim to come to know how others understand the world. But there must be a logical limit to this knowledge. Some will say that 'to know one, you must be one', meaning, for example, to understand the perspective of a fundamentalist Christian or Muslim you must become, or perhaps nearly become one. This issue was explored in an excellent novel by Alison Lurie, called *Imaginary Friends*, which follows some investigators who infiltrate a UFO, millenniumist cult and who get drawn further and further into the beliefs of the cult.

Quite apart from the issue of 'going native' in such research, the issue remains that to know another mind (or minds) you must become that mind, and therefore a philosophical impossibility.

What can we know of the world?

The great philosopher Bertrand Russell reflected upon the habits of his cat. He sees his cat in the morning, when the cat is fed, and in the evening, when the cat is fed again. Often, he does not see him between those times. Does the cat exist, when not seen? This seems totally implausible and Russell (as would you and I, in the matter of cats, relatives and politicians between elections) assumes that the cat exists when not seen.

This is a trivial example, but actually is important philosophically and in social research, practically. How far can we reason beyond what our sense data tells us? In social research, this has historically been a major source of controversy. Positivist social researchers maintained that we could not reason beyond what was measured, so if two variables (say poor educational attainment and class) were associated, we could do no more than simply report the finding and report to what extent could such an association be simply chance, whatever other evidence might point to a possible causal connection. In practice, of course, even positivists would seek to test for relationships with third and subsequent variables, to attempt to establish whether a third, or subsequent variable made any difference to that relationship. Other researchers, broadly called 'realists', would say that just because we cannot observe something (rather like Bertrand Russell's cat) it does not mean it is not there.

They, instead, argue that there are real things and processes that exist beyond our ability to 'know' them with our senses. I will not adjudicate on this historical dispute, at this point at least, other than to pose the question of what do we mean by 'sense data' anyway? If you are caught driving your car too fast, it is likely to be as a result of activating a speed camera and the 'sense' data is that of the reading on the instrument. So it is in social research. We 'observe' through the proxy of data collection instruments, such as surveys and even in our one-to-one encounters, perhaps in participant observation, we must reason from verbal or visual clues to conclusions that are not manifest from our 'observations'.

Both of these problems are 'metaphysical' at root. Metaphysics is the branch of philosophy (perhaps the most important one) that goes beyond our existing knowledge and poses questions of existence and what can be known of it. It further divides into epistemology, which is concerned with how we know what we know and our justification for claiming to know it, and ontology, which is concerned with existence and the nature of the things that exist. On reflection, quite a good description of social research! One might even be brave enough to say social research is philosophy in action, but I'm not quite brave enough to say that. Epistemology and ontology can be found as entries below.

One further example that leads to epistemological and ontological questions, but is itself a separate branch of philosophy, is that of ethics.

I won't try to define ethics here, again there is an entry later. But consider this. Because all of us, except for Robinson Crusoe (and even he found his man Friday), are social beings, we must find ways of acting toward each other that produce social harmony. If not, as Thomas Hobbes said, life would be 'solitary, poor, nasty, brutish and short' (Hobbes 1960: 82–95). Now because we are social and mostly prefer not to be hit over the head with a club, or be nuked to death, we can be said to prefer social harmony – even the most cantankerous of us! That, of course, begs the question of what counts as social harmony, but no matter. We can approach this two ways: we can say that there are certain recipes for acting that will be the right thing to do, these may be religiously grounded in the Bible or the Quran, for example, or they may have a secular basis; or we may say that we should do those things, whatever they are, that promote social harmony, often translated as happiness. Both of these approaches inform our informal codes of conduct, our belief systems, our laws and our politics. And often they go horribly wrong and lead to the horrors of conflict, cruelty, division and de-friending on Facebook. Ethics may be a branch of philosophy, but it underwrites social research in so many ways: the way we behave to those who we research, the kinds of research we will do, but most importantly it is about questions of commitment. Do social researchers commit to a set of values, beyond the communities they research, are they 'on the side' of one or other group, or is it only their duty to hold a mirror up to society? Again, I will not answer these questions here, but conclude this section with one observation: that both philosophically and as researchers, our ability to reflect upon and investigate the world and our species within it is an outcome of what we are as humans, and this leads us to reflect upon and investigate the world and our species within it.

THE SMALL PRINT: READING THIS BOOK, SOME CLARIFICATIONS AND EXCUSES

As I said at the beginning, this is not a book for philosophers. Think of it as minor triage for social researchers who need (and indeed ought) to learn a bit about the philosophical underpinnings, or as a philosophical *amuse bouche* for those social researchers who want to learn some philosophy. If you are a philosopher and have ended up with this book and really wanted to know about social research, then I can heartily recommend my own *Making Sense of Social Research*. OK, so now I have managed expectations, here's a bit more about this book and why it is like it is.

It is divided into short essays of between 1300 and 3000 words, because that is what the SAGE Key Concept books are like. But within this there are different kinds of entry. Some, like 'Epistemology', 'Ontology', 'Empiricism', might be found in any philosophy book, but they are angled toward social science and social research (and you won't necessarily need to look them up elsewhere). Other entries, though less obviously philosophical, are nevertheless a bit grandiose – for example 'Statistics'. But under this entry you will not find a comprehensive historical or technical discussion, nor will you learn how to do your statistics assignment, but you will find out a bit about the philosophical relationship of statistics to social research. Then there are the more obviously 'social research' type entries, such as 'Interpretation and meaning', where I try to relate research issues to their underlying philosophy. Some entries present an argument or arguments, but mostly it is impossible in such a few words to actually *make* an argument, so for the most part I simply summarise the arguments others have made.

There is a big overlap between concepts and I ended up with several that were really saying many of the same things as other entries, so some things are not there (e.g. naturalism, poststructuralism, agent-based modelling, reflexivity etc.), but mostly you can find them under other concepts and thus see how they fit within these other concepts. Some concepts could have had their own entry (e.g. hermeneutics, phenomenology), however, by describing them under their 'parent' philosophy, in this case idealism, it is possible to see how this philosophical position led to what we might term 'second order philosophies', which are also methodologies (or the basis of methodologies).

There were a few things that younger colleagues said ought to be in, for example posthumanism, but I either rather snootily thought these were just old wine in new bottles or some cases, such as posthumanism, I had no idea what the writers were talking about, and I suspect in some cases neither did they!

Within the concept entries themselves, there are a number of practical features. Often there are important linkages between concepts and these are indicated in the text itself and summarised at the end. Some concepts (e.g. Causality) have their own entry, but keep cropping up in other entries. Also at the end I list a few key readings, sometimes just one or two, other times several. These may amplify the concept more, or go into more depth about a particular feature of a concept. Some are debates about contentious issues, some are classics, others more obscure, but hopefully interesting. When I look through the references and key readings at the end of each concept, a few appear several times. These books might be worth broader attention. The first is Norman Blaikie's *Approaches to Social Enquiry* (2007), which is an excellent and accessible bridge between philosophical issues and the methodology of social research. A very clear introduction to philosophical issues in science is William Newton-Smith's *The Rationality of Science* (1981). My own *Science and Social Science* (2000) examines in a little more depth many of the concepts presented here and attempts to make the case for a moderate scientific social science. Finally, there are many very good introductions to philosophy more generally. Bertrand Russell's *A History of Western Philosophy* (1979) is clear and comprehensive.

Also at the end of each concept entry is a list of 'key thinkers'. I struggled with this one. Some concepts are clearly associated with famous philosophers (e.g. Empiricism with Hume, Falsification with Popper), but sometimes more contemporary and less well-known figures are, at least in my view, 'key', so sometimes the list is a bit idiosyncratic, containing household names from philosophy and social science and a few Johnny-come-latelys. Also, just because someone is listed as a 'key thinker' does not mean they take the same view as others in the list on a matter, and indeed they might be quite opposed to each other. The penultimate entry in the book is 'Theory'. I have listed a few thinkers I think are key for this entry, but here the list could have gone on for pages!

In this book I have tried to be fair to positions that are often contentious, but this does not mean I have adopted a position of lofty disinterestedness. Like all social researchers, I have my views on technical issues and on good practice, and like all those who are concerned with methodological and philosophical matters, I have particular views on these too. Inevitably these views will become apparent, so it's better that I confess now. To begin with, I do not think there is any neutral or Archimedean position on knowledge; all knowledge, including that of the social world, is from a perspective. However, it does not follow from this that all knowledge has epistemological equivalence. It is a fact that I know more about the wines of Bordeaux than my postman, who refers to it as that 'French jollop', though I know a lot less that Robert Parker about the matter! Similarly, the scientific and social scientific knowledge of scientists and social scientists is greater than that of most lay people. It does not make scientists and social scientists always right, and certainly not superior in any moral sense. Scientists in particular can prove they know more, more readily, because they can do wizzy stuff that lay persons can't. So, I'm in favour of science (as Raymond Tallis (1995) argued, what is the alternative?), but a moderate and falsifiable science and this view equally applies to social science. Yet, whilst I reject the epistemological relativism, which often arises from more humanistic approaches to social science, I can also see the enormous importance of humanist approaches to knowing the social world. Additionally, I am a realist, which means I believe there is an actually existing world (physical or social) that transcends what we can know of it (and anyway, how would we know that we 'knew' it?). This puts me at odds with the positivists, because I believe in complex causality and mechanisms and not just associations, and also at odds with the more militant social constructionists, because I believe that whilst the social world is constructed, it is nevertheless 'real' in its consequences and it is grounded in a largely non-negotiable physical world.

The positions I have outlined also make me a member of a philosophical tribe, called 'analytic philosophy', which includes such luminaries as Hume, Popper, half of Wittgenstein, Russell, Carnap, Hempel and Ayer. The other tribe are called 'continental' and include heavy-duty thinkers such as Hegel, Heidegger, Nietzsche, Derrida and Foucault. There are others, particularly Kant, who are claimed by both sides. The differences between these tribes are of substance and style, but in my view the style of the latter often obscures the substance, but you must decide. Indeed I must confess, that most of the entries in this book are conceptually about debates in analytic approaches, but that is because historically analytic approaches to philosophy have been more concerned with questions of the possibilities and limitations of science (and by extension those presented by social research). For example, analytic philosophy has much to say about both statistics and language, but mostly continental philosophy is silent, or even contemptuous of the former.

I confess that the rest of the book is a bit less light-hearted than this Introduction, nevertheless I hope you enjoy reading about the concepts as much as I enjoyed writing about them.

There are a few people I would like to thank for helping to bring this book to fruition. First SAGE publications, particularly Chris Rojek for the idea for the book and Delayna Spencer for her patience in the long wait from idea to completion. Katherine Haw and Michael Ainsley expertly guided the manuscript to publication. Four anonymous reviewers read the manuscript and made lots of supportive and useful comments. Space did not permit my taking up all of these. Finally, I would like to thank a number of people for conversations and ideas that make it all worthwhile, particularly Will Baker, David Byrne, Wendy Dyer, Martyn Hammersley, Tim May, Ray Pawson, Luke Sloan, Emma Uprichard, Paul Vogt and Dick Wiggins.

REFERENCES

Blaikie, N (2007) *Approaches to Social Enquiry*, 2nd edn. Cambridge: Polity.

Hobbes, T (1960) *Levithian* (edited and with an introduction by M Oakeshott). Oxford: Blackwell.

Newton-Smith, W H (1981) *The Rationality of Science*. London: Routledge.

Russell, B (1979) *A History of Western Philosophy*. London: Unwin Hyman.

Tallis, R (1995) *Newton's Sleep: Two Cultures and Two Kingdoms*. London: Macmillan.

Williams, M (2000) *Science and Social Science: an introduction*. London: Routledge.

Causality

Causality (sometimes described as causation) is a cornerstone, albeit a controversial one, of philosophy and science. It might be simply described as 'what makes something happen', or in social research 'how does change in one variable create change in another'?

> *In this section some key philosophical issues are examined and four possible strategies are set out: abandoning causality, causality through sufficient conditions, causality through necessary conditions and causality as probability. Causes in social research as singular and aggregate and the relationship to complexity and mechanisms.*

In our everyday lives we constantly use causal language. Sometimes this employs the word 'cause' (or its derivatives), for example 'She went through a red light and caused an accident', or language that implies that something was caused, 'I arrived late because I missed my flight'. In common speech we do not distinguish between things caused by human behaviour or non-human events (e.g. the brakes failed and this caused the car to crash). Our everyday causal language is good enough for everyday events. However, in the sciences we require more precision. Pharmacologists must specify a precise dosage of a drug that will cause the desired effect, or indeed the maximum safe dosage; similarly accident investigators are required to closely specify the circumstances that caused a crash. Though in the social sciences such precision is not required, or indeed possible, a causal explanation is expected to go beyond common sense. Indeed causal explanation is a central feature of social science because many, if not most, questions are about why something is the case. Yet specifying what a 'cause' is that goes beyond common sense is not straightforward.

One of the foremost philosophers of causality, Paul Humphreys, has written 'objects do not cause anything; it is the properties possessed by them that do the causing' (2001: 31). The social world has particular properties, that it is made up of consciously aware individuals who can bring about change in the world through acting, speaking and even thinking. In this respect causes in the social world take on a different character to those in the physical world, though some of the ways of thinking about causes have applicability in each of these domains.

CAUSES AND METAPHYSICS

Before we can consider the special circumstances of causes in the social world we need to think about some of the properties of causality from a philosophical perspective.

The common-sense version of causality has two key properties: that event A (cause) was prior in time to event B (effect); and that B would not have happened if A had not happened. This model of causality was drawn into question by the 18th-century philosopher David Hume and most debates since have referred to his scepticism.

Hume illustrates his argument with the example of billiard balls (see **empiricism**). In his example all we see is one ball hitting the other and the second ball moving. To say that a cause was present requires us to infer beyond what we observe: that if a billiard ball is hit by another and moves that, the first caused the second to move.

This may seem pedantic, yet there are plenty of examples where events fulfil the time condition, but one did not cause the other. Eating your breakfast before leaving home is a common association, but there is no causal connection. In social research two variables may be associated in a study, but they may or may not be causally connected, though there is a temptation to read a causal connection into what we know of the circumstances.

The media commonly point to links between watching violent TV or video images, or playing violent media games and subsequent violent acts. It is possible that the prior behaviour caused the second, but it is equally possible that persons prone to violence are attracted to violent media representations. As a friend of mine often says, many violent people eat hamburgers, but the media rarely cite this as a cause of violence.

The philosophical problem is that we can easily show association and contiguity in time, but to claim a cause–effect relationship requires us to draw upon knowledge of non-observables.

Hume's problem is perhaps irresolvable, but there are four strategies that are employed to circumvent it:

1. *Abandon causality altogether.* This was famously advocated by Bertrand Russell (1992). Scientists would simply talk about statistical association. Indeed this was a key feature of positivism: that there are no 'causes' in nature, simply regularities (see **positivism**). To explain an observed event, it is only necessary that it is located in a pattern of regularities. A few sociologists, notably Paul Lazarsfeld and Stuart Dodd (see Platt 1996: ch. 3) tried to go down this road, but whilst theoretical physics can do without causal language, in most sciences causal inference (however informal) seems unavoidable. Even positivists eventually embraced 'causal analysis' in social science (see Blalock 1961).
2. *Sufficiency.* We can think of causality at the aggregate or individual level. At the aggregate level the ideal scientific claim is that whenever A occurs B is the outcome, a very difficult matter to establish because even if we have good reason to infer A caused B, the problem is that rarely, if ever, are there circumstances where A *always* causes B. However, at the individual level, it is possible (as lawyers will tell you) to establish that A caused B. If there are witnesses to Garfield hitting Denzil and Denzil falling over and hitting his head on the curb, then few people would have a problem saying that Garfield hitting Denzil, and the presence of the curb, caused Denzil to fracture his skull. Humean philosophical niceties would not save Garfield from the judge and jury! In the individual case, in singular instances, we can establish causality, *de facto* if not *de jure*. A variation on this is that one should be able to cite the conditions that are both necessary *and* sufficient for something to happen, an altogether stronger set of conditions. That philosophers of social science struggle to find examples in social world, rather than physical world, is perhaps an indication of the difficulty in achieving this (Papineau 1978: 50–52).
3. *Necessity.* Despite Hume's stricture, many still claim that necessary conditions can obtain such that A has the property, or disposition, of bringing about B and this is a necessary relationship. This does require a particular set of circumstances obtain. For example, we may say that a substance when placed in water will always dissolve and this is a necessary relationship that arises from the properties of that substance and water. However, it does require that the

circumstance of placing the substance in water is enacted. Such necessity is claimed for deterministic laws of nature, such as gravity or thermodynamics. Exceptions will only be local and can be accounted for. Gravity dictates that a person jumping off a tall building will fall to the ground, but locally a flagpole may break that fall. Whilst necessity may be defensible in natural science, in the social sciences this may not be the case (see **contingency and necessity**).

4. *Probability*. Even if necessity-based versions can work in a subset of circumstances, say when there are deterministic physical laws, for the most part they do not work for aggregate phenomena in the social world, because the latter is far too complex (see **complexity**). Probabilistic versions of causality are by far the commonest and in my view, the most useful. Probabilistic versions have their origin in Hume, and what is sometimes called 'Humean' causality is in fact probabilistic association. This can be between two variables, but only when a circumstance or action conjoining them can be established. For example, if you have a headache and take an aspirin and the headache disappears, then you will usually attribute its disappearance to taking the aspirin. This seems to work for many (or most people). If we make the proposition 'aspirin cures headaches', evidence for this assertion might be base on observing *n* cases, in which 80 per cent find a cure through aspirin. However, a fuller account would control for other pharmacological or physiological variables to demonstrate which are present to make the aspirin efficacious. Probabilistic versions of causality usually work by saying the addition of variable X raises the probability of an association of A and B, and thus we might infer that A caused B. In practice, most causal models in complex systems will actually rely on several variables.

CAUSES IN SOCIAL RESEARCH

With the exception of the first strategy (which is now rare in social science) all three of the others, sometimes in combination, are used. But there are special circumstances in the social world that limit their efficacy. Frankly, our causal accounts are often weaker than those in the natural sciences (especially physics and chemistry).

First, direction of causation is often hard to establish, especially in aggregate data from surveys when the data are gathered at the same time (rather than through longitudinal studies). We may find an association between low educational achievement in children and a reluctance to read, but which way does the causal arrow flow? Indeed other variables, such as poverty or poor parental education, may contribute to the explanation. Also, an explanatory model may add in other variables, say ethnicity. No one would claim that being a member of a particular ethnic group *causes* under-achievement, but rather it is a proxy for saying that the social circumstances experienced by such group membership do.

Second, even when causes can be identified they exist within a complex feedback mechanism. For example, a plausible case can be made to show that unemployment is a cause of homelessness, but equally being homeless can be said to be a cause of unemployment. Actually, the relationship between unemployment and homelessness is dynamic and complex, not least because homelessness itself is a changing and multi-faceted state, and unemployment may be differently defined (Williams 2005).

Third, humans 'cause' things to happen (see the 'Garfield and Denzil' example above). We do this on the basis of reasons. Garfield hit Denzil because he was angry with him. Some years ago there was a debate in social science literature about whether reasons could be causes (Papineau 1978). Arguments either way were complex, but even though the consensus is nowadays that if we can identify a reason for action, it can be deemed to be the cause of that action. The difficulty lies in separating out complex reasons in individual accounts of actions. Similarly, attitudes and behaviours, when recorded in surveys, will have a 'fixed' quality that may lead to the identification of causal patterns, but the best we can say is that these stand in for more complex patterns of behaviour that might be further explored through qualitative methods. Nevertheless, even then, informal causal inference is unavoidable in drawing explanatory conclusions (see Hammersley 2014: 17–32 for a discussion of causality in qualitative research).

COMPLEXITY, MODELS AND MECHANISMS

The social world is a quintessentially complex system, or systems (see **complexity**) and our identification of causality requires sophisticated strategies. It is very difficult to clearly identify causes in dynamic and complex patterns of social being, but in recent years there have been advances in causal explanation that aims to demonstrate causality through models, either statistical or theoretical. This is rarely of the simple A → B variety, but more likely causal outcomes will be explained through statistical models or through explanatory mechanisms (or indeed both). Such models are essentially 'heuristics' that help us explain the world. These are discussed further in the sections on **probability, mechanisms and models** and **realism**.

REFERENCES

Blalock, H (1961) *Causal Inference in Nonexperimental Research*. Chapel Hill, NC: University of North Carolina Press.

Hammersley, M (2014) *The Limits of Social Science: causal explanation and value relevance*. London: Sage.

Humphreys, P (2001) 'Causation', in Newton-Smith, W H (ed.), *A Companion to the Philosophy of Science*. Oxford: Blackwell.

Papineau, D (1978) *For Science in the Social Sciences*. London: Macmillan.

Platt, J (1996) *A History of Sociological Research Methods in America 1920–1960*. Cambridge: Cambridge University Press.

Russell, B (1992 [1912]) 'On the notion of cause', in Slater, J (ed.), *The Collected Papers of Bertrand Russell. Volume 6: Logical and Philosophical Papers 1909–1913*. London: Routledge, pp. 193–210.

Williams, M (2005) 'Definition, measurement and legitimacy in studies of homelessness' in Romero, M and Margolis, E (eds), *Social Inequalities* (Blackwell Companion to Sociology Series). Malden, MA: Blackwell, pp. 190–210.

KEY READINGS

Blalock, H (1961) *Causal Inference in Nonexperimental Research*. Chapel Hill, NC: University of North Carolina Press.

Goldthorpe, J (2001) 'Causation, statistics and sociology', *European Sociological Review*, 17 (1): 1–20.

Harré, R and Madden, E (1975) *Causal Powers*. Oxford: Blackwell.

KEY THINKERS

Hubert Blalock; Rom Harré; David Hume; John Stuart Mill; Donald B Rubin

See also: *Complexity; Contingency and Necessity; Empiricism; Explanation; Generalisation and Laws; Mechanisms and Models; Positivism; Probability; Realism; Time*

Complexity

Complexity (sometimes described as 'Chaos'[2]) refers to the behaviour of non-linear systems in the physical and social world.

Complexity describes a relatively recently identified ontological characteristic of many phenomena in the natural and social world. This section initially outlines what is meant by complex behaviour and then goes on to describe this in the social world. Although empirical methods, to research complexity in the social world are in their infancy, simulation and the analysis of 'big data' provide new and insightful methods for understanding social behaviour.

WHAT IS COMPLEXITY?

In a number of places in the present book there are references to the social world as 'open' or 'indeterminate'. This ontology, though now almost universally adopted, is relatively new (see **positivism**) and arises out of the philosophical insights of chaos theory and its later development complexity.

The 'discovery' of chaos was initially through the modelling of weather patterns (Gleick 1987: 14–15) in the 1960s. Alternative models, which began with only slightly changed initial conditions, could produce very different outcomes. Non-mechanistic systems, eventually termed 'complex', were seen to be sensitive to small changes, either initially or during their evolution a small change could 'tip' them into very different states. Researchers noted how relatively stable systems in weather, oceans, and biological systems could change suddenly or descend into apparent disorder, and conversely, how apparently stochastic systems could become ordered. Complex systems, exhibiting such

[2] The term 'Chaos' is much less used nowadays and hardly at all in social science, but the history of Complexity is located in 'Chaos Theory'. See, for example, Gleick (1987). The distinction between the terms is not altogether clear.

characteristics, exist throughout nature in the development of galaxies to cell division (Kauffman 1995).

The social world as a whole and parts of it are quintessentially complex, though unlike the natural sciences, the social sciences have been slow to develop new methods to research complexity. With some exceptions (see below) complexity has remained more of an ontological assumption with great potential to enrich other methodologies, in particular **realism** and our thinking about **causality** (Byrne 2011).

It was never denied that the social world was complicated, but complexity means something rather different. Two simple illustrations show the difference:

- Paul Cilliers (1998) provides the analogy of a jumbo jet, which is hugely complicated, but its parts fit together in an ordered and linear way. You can build it and take it apart. However (apart from flavourings), mayonnaise has only two ingredients: egg yolks and oil, yet there is a complex chemical process which binds them together to produce an emulsion, which is not just a sum of its components, but is emergent as something quite different, that cannot be undone. The components and structure of a jumbo jet are of a different kind to mayonnaise.
- Some years before the ideas of chaos or complexity entered the scientific lexicon, Karl Popper (1979) contrasted clocks with clouds. Clocks are stable, mechanistic (nowadays also electronic) and have entirely predictable patterns of behaviour. Clouds, though identifiable as such, emerge, change shape, become denser and finally dissipate. Some systems are closer to clocks, others closer to clouds. Note that it is not being said that clouds do not have shape or form, that their behaviour cannot be predicted. 'Cloud like' systems can only be described qualitatively or probabilistically – unlike 'clock like' systems, in which future behaviour can be predicted with great accuracy. The simple test for complexity is to look at an entity and ask what kind of system produces that outcome – is it more clock/jumbo jet like, or more cloud/mayonnaise like?

COMPLEXITY IN THE SOCIAL WORLD

The social world and its components are much more cloud like than clock like, though some outcomes can appear fairly mechanistic, in Popper's sense (though see **mechanisms and models**).

Although social science has been relatively slow to adopt complexity approaches empirically, they do actually have a longer pedigree in social science than the natural sciences. Talcott Parsons' later structural functionalism was influenced by cybernetics. He theorised that social systems, like biological ones, could be described and understood through the exchange of control and information within systems. Indeed the key question at the heart of structural functionalism was 'how is social order and reproduction maintained?'.

Societies are complex configurations of people, whose actions overlap and produce new configurations. Actions are performed on the basis of information, and these actions in turn create new situations with other possibilities or constraints. So where is the 'chaos' in social systems? Can social systems become ever increasingly stochastic? The answer, fortunately for social research, is 'no'. The upheaval of dramatic revolution will have relatively predictable dynamics and will largely rely on information and behaviours that pre-date it, and in due course it will become a stable (though dynamic) system.

Social systems are complex and they are dynamic, but also adaptive and often become more ordered in time. The French Revolution in 1789 was one of the most dramatic in history, heads literally rolled and even the calendar was renamed. But within half a century the cultural and political norms that are today the basis of French society and government were established. Periodically, events such as the 1870 war with Prussia and more especially the initial defeat in the Second World War, and the Vichy regime deeply challenged this order, but each time these perturbations created turbulence and change, without destroying the system in the long term. Virtually every system or institution we can name will embody both longevity and change.

THE ONTOLOGY OF COMPLEXITY IN THE SOCIAL WORLD

At the risk of simplification, we can perhaps characterise complexity as an ontology of relationships, rather than things. Yet most social science is an ontology of things, and social research is mostly a battery of methods to research things. This is more than language. Even when we talk of relationships between variables our models and methods specify those variables, as if they were fixed, and then we seek to specify the linear relationships between them. Dave Byrne, provocatively, has pronounced 'death to the variable' (2002: 29) and he is quite right, they exist only as heuristic fictions. But let us not go too far! There are 'things' – people – and there are other relatively fixed objects and properties in the physical world that enable and constrain the social world. So 'variables' (or as Byrne calls them 'variate traces' that name them: sex, age, location, type of housing, diagnosed illnesses) are assuming they are accurately measured, relatively fixed. But everything else is a relationship, between relationships in time! How we capture these relationships, both in descriptive language and crucially methods, is difficult, particularly if we want to do research on actual people, rather than through (perfectly legitimate) simulations (see below).

This way of thinking about the social world leads to two apparently contradictory conclusions. First, I have argued elsewhere that there is no natural necessity in the social world (Williams 2011). Certainly some things are much more likely to happen than others and on some we could safely place a wager, but they are not necessary. That there is such a range of likelihoods from the near, but not absolutely, certain to the very unlikely explains both stability and change (see **probability**).

Second, though the relationships are characterised by their probabilistic nature, they are nevertheless real, in so far as their outcomes will raise or lower the probability of other things happening (see **causality**).

One final point that underscores the need to think differently about complexity is that throughout this section so far I have talked unproblematically of 'systems', as if like the mechanism of the clock they were discrete and identifiable. They are not, they are much more noumenal (see **idealism**) in character. We identify a system, only because we look at social phenomenon in a specific way and describe it accordingly. We could look at it very differently and describe different 'systems'. We could, for example, describe a system of organised crime in a country and the judicial system of that country as two systems, but each are actually manifestations of complex changing social processes that overlap, though certainly have identifiable features and causal consequences. But the 'system', like the 'variable', is pretty much a fiction.

So how can we research complexity?

RESEARCHING COMPLEXITY

The first of these is simulation, in which artificial computer models are built to emulate aspects of the social world. The second is theory driven, heuristic and uses traditional methods in new ways. The third is the most revolutionary and uses simple, but large-scale data (big data) to find patterns in actions and interactions.

Simulation

Simulation takes many forms, including some that are entirely abstract, such as system dynamics or artificial intelligence (Grune-Yanoff 2011: 612–615). However, in social science, the commonest form of simulation is agent-based modelling (ABM), sometimes referred to as agent-based simulation. These models can be predictive, or explanatory, but for the most part they explore what happens when (artificial) agents begin interacting, given some usually quite simple rules.

A precursor of ABM is cellular automata (CA). CAs consist of cells in regular grid, which may have one to three dimensions. Each cell has a number of states which change over time. One of the most famous CA models is Conway's 'Game of Life' (Berkelcamp et al. 1982), in which each cell in the grid is either 'dead' or 'alive', but dead cells with exactly three neighbours become 'live', whereas 'live' cells with less than two, or more than three neighbours become 'dead'. These very simple rules lead to evolving systems, the future states of which cannot be known a priori, and are an excellent example of how complex patterns can emerge from simple systems.

There is controversy about to what extent simulation offers new philosophical challenges (Frigg and Reiss 2009), but three characteristics make it different to other kinds of models and may also be helpful in our understanding of emergence and thus complexity.

First, they are epistemologically different in so far as they cannot be analytically broken down into components or readily expressed as a mathematical algorithms.

Second, they incorporate a dynamic element of time. In a static (traditional) model, elapsed time is represented only by variables measured at different time points. Simulation can help us to understand how complex systems change through time – not the least because we can use visualisation techniques.

Third, and possibly more of a challenge, they cause us to question what we mean by an 'agent' or the 'social'. In simulations agents are given characteristics and they interact, but they are (unlike agents in the real world) goal directed. Yet what emerges can often be artificial societies that have huge verisimilitude to 'real' ones. So how important to the social is goal directed, or teleological behaviour to the creation of social entities (see **functionalism**) and therefore to what extent are the social entities independent of particular agency?

Mechanisms and cases

I have talked about this in more detail in the section on **mechanisms and models** and here I just want to make the point that whilst we can think of variables and systems as ontological fictions, epistemologically and methodologically they can be useful in specifying and testing for the existence of phenomena in the social world. No one really believes that a 'mechanism' exists in the social world in the way we would think of a clockwork mechanism, but it is shorthand for a relatively stable cohering alignment of characteristics that produce outcomes that we can measure.

As I noted above, whilst the social world does not possess natural necessity, much of what we do or happens to us is grounded in the physical world. Moreover, the 'we' is you and I, and individuals have potentially measurable trajectories through time, in other words stuff happens to us! So, instead of beginning with the variable, which represents the characteristics or the things that happen to people, we can begin with the individual – the 'case'. A different, though admittedly limited, battery of methods are open to us, such as case-based cluster analysis (Williams and Dyer 2009; Uprichard 2009; Castellani and Rajaram 2012) or qualitative comparative analysis (QCA) (Ragin 2009). The latter is gaining adherents quite rapidly, and both have the potential to capture the ontology of complexity I outlined above.

Big data

At the time of writing 'big data' is a fashionable but often ill-defined concept. Social scientists have used 'big data', in the form of large administrative or survey datasets, for decades. Mostly these rely on sample data/panel data and their analysis has assumed that the data are a relatively accurate and stable representation of the real world. However, 'big data' has come to mean something much more than large sample datasets with many variables. Certainly size is foremost, because the search for patterns in data require enough of it. But it has other characteristics, such as the speed of its generation and that it often is naturally occurring in real time. Big data, in the social world, is heterogeneous. It might refer to the everyday 'transactional' data generated through individual economic behaviours (credit cards, loyalty cards, buying patterns), or social behaviours (such as travel, social media etc.). The commercial sector has been aware of the characteristics and potential of big data for quite some time (through consumer choice linkages in Amazon, or through the profiling of shoppers through their buying patterns), but in the last few years social behaviour has become a candidate for big data analysis. Typical of such research was that of Burnap et al. (2014) who analysed Twitter data following a terrorist incident in London, in 2013. Their models were able to show the size and survival of sentiments expressed through tweeting and re-tweeting over time. New social media postings are a good example of large-scale, rapidly changing and evolving social phenomena. This kind of change and evolution has always existed, though the speed and saturation of information can change behaviours faster, more comprehensively and across more people than ever before. Crucially, social scientists can capture this behaviour across potentially millions of people (the Burnap et al. sample was relatively small at 427,330 tweets/re-tweets) and can identify complex patterns, stochasticty, stability or increased/decreased velocity of behaviours or sentiments. Indeed big data may lend legitimacy to 'theory neutral' analyses that simply look for patterns in complex data and seek to make sense of them theoretically post hoc.

REFERENCES

Berkelcamp, E, Conway, J and Guy, R (1982) *Winning Ways for your Mathematical Play. Volume 2: Games in Particular*. London: Academic Press.

Burnap, P, Williams, M L, Sloan, L, Rana, O, Housley, W, Edwards, A, Knight, V, Procter, R and Voss, A (2014) 'Tweeting the terror: modelling the social media reaction to the Woolwich terrorist attack', *Social Network Analysis and Mining*, 4: 1.

Byrne, D (2002) *Interpreting Quantitative Data*. London: Sage.

Byrne, D (2011) 'What is an effect? Coming at causality backwards', in Williams, M and Vogt, W P (eds), *The Sage Handbook of Innovation in Social Research Methods*. London: Sage. pp. 81–91.

Castellani, B and Rajaram, R (2012) 'Case-based modeling and the SACS toolkit: a mathematical outline', *Computational and Mathematical Organizational Theory*, 18(2): 153–174.

Cilliers, P (1998) *Complexity and Postmodernism: understanding complex systems*. London: Routledge.

Frigg, R and Julian Reiss, J (2009) 'The philosophy of simulation: hot new issues or same old stew?', *Synthese*, 169: 593–613.

Gleick, J (1987) *Chaos: making a new science*. Harmondsworth: Viking Penguin.

Grune-Yanoff, T (2011) 'Artificial worlds and agent-based simulation' in Jarvie, I and Zamora-Bonilla, J (eds), *The Sage Handbook of the Philosophy of the Social Sciences*. Thousand Oaks, CA: Sage. pp. 613–631.

Kauffman, S (1995) *At Home in the Universe: the search for the laws of self-organization and complexity*. Oxford: Oxford University Press.

Popper, K (1979) *Objective Knowledge: an evolutionary approach*, 2nd edn. Oxford: Oxford University Press.

Ragin, C (2009) 'Reflections on casing and case orientated research', in Byrne, D and Ragin, C (eds), *The Sage Handbook of Case Based Methods*. London: Sage. pp. 522–534.

Uprichard, E (2009) 'Introducing cluster analysis: what can it teach us about the case' in Byrne, D and Ragin, C (eds), *The Sage Handbook of Case-Based Methods*. London: Sage. pp. 32–147.

Williams, M (2011) 'Contingent realism – abandoning necessity', *Social Epistemology*, 25 (1): 37–56.

Williams, M and Dyer, W (2009) 'Single case probabilities', in Byrne, D and Ragin, C (eds), *The Sage Handbook of Case-Based Methods*. London: Sage. pp. 84–100.

KEY READINGS

Byrne, D (1998) *Complexity Theory and the Social Sciences: an introduction*. London: Routledge.

Sloan, L, Morgan, J, Housley, W, Williams, M L, Edwards, A, Burnap, P and Rana, O (2013) 'Knowing the Tweeters: deriving sociologically relevant demographics from Twitter', *Sociological Research Online*, 18 (3): 7.

KEY THINKERS

Dave Byrne; Brian Castellani; Paul Cilliers; David Harvey; David Ruelle; Emma Uprichard

See also: *Causality; Idealism; Mechanisms and Models; Positivism; Probability; Realism; Time*

Necessity is the claim that within particular domains some things are inevitable, whereas contingency refers to one fact being contingent upon another, or that there is an uncertainty in the relationship between two or more facts.

Social science is concerned with discovering and explaining different kinds of connections in the social world. These connections indicate relationships, some would say causal ones. But are these relationships necessary outcomes, or could things have been different? Empiricists have denied that we can ever discover necessary relations in the social world, but critical realists have argued quite the opposite, that there is natural necessity in the social world as much as the physical world. To assess these competing claims, the section explores what can be meant by necessity and contingency and finally concludes that natural necessity has not been shown to exist in the social world.

Throughout its history, the social sciences have sought to discover connections between phenomenon, and often this has been a search for a causal connection. In grand theory (see **theory**) or historical theory causes – say the 'cause of the First World War' – are often specified only in the broadest terms and when examined in detail, the necessary or sufficient conditions of the form X → Y are found to be lacking. Indeed social science positivists (see **positivism**), such as Lazarsfeld (1948) and Dodd (1948) have explicitly denied the possibility of discovering causal connections in the social world and maintained only that we can establish statistical correlations between phenomenon (see **causality**). David Lewis neatly sums up this view that 'It is the doctrine that all there is to the world is a vast mosaic of local matters of particular fact, just one little thing then another' (1986: ix–x). The somewhat extreme view of Lazarsfeld or Dodd (see Platt 1996) is rarely expressed today, but the problem of connections remains. Are there any connections between phenomena in the social world that are *necessary*, that must be the case? The counterfactual,[3] that there are no connections at all, is offended by everyday experience. Although trains may be late, or cancelled on occasions, there is nevertheless some kind of relationship between the arrival and departure of trains and their scheduling in timetables. We can see the connection between the expression of a desire for something (say a desire to eat chocolate), our actions (to buy chocolate) and the satisfaction of that desire. In social science, however

[3] The term 'counterfactual' was first used by Nelson Goodman (1947). Simply put, it refers to other possible logical states that could exist, but may not be suggested by the evidence.

sceptical one might want to be about the possibility of social explanation, it is the case that social scientists can predict events and trends on the basis of their data. Otherwise polling and market research companies would go out of business. Thus at the very least, we can say that relationships where X happening is, in some sense, *contingent* upon Y happening. However, as is so often the case in philosophy, the devil lies in the detail. What do we mean by contingency and what do we mean by necessity? Before examining what these concepts might mean for the social world, it is helpful to see if the problem I have outlined above exists in the natural world.

NECESSITY AND NATURE

When we tell common-sense stories about causes in the social or natural world, we do not usually distinguish between the social and physical components, the causal language is the same. For example, 'She divorced him *because* she did not love him', or 'the lights did not work *because* there was a power cut', or '*because* of the power cut the school was closed'. Notice in the third example the social act of not opening the school was attributed to the physical absence of electricity. I will return to this 'mixing' of the natural and the social below, but for the moment it is enough to note that locally physical and social phenomena are interconnected (e.g. the power cut may have happened because there was a strike). But are there any things in the physical world we can say must happen under particular circumstances?

In metaphysics there has long been a debate about, whether or to what extent the world is determined a priori (Honderich 1979), but philosophers of science have rarely troubled themselves too much with such debates, concluding that this would render impossible most reasoning about the epistemological and ontological conditions for the possibility of science. Thus, most philosophers of science would accept that what are known as fundamental laws, such as gravity or thermodynamics, will operate under all of the conditions humans can experience. They will bracket off local variation, or that in certain extra terrestrial conditions, such laws will break down. For example, a fundamental principle of gravitational attraction is that objects will fall towards the Earth. But this is subverted by (say) aeroplanes – though as is sometimes said taking-off is voluntary, landing is compulsory! We also know that the laws of gravity break down past the 'event horizon' of a black hole.

Yet, *ceteris paribus,*[4] and in the universe we inhabit, these fundamental laws will always assert themselves and this allows scientists to assert that, in given circumstances, phenomena must *necessarily* behave in particular ways. This kind of *natural necessity* is a fundamental pillar of natural science. Yet, however important fundamental natural laws are, as a final guarantor, they are only invoked in a relatively small number of scientific investigations. Much of natural science is concerned with explaining more local manifestations of connections between phenomena, often in the complex systems (see **complexity**). Indeed, of all of the laws of nature, very few are 'deterministic' and many more either operate only certain conditions or, like the law of gases, are probabilistic. In practice, natural scientists do not trouble themselves too much with matters of necessity, unlike social scientists for whom it is often a more pressing matter, because a reasonable question to ask is, 'are there any instances of necessity in the social world in which we can ground other more contingent behaviour?'.

CRITICAL REALISM, NECESSITY AND DISPOSITIONS

One social science doctrine insists that there is necessity – indeed natural necessity in the social world is critical realism (see **realism**). Natural necessity explains the dynamic relations between states, powers and natures of things in the world (Harré and Madden 1975: 8) and is usually seen as fundamental to a realist theory of causality. No distinction, in principle, is made between necessity in the physical world and the social world. They do, of course, distinguish between the ways in which necessity operates in each world and allow for weaker modulation of causal powers or liabilities in the social world. As Andrew Sayer puts it, 'People have the causal powers of being able to work ('labour power'), speak, reason, walk, reproduce etc.' (1992: 105). They may not choose to exercise these, or such powers (e.g. labour power) may inhere in social relations or structures, but when they do there is a necessary link between the causal power or liability and a particular outcome. These causal powers or liabilities are conceptually the same as what philosophers of science describe as dispositions in the physical world.

[4] *Ceteris paribus* is a term commonly used by philosophers as shorthand for all other things being equal. It allows for exceptions to a rule (or in science, a law or theory).

For example, solubility in water is a disposition, though it does not follow that because something can be dissolved it will be dissolved, nevertheless as Stephen Mumford notes 'the properties of being soluble and being dissolved would have some degree of necessity connecting them' (2007: 74). For social science realists there is no in principle difference, in respect of necessity, between (say) solubility and labour power.

Dispositions (causal powers, liabilities) are important here because the argument for necessity turns on whether, under the right conditions, some particular state of affairs *must* come about. Now, in the solubility example, a chemist can specify precisely the conditions in which a given substance, known to be soluble in water, will dissolve in water (in other words, there may be ambiguity about the properties of certain substances). The test condition for a similar claim in the social world is whether there is any matter of fact that must come about in every circumstance, where a specific condition, or conditions are met? If, in Sayer's example, labour power is to have any social meaning beyond physiological capabilities, then there would have to be a specific set of circumstances in which the property of labour power must be exercised. It is hard to think of any, because the concept of labour power is itself not a fixed one. Nevertheless, the idea of 'labour power' as a potentiality (however defined) is a useful social science construct. Indeed it is hard to see how we could do social science without such constructs. Dispositions may not be necessary in the way critical realists wish, but they are useful.

DEFINING NECESSITY

Harré and Madden provide a clear definition of what is meant by necessity:[5]

> To attribute necessity to items as various as a condition, an outcome, or effect, the truth of a statement, a conclusion, is, we contend to indicate that within the relevant context no alternative to that condition, outcome, or effect, truth-value or conclusion is possible. (1975: 19)

[5] Some caution around definitions is required in this, as many other cases. Necessity is a contested definition in philosophy. The Harré and Madden one is not the only one, but because it is an explicitly realist one, it is the most useful for a discussion of necessity in social science, where contemporary critical realists are the staunchest defenders of necessity in the social world.

Note here, that a number of qualifying adjectives are used (condition, outcome, effect, truth value) which move beyond a common-sense understanding of necessity. They elaborate this definition through a description of modes of necessity, which are themselves divided into a priori and a posteriori modes:

- The *a priori* mode consists of logical necessity, whereby conclusions must follow from premises and transcendental necessity, whereby certain conditions must obtain for a rational human to have knowledge of the world.
- The *a posteriori* mode is divided into conceptual and natural necessity. The first of these is that which is necessitated conceptually as a property of a thing, which for that thing to be what it is must obtain. A chair cannot simultaneously be a dog, its properties of 'chairness' conceptually necessitate it being a chair and not something quite different.

The third mode is natural necessity, which they define as:

> When the natures of the operative powerful particulars, the constraining or stimulating effect of conditions and so on are offered as the grounds for the judgement that a certain effect cannot but happen, or cannot but fail to happen, we have natural necessity. (1975: 19)

One can immediately see how, of these three modes of necessity, two frequently apply in the social world (and in social science). Logical necessity is present in deductive argument (see **logic and truth**), where there must be agreement between premises and conclusions, but also in the symbolic form of statistical formulae. Similarly conceptual necessity is ever present, though subject always to definition and re-definition. In the conceptual schema of Marxism, a proletarian cannot simultaneously be a capitalist. In reading the work of critical realists, it is not always clear whether they intend to mean 'conceptual' or 'natural necessity' in their descriptions, particularly as they mostly use the latter term.

CONTINGENCY AND SOCIAL RELATIONS

Like necessity, contingency can be used more than one way. Its commonest use in social science is in the 'contingency table', which is a table showing the statistical relationship between two or more variables.

Within a given data set of *n* number of cells, created from a finite number of values within variables and a finite number of cases, the number of possible relationships is limited to one multiplied by the other; moreover, because the variables are arranged in a particular way with each case, there is a logically necessary finite set of possibilities. There will also be a conceptual necessity in the statistical relationships that can be shown. Conceptual and not natural, because the definition of the variables measured is a conceptual operationalisation of social properties. In a census, which has measured the properties of *every* member of the population (to capture everyone in a census is, however, rare), the conceptual necessity will also match the logical necessity, because these are the total, actual properties of individuals (as operationalised and measured). If the dataset is a sample, then the properties measured represent those which are probabilistically held to represent the population.

Statistical relationships are not magic and are prone to error, particularly that accrued in their gathering, yet they really do seem to describe social relationships within a society (see **statistics**). Often they also mirror the common sense or everyday observed relationships, such as that (say) between obesity and poverty that can be seen in many Western communities. Other times they may show surprising and novel relationships, which were not immediately apparent. However, the key word here is 'relation'. Leaving aside claims to natural necessity, it really seems to be the case that many things in the social world come about as a result of other things happening. This is where contingency comes in. We may think of it in two further ways (and leaving aside the previous definition):

- As the absence of certainty in the occurrence of events.
- Dependent on, or conditioned by prior events.

These definitions are not mutually exclusive. In the social world, the first applies in all relationships where human agency is involved. A simple example suffices: in an election you choose to vote for the candidate of the 'red' party. The 'red' party wins the election and that is just what the pollsters predicted. Prior to the vote, the pollsters could predict, but there was always uncertainty present, because each individual had to make her or his choice, and this was not determined until each vote was cast. Political polling mostly involves fairly accurate predictions, but especially at a micro level, the uncertainty of the outcomes of human agency will always involve an absence of certainty.

I continue with this simple example to illustrate the second usage of the term 'contingency'. In order to form an administration, a party must win the election, thus we can say that the red party forming an administration was contingent upon their winning the election. It is fairly easy to think of plenty of examples where event B in the social world was contingent upon event A. But does this make B necessary? Well we can concede that it is highly likely and definitely worth a flutter with Bob the Bookie, if he could be persuaded to give you any odds at all. One can think of all sorts of (admittedly) unlikely scenarios where the Red party did not form an administration: the margin of victory was too slender to provide a big enough majority, some Red candidates were disqualified or defected to the Blue party, the leader of the Red party invites the leader of the blue party to form a grand coalition and so on. All of these things have historical precedent, indeed social life is replete with 'outliers', unlikely exceptions to the rule.[6]

All of this must lead us to the conclusion that contingency, in both the latter senses, is the ontological rule of social life. Social life does indeed cohere into measurable (and I would say explicable) patterns. Some events make subsequent events very, very likely and further we can often distinguish causal relationships, but natural necessity in the social world seems to be an elusive beast.

There is one exception. Many agent decisions or social events precipitate events in the physical world, which are subject to physical natural necessity. A driver makes the decision to break the rules of the road and overtake on a blind bend. The subsequent collision with another car, or the wall, is subject to necessary laws of nature, at least in the final outcome.

REFERENCES

Dodd, S (1948) 'Developing demoscopes for social research', *American Sociological Review*, 13: 310–319.

Goodman, N (1947) 'The problem of counterfactual conditionals', *The Journal of Philosophy*, 44 (5): 113–128.

[6] At the time of writing the British Conservative Party won a surprise majority in the 2015 general election. For many months all of the political polls predicted that neither they or the main opposition Labour party would win a majority. In fact, the final result was, for many of the polls, within the 3 per cent margin of error.

Harré, R and Madden, E (1975) *Causal Powers.* Oxford: Blackwell.
Honderich, T (1979) 'One determinism', in Honderich, T (ed.), *Philosophy As It Is.* Harmondsworth: Penguin. pp. 239–276.
Lazarsfeld, P (1948) 'The use of panels in social research' *Proceedings of the American Philosophical Society*, 92: 405–410.
Lewis, D (1986) *Philosophical Papers II*. Oxford: Oxford University Press.
Mumford, S (2007) 'Filled in space', in Kistler, M and Gnassounou, B (eds), *Dispositions and Causal Powers*. Aldershot: Ashgate.
Platt, J (1996) *A History of Sociological Research Methods in America 1920–1960.* Cambridge: Cambridge University Press.
Sayer, A (1992) *Method in Social Science: a realist approach*, 2nd edn. London: Routledge.

KEY READINGS

Cartwright, N (1989) *Nature's Capacities and their Measurement.* Oxford: Oxford University Press.
Harré, R and Madden, E (1975) *Causal Powers.* Oxford: Blackwell.
Kistler, M and Gnassounou, B (eds) (2007) *Dispositions and Causal Powers*. Aldershot: Ashgate.
Popper, K (1995) *A World of Propensities*. Bristol: Thoemmes.
Williams, M (2011) 'Contingent realism – abandoning necessity' a *Social Epistemology*, 25 (1): 37–56.

KEY THINKERS

Nancy Cartwright; Rom Harré; Stephen Mumford

See also: *Causality; Complexity; Empiricism; Probability; Realism; Statistics; Time*

Empiricism

Empiricism is a philosophical movement which holds that the only legitimate knowledge claims are those that can be established by inference to sense data.

Empiricism as a core doctrine in philosophy and came to influence a number of 20th century philosophers, known as logical empiricists, or logical positivists. This section begins by describing the core empiricist doctrines of Hume, particularly his 'psychology' of perception. It goes on to discuss other key elements in empiricist thinking such as causes, induction and 'is' and 'ought' problem. Empiricism has been influential in the social sciences and the final parts of the section discuss this influence, the limits of empiricism and its legacy in social research.

The core doctrine of empiricism is one of the simplest, but also most influential in philosophy. It is that all of our knowledge of the external world comes from the interaction of our five senses with the world. It is associated with thinkers such as Berkeley, Locke, Hume and in the 20th century with Ayer, Carnap, Hempel and most recently Bas Van Frassen. For social researchers David Hume (1711–76) (Russell 1979: ch. 17) is the most important founding philosopher, because his thinking has underlain much of the development of the methodology of quantitative methods, particularly causal reasoning.

Hume was not a social scientist (because social science did not yet exist), but he was a keen observer of the physical and social world. At least some of his observations derived from playing billiards and an enduring example from that game encapsulates the essence of his argument. Imagine that with your billiard (or indeed snooker/pool) cue you strike a ball and that ball travels toward a second ball and strikes it. The second ball moves and this is obviously caused by the first ball hitting it. Good enough for the billiard player, but Hume the philosopher maintained that this reasoning was just down to our habit of expecting this to happen and said more about our psychological state than what we can actually observe, which was one ball hitting another and the second moving. Anything else was down to our reasoning, not observation. This example is discussed further in **causality**.

Hume did not deny the importance of such reasoning in billiards and everyday life and he did not advocate scepticism, except in philosophy. But his scepticism went beyond abstract philosophising to influence both the natural and social sciences. Before considering the influence on science and social research, let us consider the implications of the empiricist maxim, all knowledge derives from sense impressions.

- *Causes*: When we observe one event followed by another we see only that. Anything beyond that, such as the claim that the first event caused the second, is a product of our reasoning from experience (see **causality**).
- *Induction*: We come to expect things. We expect fire to be hot, we expect the sea to be salty, unemployed people to suffer poverty and so on. Inductive reasoning (as in the billiard ball example) expects things to happen as they have in the past, assuming all others to be equal. Again, there is nothing in the events themselves that can provide grounds for believing they will repeat, we are just reasoning from experience.
- *Is and ought*: If, strictly speaking, we cannot derive causes from observed events, or what will happen in the future from observing present events, equally there is nothing in any observed event that allows us to say what should be the case. You cannot derive an 'ought' from an 'is'. Moral reasoning is independent of sense data (see **ethics and morality**).

Hume himself certainly did not advocate that such scepticism should guide our lives; indeed he took quite the opposite view, maintaining that our senses should be slave to our passions, but since Hume in philosophy, science and social science has adopted varying levels of militancy in this regard. Perhaps the most militant of all were the logical empiricists (often called 'logical positivists') who aimed to build a body of science from basic observation statements, uncontaminated by prior reasoning or assumptions. Their fundamentalism (with a few exceptions) was never much taken up by natural scientists and still less by social scientists, but they were the vanguard of a wider positivist movement in natural and social science that prioritised observation, association rather than causation and value freedom.

Indeed militant empiricism makes science impossible. Sense data is always mediated through psychological and social processes. We need to know what to look for, or indeed what we are looking at. Scientists may accidentally 'discover' something, but mostly they are actively looking for something. An X-ray plate is often unintelligible to the lay person, without interpretation. As Theobald succinctly put it, the assertions of science 'are justified by experience, but this is not at all the same thing as to say that they are entailed by experience, or that its assertions are about experience' (1967: 19).

Further, in the matter of causes, there would be very little point to science unless we could say that something causes something else, indeed many would say that the goal of science is causal explanation. Finally, whilst it is quite possibly true that we cannot derive moral judgements from observing events, the events themselves often come about as a result of moral decision making. That we do science at all is a moral judgement that we should.

But even in his philosophy Hume gave us room for manoeuvre. Along with sense impressions go ideas. No one sane or sober has seen a unicorn, but the observation of a 'horn' and a 'horse' allows the derivation of that idea.

Modern empiricism is sophisticated and whilst retaining the fundamental primacy of empirical data, it allows room for both theorising and the development of logical reasoning based on data. In social science empiricists, or perhaps more accurately 'neo empiricists', rarely invoke Hume and the days of positivist orthodoxy have passed. But empiricism lives on in social research, especially in the social survey and what is termed 'causal analysis' (see **causality**).

In the social survey, researchers still emphasise the importance of the rigorous derivation of indicators to measure phenomenon in the process of the operationalisation of variables. Inductive reasoning underpins probability theory, whereby we can calculate the probability of some kind of event, given the probability of others. Indeed in modern empiricism probabilistic reasoning is the basis for causal reasoning and analysis. Suppose we have many observations of X and Y being associated together. Whilst we cannot reason that X caused Y (or indeed if they are observed at the same time vice versa), if they continue to associate, even when we 'control' for many different circumstances, then we may infer a causal connection. For example, we may observe that graduates with science or engineering degrees earn more than those with humanities degrees. To make a causal statement about this would require us to test this association (and possible counterfactuals) by adding in several independent variables to the model, such as university attended, sex, time elapse from graduation, sector and so on.

Empiricism has always been controversial in social research, especially in its 'positivist' variant and various aspects of it have been wholly or partially refuted by realists, critical rationalists and interpretivists, but it remains important not just for its historic value in influencing social research, but also for its enduring legacy in causal analysis in particular.

Less specific, but no less important, has been the role of empiricism in the establishment of scientific values such as logical coherence, parsimony and objectivity.

REFERENCES

Russell, B (1979) *A History of Western Philosophy*. London: Unwin Hyman.

Theobald, D (1967) *An Introduction to Philosophy of Science*. London: Methuen.

KEY READINGS

Losee, J (1980) *A Historical Introduction to the Philosophy of Science*. Oxford: Oxford University Press.

KEY THINKERS

David Hume; Carl Hempel; John Locke; Bas van Frassen

See also: *Causality; Ethics and Morality; Induction; Observation; Positivism; Probability; Rationality; Realism*

Epistemology

Epistemology is the branch of philosophy concerned with the study of knowledge. Different positions on what counts as knowledge and how we can derive shape both science and social science and are often at the root of controversies in both. Contrast with **ontology**.

The section begins with a review of the modern origins of epistemology in rationalism and empiricism. Epistemological positions have shaped the debate about the authority and possibility of the science and some of these issues are considered, along with their implications for social science and the foundations of knowledge of the social world.

'Epistemology' is a term frequently encountered in social research to indicate the philosophical underpinnings of methodology. It can both refer to the knowledge assumptions underlying the researcher's methodology, but also to those of the researched. So, for example, in classical anthropology the epistemological basis of the researchers' methods were not those of the researched in the non-Western societies studied. In more recent decades many interpretivist researchers have taken the view that there should be, or at least we should aim for, an epistemological unity or equivalence between researcher and researched. The reasoning for this might be on grounds of maximising validity, or on the grounds of the unequal power relations between researcher and researched (Oakley 1981).

Yet epistemology was the invention of Western philosophy, post Enlightenment, as enquiry into the nature, scope and justification for human knowledge. It was a reflection upon what we know and how we know it and therefore to be distinguished from faith, belief or prejudice. So to speak of 'the 'alternative epistemologies' of a particular group who do not share this value of critical enquiry is perhaps an oxymoron? Roger Trigg goes as far as to say 'Epistemology flounders once the tight constraints of empiricism are loosened' (1993: 12).

Trigg perhaps goes too far here. What he wants to preserve is a foundationalist account of knowledge, upon which enquiry can be built. The opposite of this is relativism – more specifically epistemological relativism, the view that all knowledge is context dependent and that there are no truths which transcend particular contexts (see **relativism**). However, what we mean by a 'foundation' for our knowledge is not necessarily that of empiricism, which has itself been challenged even by those who would nevertheless adhere to the post-Enlightenment concept of epistemology.

Indeed epistemology arose from two separate traditions, that of rationalism and that of empiricism. The former is epitomised by the work of Descartes and the desire to produce a true foundation for knowledge, through reason alone, in much the same way as was shown to be possible in pure mathematics. Empiricists, on the other hand, began from the view that only our senses could provide firm knowledge of the world. Kant attempted, many would say successfully, to unite these views. Somewhat crudely we can describe Kant's philosophy as a synthesis between the former two positions. He distinguished between the analytic, whereby something would be true in any possible world, and the empirical, which is sense dependent. The former is the basis of modern logic (see **logic and truth**). However, he went much further. He maintained that in order for humans to make sense of the world and impose some order upon it, it must make judgements (what he called 'categories'), for example: cause and effect, substance, necessity, possibility, reality, negation. These can only be applied within space and time, which he saw as human intuitions.

If then, we hold on to the notion of epistemological foundations for social research, we can distinguish three traditions, though there are many hybrids of these, arising from empiricism (e.g. positivism, pragmatism), rationalism (phenomenology) and Kant's 'transcendental idealism' (Weberianism, critical realism). However, cross-cutting these are the ontologies (see **idealism**, **materialism**, **ontology**) of idealism and materialism. Thus many social scientists, in the idealist tradition, will reject the idea of any foundationalist epistemology; they will nevertheless use the term to denote alternative justifications for knowledge claims.

EPISTEMOLOGY AND SCIENCE

Though epistemology and science are Western post-Enlightenment constructs, this does not imply epistemological relativism. It does not if one subscribes to the view that science and its underlying epistemology have delivered testable truths about the world, which in turn have produced technologies that could not have existed without modern science (Williams 2000: 8–27). This, however, begs a question: to what extent is the knowledge that we have (even accepting it came about through social processes) knowledge of a mind independent reality, or simply knowledge that is contingent upon those social processes which produce some kind of convergence with the world as we experience it? This question leads us to a classic problem in epistemology identified by Edmund Gettier (1963). What is sometimes called the 'standard analysis' of propositional knowledge (associated with Kant and other philosophers) implies that justified true belief, that if *p* is the case and we believe *p*, then our knowledge of *p* is true. Gettier proposed scenarios whereby *p* was the case and someone believed it to be so, but on the basis of wrong assumptions. This problem is actualised empirically in science. For example, an economist may predict a recession on the basis of deflationary tendencies in an economy.

The recession may come about, but as a result not of deflation in that economy but of an external market collapse. More generally, scientific theories may predict phenomena, but on the basis of a wrong explanation. Indeed two or more theories may predict a particular outcome and therefore not all of them can be correct and are therefore said to be *underdetermined* (see **theory**).

The Gettier problem has never been successfully resolved (at least in terms of its own problematic about justified true belief). In mathematics and logic, proofs can be shown, but in empirical science this is all but impossible.

What became known as the 'science wars' (Baringer 2001) in the 1970s and 1980s pitched those who denied the possibility of a foundationalist epistemology with those who tried to cling to the key tenets of such. This made a difference, particularly in the social sciences, where the normative position was the denial of foundationalism and the justification for knowledge shifted to social location. Typical of these were feminist epistemologies (see **feminism**) which began from the position that knowledge was social, was the product of particular social arrangements and finally, that those particular social arrangements in our society (and its ensuing science and technology) were androcentric (Hartsock 1983). One can immediately see that this argument can be extended to dominance/marginalisation of other social groups defined by ethnicity or class. In feminism, there were a number of influential attempts to rescue epistemology from the relativism implied by according equivalence to different knowledge positions, notably the feminist standpoint theories of those such as Sandra Harding (1986), or the 'feminist empiricism' (actually closer to pragmatism) of Helen Longino (1990). Others, such as critical realists (see **realism**), sought to rescue analytic approaches by placing emphasis on ontological structures, the assumption of which was that there was an actually existing world beyond anyone's particular knowledge of it and the aim of science was to connect our theories with that actuality.

FOUNDATIONS AND THE POSSIBILITY OF KNOWLEDGE

I paraphrase realism drastically in the above, but it does seem that the realist (and indeed critical rationalist – see Popper 1983) view that knowledge of the world, independent of specific context, is possible. Perhaps one way of looking at the problem is to accept that knowledge arises in a social context (and feminists and others are quite correct in this), but we can transcend that social context. Social scientists are capable of grasping the 'realities' of others through methodological strategies, such as *verstehen*, and despite the claims of Winch and others (see **rationality**) we can do this from the basis of our own epistemological position, simply because we can find referents in common across cultures.

Second, although the problem of theory under-determination never goes away, theories and evidence are not one-shot attempts at knowledge. Assuming a Gettier situation where a theory predicts an outcome from the wrong premises, it is unlikely that in slightly different circumstances the theory–outcome relationship will hold and the theory itself will be found wanting and will be modified and again tested. If the newer theory can predict the same as the old one and more, then it is an adequate replacement for its predecessor (Newton-Smith 1981: 226–232).

Third, knowledge foundations can be relatively localised, without lapsing into relativism. For example, we may say that in Western societies urban to rural migration (counterurbanisation) is the commonest migration pattern, but there are exceptions to this. Both the practice and its exceptions may be explained and encapsulated in a broader explanation of migration flows.

Fourth, it is true that scientific knowledge claims exist in something like a web of theory. Willard Van Orman Quine (1980) maintained that there is a logical interconnection between theories, and the falsification of one theory has implications for all others (see **explanation**). However, in practice, we do not expose our entire knowledge base in an area to empirical scrutiny. We can, for example, test whether a particular form of classroom assessment is effective, without testing or calling into question all of the pedagogic practice of a school or education system. These can be held as 'constants', though are nevertheless open to other later scrutiny.

Fifth, the claim that there are no truths which can transcend social context is falsified, not just by analytic truths, or Kantian categories of thought (which seem to be universal), but empirically through knowledge that has been transferable through time and across cultures.

Sixth, there is not an epistemological equivalence between all knowledge claims. Some knowledge stands on better ground than other knowledge. For example, attitudinal data drawn from several thousand respondents is likely to be a better reflection of that society's attitudes than the punditry of a politician or cleric who thinks differently.

As I noted above, the Gettier problem, like so many in philosophy, is probably not resolvable, but empirically it does seem possible to hold on to the enlightenment value of epistemological scrutiny. Furthermore, though it is possible to agree that epistemology itself is a social construct, it does not follow from this that can be no truths that can transcend particular social contexts.

REFERENCES

Baringer, P (2001) 'Introduction, the 'science wars", in Asman, K and Baringer, P (eds), *After The Science Wars*. London: Routledge. pp. 1–13.

Gettier, E (1963) 'Is justified true belief knowledge?', *Analysis*, 23: 121–123.

Harding, S (1986) *The Science Question in Feminism*. Milton Keynes: Open University Press.

Hartsock, N (1983) 'The feminist standpoint: developing the ground for a specifically feminist materialism', in Harding, S and Hintikka, M (eds), *Discovering Reality: feminist perspectives on epistemology, metaphysics, methodology and the philosophy of science*. Dordrecht: Reidel.

Longino, H (1990) *Science as Social Knowledge: values and objectivity in scientific enquiry*. Princeton, NJ: Princeton University Press.

Newton-Smith, W (1981) *The Rationality of Science*. London: Routledge and Kegan Paul.

Oakley, A (1981) 'Interviewing women: a contradiction in terms', in Robertsm, H (ed.), *Doing Feminist Research*. London: Routledge and Kegan Paul. pp. 30–61.

Popper, K R (1983) *Realism and the Aim of Science* (from the Postscript to the Logic of Scientific Discovery). London: Routledge.

Quine, W Van O (1980 [1953]) *From a Logical Point of View*. Cambridge, MA: Harvard University Press.

Trigg, R (1993) *Rationality and Science: can science explain everything?* Oxford: Blackwell.

Williams, M (2000) *Science and Social Science: an introduction*. London: Routledge.

KEY READINGS

Morton, A (1997) *A Guide Through the Theory of Knowledge*. Oxford: Blackwell.

Williams, M and May, T (1996) *Introduction to Philosophy of Social Research*. London: Routledge. ch. 2.

KEY THINKERS

Sandra Harding; Willard Van Orman Quine; Karl Popper; Bertrand Russell

See also: *Idealism; Materialism; Ontology; Relativism*

Ethics and Morality

'Ethics' is a term used in several different, but overlapping ways both in philosophy and in professions, such as social research. In a broad philosophical sense, it is a study of morality and often a search for universal forms of morality. In the professions ethical codes of conduct are usually grounded in broader ethical principles.

The section begins with a description of how the term 'ethics' is used in social research. This is a practical or narrow application and the section goes on to discuss the relationship between ethics and science and how the emergence of the latter disturbed the hitherto theist moral order. The final part returns to the philosophical relationship of ethics to social research through a consideration of the relationship of ethics to objectivity and subjectivity.

ETHICS – THE NARROW VIEW IN SOCIAL RESEARCH

Virtually all general textbooks on social research will contain a section on ethics and a few will additionally discuss the politics of research. However, for the most part, ethics is rather narrowly conceived as appropriate behaviour toward those who we are researching and is a model that has been appropriated, mostly, from psychology, and has become institutionalised in the forms and ethical procedures of universities and other research organisations. Researchers are asked to explain such things as how they will avoid harm to participants and how they will obtain informed consent etc.

But ethics goes far beyond this and is a branch of philosophy concerned with how we should live and how philosophers may study the various moral principles that have been adopted in different societies. It may be a study of meta principles, or it may be a study of particular forms of ethics, for example medical ethics. Indeed the ethical protocols I describe above might be taken as an 'ethics of social research', albeit a rather narrowly focussed one, but nevertheless an example of a particular set of moral rules for how we should behave towards those we research. However, implicit in these codes of practice are particular moral principles about how human beings should behave toward each other, for example that we should not, through our actions, cause physical or mental harm to others, or that researchers should not dupe those they research. These entirely laudable practices have arisen from the experience of past research, much of it in psychology, where researchers have not been deemed to have acted properly toward those whom they research (see e.g. the Zimbardo experiment: Haney et al. 1973; McLeod 2008). Yet the ethical principles could be otherwise, or other principles emphasised over these.

ETHICS AND SCIENCE

For reasons I discuss at various places in this volume, social *science* research might be treated as a subset of science, and its ethical issues are mostly those faced by scientists in general.

All societies are guided by moral principles that may be enshrined in laws or codes of practice, or may simply be informal or historical custom, although anthologists will point to practices and taboos that are common across many societies. However, for the most part these moral principles are normative prescriptions for living. In many societies, perhaps until the 20th century, they were grounded theist principles, such as those found in the Bible or the Quran. That, even within religions, these principles could conflict with each other was less important than their legitimation in application, as 'God's will'.

The scientific enlightenment, from the 16th century, increasingly legitimated scientific thought, as providing answers to metaphysical questions through its success in solving those of physics and providing workable technology (Williams 2000: ch. 1). The position of 'God' in philosophy was relegated to the gaps in the knowledge of science. This led to many philosophers, at least implicitly, considering whether there could be moral reasoning without a theist guarantee. Ethics began to change from an interpretation of 'God's will' to an investigation of what might constitute the 'good life'. This task remains an ongoing project in philosophy.

Two of the most famous approaches are those based on rights and duties and those based on the utility or consequences of actions. The former is principally associated with Kant's categorical imperative, usually expressed as 'Act only on that maxim which you can at the same time will to become a universal principle' (Körner 1955: ch. 6). This might be seen as a necessary, though not sufficient, starting point for a moral principle that you should only adopt or act on the principles everyone can accept. So many actions or advice might be grounded in circumstances: for example, we may express the imperative 'if you want to stay healthy you should eat plenty of fruit and vegetables', but this is not a moral imperative, whereas 'you should not tell lies' is, and its observance is not contingent upon circumstances but something to be observed under all circumstances. The divide between the two kinds of imperative is far from straightforward and since Kant there have been many attempts to derive ethics based on rights and duties, for example the work of John Rawls (1971) and Robert Nozick (1974).

Utilitarian ethics (associated with Jeremy Bentham, John Stuart Mill and G E Moore) conversely hold either a) in its consequentialist form, that the rightness of any action must judged by its consequences and the greater the good the better the action, or b) in its 'hedonistic' form, that the only thing that is good is happiness and an absence of pain. The emphasis in utilitarian ethics then, is on maximising the sum of goods in society.

The problem with both approaches to ethical reasoning, quite apart from their interpretation and implementation, is that they begin from reasoning that is either circular or leads to infinite regress. For example, Robert Nozick's philosophy begins from a respect for the personhood of the individual. This sounds like a good starting point, but possibly only for those of us who have been socialised in such a general principle in Western liberal societies. Other starting points are available!

The ascendance of scientific thinking in society led to a search for a meta-ethic that could be derived, not from how we thought the world ought to be, but from how the world is. Philosophers began to seek clarification of what can be meant by 'duty', 'rights' or 'virtue' (Smart 1984: 2), in effect a scientific investigation of ethics, with a view to producing a naturalistic 'meta-ethic'.

The problem with using scientific reasoning as a source of ethics, or the language of science to derive ethical principles, is that it is tautological with regard to the way science and scientists should behave. Thus if it is held that scientific practice must be ethical and the source of that ethic lies either in it being scientifically established as natural, or scientifically reasoned as deriving in some other way, then the ethic itself can only be validated by the science that is supposed to be ethical! Ethical decisions are about how humans should treat each other,[7] they are then recipes about how social life should be.

Quite apart from the evident risk of devolving ethical decision making to the scientists themselves, it ignores the fact that science itself is a social product and though its discoveries can transcend its social relations (Williams 2013), it exists in a set of social relations that are themselves different in time and place. For example, at the time of writing, the UK parliament is in the process of approving a technique called 'mitochondrial DNA replacement therapy' that can allow women who carry disease-causing mutations in their mitochondrial genes to give birth to genetically related children free of mitochondrial disease. In practice this involves the replacement of an egg's defective mitochondrial DNA with healthy DNA from a female donor, producing 'three-parent babies'. If approved, the UK would be the first country to permit such practices. A utilitarian argument in favour is that this will benefit many women who carry genes likely to lead to life-threatening disease in their offspring. However, as one can imagine, this is hugely controversial and its opponents are mostly against it on moral grounds, or that 'three-parent babies' are not 'natural'. Opposition is also on the unknown consequences, for future generations, of such genetic 'engineering', and with a new kind of hybrid imperative introduced, a concern about the 'herd' consequences of the science. This latter derives both from scientific doubt and a more generalised concern about societal consequences

In practice there is often a symbiosis between the ability of science to do things and moral principles outside of science, usually with moral principles, or the law, adapting to scientific ability, albeit with a time lag. Yet a meta-ethic, derived from scientific rationality, which can guide decisions beyond scientific ability still seems very far away and possibly not even desirable.

ETHICS AND SOCIAL RESEARCH

Social research, like the natural sciences, is investigative. Its practices and results, like those of natural science, have the ability to change society. If it is both the case that all ethical principles are normative and that social research (like science itself) is a social product, and indeed in its concerns and practices will be different in time and place, then a conclusion of

[7] Some ethicists extend the principle to animals or nature itself. See for example Singer (2009).

moral relativism would seem to follow (see **relativism**). But this conclusion would surely depend on social research existing in a society that was also morally relativist. Such a society has never existed and probably never will, so it follows that when we do social research we will be subject to some kind of social norms and moral imperatives. This is not simply in the narrow practice of research in the field, but the social and political context of the research itself.

Ethics is inextricably linked to issues of objectivity and subjectivity (see **objectivity – subjectivity**). Social research is never value free, but will be shaped by internal and external values. The latter are themselves grounded in (often implicit) moral values. The moral values of the society in which the research is conducted will shape the ethical basis of the research. It may do so through prescribing what a researcher may do or not do, or through the policy imperatives of funding. Alternatively, the research we conduct may be driven by, or produce results, that challenge the moral order. The very act of doing research at all is to commit to a value of investigation, and virtually all social research will be driven by commitments that go beyond mere inquisitiveness.

REFERENCES

Haney, C, Banks, W C and Zimbardo, P G (1973) 'A study of prisoners and guards in a simulated prison', *Naval Research Review*, 30: 4–17.

Körner, S (1955) *Kant*. Harmondsworth: Penguin.

McLeod, S A (2008) *Zimbardo – Stamford Prison Experiment*. Available at www.simplypsychology.org/zimbardo.html (accessed 11/1/16).

Nozick, R (1974) *Anarchy, State and Utopia*. Oxford: Blackwell.

Rawls, J (1971) *A Theory of Justice*. Oxford: Oxford University Press.

Singer. P (2009) *Animal Liberation: a new ethics for our treatment of animals*. 4th edn. New York: HarperCollins.

Smart, J (1984) *Ethics, Persuasion and Truth*. London: Routledge and Kegan Paul.

Williams, M (2000) *Science and Social Science: an introduction*. London: Routledge.

Williams, M (2013) 'Situated objectivity in sociology', in Letherby, G, Scott, J and Williams, M (eds), *Objectivity and Subjectivity in Social Research*. London: Sage.

KEY READINGS

Journal of Information, Communication and Ethics in Society, available at www.emeraldinsight.com/journal/jices (accessed 11/1/16).

Ransome, P (2012) *Ethics and Values in Social Research*. London: Palgrave.

Williams, M (2003) 'The ethics of social research', in Williams, M (ed.), *Making Sense of Social Research*. London: Sage.

KEY THINKERS

Immanuel Kant; John Stuart Mill; G E Moore; John Rawls

See also: *Epistemology; Objectivity – Subjectivity*

Experiments

Experiments were originally procedures, in the natural sciences, carried out in laboratories to test a hypothesis, usually in order to establish a cause–effect relationship. In the laboratory they depend on manipulation, but in the social world where they are carried out in open systems, they rely on randomisation, or in quasi-experiments which employ more informal controls.

The section begins with a description of the logic of experiments, their history and relative absence in the social sciences. Laboratory experiments in physics are contrasted with randomised control trials in open systems. Criticisms of experimental method in the social world are assessed against the possibility of experimentation that can help us accumulate knowledge of causal processes in complex mechanisms.

Experiments, or at least the logic of experiments, are at the heart of natural science and have been the method of choice in psychology for over a century. In the social sciences, the work of Donald Campbell was seminal in establishing the experiment as a legitimate research strategy in the evaluation of social and education programmes in the US (Cook and Campbell 1979). These were often large-scale social programmes in areas such as income maintenance, housing subsidies, prisoner rehabilitation programmes, educational performance and so on (Oakley 2000: ch. 9).

Yet historically, experiments have not played a major role in social science, where longitudinal, cross-sectional and case-study designs, using variants on the social survey and interpretive methods, have dominated. Indeed experiments have been much criticised. Yet through the much commoner strategy of the testing of statistical hypotheses (see **hypothesis**), one might say the logic of the experiment is preserved.

THE LOGIC OF EXPERIMENTS

The logic of experimental method is closely related to causal reasoning (and has come to mean a test of observations predicted by a theory (see **causality** and **theory**). Experiments seek causes. Their set-up is intended, if successful in its outcome, to show that A was the cause of B.

Laboratory experiments begin with a hypothesis derived from a body of theory, or law (see **generalisation and laws** and **explanation**). In the laboratory all extraneous influences are controlled for (or at least those that are known) and an operation is performed. The experiment is an active intervention by the scientist and not simply a passive observation of nature. The classic two-slit experiment in physics tested the hypothesis that light can behave both as a wave and as particles. A light, such as a laser, is shone through two parallel slits onto a thin plate and is captured on a screen behind. As the waves pass through the slits, they interfere with each other and produce dark and light bands on the screen (an effect that would not happen if light was composed of particles), but the absorption of the light as photons on the screen is that of particles. The experiment demonstrates the wave–particle duality of light and is a key observational feature of quantum theory. This account is a simplification, but demonstrates how the scientist must intervene to show how nature works. This relatively simple experiment also demonstrates that controlling for extraneous conditions (e.g. other light sources, the composition of the screen materials, the distance of the laser from the slits) is achievable in the laboratory.

In the human sciences, psychologists come closest to the classical laboratory model, or at least they attempt to emulate it as closely as possible. Psychologists are usually testing some theory of relatively identifiable mental processes, which can be isolated through specific experimental treatment. Extraneous 'noise' from other stimuli can be relatively easily controlled for, or statistically accounted for, through error terms (see **statistics**).

THE EXPERIMENT IN AN 'OPEN SYSTEM' AND RANDOMISATION

The social scientist rarely has such luxury and though some behavioural experiments that use game or role play (Güth et al. 1982; Evans and

Crocker 2013) can come close to such controlled conditions, these are inevitably at a micro level and can only seek relatively limited causal explanations of a narrow range of phenomenon, such as bargaining behaviour, or specific forms of rationality. If experiments are to be valuable more broadly in social science, they must be set up to provide adequate causal explanations in open systems.

The term 'open system' refers to an environment outside of the laboratory where extraneous effects are either unaccounted for or cannot be controlled (see **complexity**). Indeed this is the case even in some laboratory experiments, for example those in social psychology.

The alternative to the physical controls of the laboratory is that of randomisation and is the methodological principle underlying the open-system experiments that comprise clinical trials. In this the probabilistic selection of cases into either an experimental or control group is the substitute for physical manipulation. Let us assume a drug company has developed a pill to reduce cholesterol. After suitable trials (often with animals) to test its safety, a sample from a target population suffering from high cholesterol levels will be selected (there may be prior stratification by age, sex, body mass etc.). The sample is (say) 2000. One thousand will be randomly assigned to the experimental group and 1000 to the control group. The trials are usually conducted 'blind' with the subjects not knowing whether they are in the control or experimental group. Each will be administered a pill, under the same conditions, with same dosage and so on, but those in the control group will receive a placebo. At the end of the trial, the success of the treatment will be measured. The tests (in this case) might be the amount of blood cholesterol present before and after treatment. Rarely will a successful trial show a uniformly positive effect in the experimental group, and often a proportion of the control group will show positive results. However, a successful trial will demonstrate a difference that is statistically significant. This approach is called the randomised control trial (RCT for short).

The trials are conducted on people who go about their normal lives; they are unobserved and may well begin the trial with quite different circumstances. The experimenter will attempt to control for as many of these as possible, thus 'standardising' the treatment as much as possible, and will often introduce 'double blinding' whereby membership of the experimental or control group is unknown to the experimenter until after the fieldwork is completed. The experimenter will make certain assumptions about the controls in the experiment, but these assumptions are nearly always violated to some degree. In this example a number of things may happen to the subjects: those in the experimental group may forget to take their pill, they may change their diet and thereby increase or reduce cholesterol, there may be other health factors present and, of course, they may leave the study. Leaving the study causes 'attrition' in the sample and is a particular problem if those leaving have similar characteristics (e.g. a particular age group, or more men that leave than women).

But what of the control group? They too may exhibit raised or lowered cholesterol and for many of the same reasons. Therefore the experimenter needs to account for these kinds of random error in both groups, but in those trials where the treatment is only marginally positive, the amount of error may cancel out the effect, or indeed other things may conspire to show a greater positive effect than may be accounted for by the treatment.

The experiments of Campbell and his colleagues, in the US Headstart programmes, randomised participants into control and experimental groups and (for the period) used quite sophisticated modelling techniques (Cook and Campbell 1979). However, the results, though often valuable in informing knowledge of context and policies, were rarely unequivocal. This apparent failure has often been cited since as evidence of their lack of efficacy or precision. Yet these social experiments were often with small samples and posed more complex questions than more straightforward clinical trials.

In open systems, most confounding factors are psychological or social. One of the most important of these is the 'placebo effect', which refers to a psychologically-induced (usually positive) change in those in the control group who believe that the 'treatment', in fact a placebo, is having an effect on them. A famous variant of this, in a social setting, is known as the 'Hawthorne effect'. This refers to a series of productivity experiments conducted in the Hawthorne Plant of the Western Electric Company, in Chicago in the 1920s and 1930s (Adair 1984) and demonstrated that social effects over time were crucial factors in production and these often outweighed any physical changes in working conditions introduced by the experimenter.

EXPERIMENTS IN THE SOCIAL WORLD: INTERACTION, COMPLEXITY AND CAUSALITY

My 'cholesterol' example was a deliberately simple one. Even in clinical RCTs the violations of assumptions will produce unclear results, with one trial often indicating contrary outcomes to others. Increasing the numbers in the samples can produce clearer outcomes, but in more complex interventions the number of possible violations of assumptions can increase exponentially.

There are several arguments that challenge the effectiveness of controlled experiments in the social world.

That randomisation is rarely possible and 'blinding' even less so. The experiments are often about 'social effects' and although the unit of analysis may be an individual, the 'treatment' is often on a social group (e.g. pupils in a class). Blinding is all but impossible, because the membership of the experimental and control group is usually known by the members of each and/or those administering the treatment.

Randomisation notwithstanding, it is rarely possible to have a social group big enough to experiment on, because the bigger the group the greater the number of violations of assumptions.

Actually carrying out the experiment itself can often bring about unanticipated consequences. This goes beyond the Hawthorne effect and might actually be the treatment itself, say a teaching technique administered differently by individuals, the means of assessing the effect through a survey questionnaire, an interview, or observation. Interviewer effects, or differences in observation technique and so on, may skew the results in ways that cannot be known from the resulting data.

The social world is complex and within that complexity there are feedback mechanisms (see **complexity**). Over time small changes of conditions or behaviour can become big enough to change the set-up completely. A longitudinal experiment, such as that in the Hawthorne plants, could not anticipate the nature and scope of social change affecting the groups over time. Arguably, mass communications, new forms of sociability, effect even more rapid social change now than the early to mid-20th century. These changes are not received passively, but result in interactions which accelerate or dramatically change behaviour in the experimental or control groups. The sheer number of variables, which change over time, produce far too much 'noise' to demonstrate any observed effects from the treatment.

Realists would argue (see **realism**) that outcomes observed can be explained by mechanisms, themselves often complex and changing, but more importantly only operating in particular ways under particular conditions (see e.g. Pawson 2013: ch. 4). Thus, cause–effect relationships, even when occurring 'naturally', do not arise *ex nilhio* and their explanation requires a knowledge of the mechanism. Realists do not always oppose experimentation outright, but a 'crucial experiment' that would provide closure on a hypothesis would require the manipulation of a particular mechanism, hardly ever straightforwardly achieved in the laboratory and less so in an open system.

Ann Oakley (2000: 233) notes that critics have often (in small sample research) confused no evidence of effect with evidence of no effect, wrongly inferring the latter from the former. Knowledge from experimental manipulations can 'cumulate' and over time a systematic review of many experiments may eventually provide evidence for a hypothesis. Even in relatively small sample research, repeated experiments on broadly similar populations may begin to show clearer results, but if a mechanism is hypothesised, then additional experiments to test the other assumptions of the mechanism will be required. Experiments and even RCTs are beginning to attract followers and funders in the UK, at least, and given the caveats above can be a useful addition to the methodological toolkit (see e.g. work conducted at the UK DECIPHer centre: http://decipher.uk.net/).

Myself and colleagues recently conducted a quasi experiment (no randomisation was possible) (Williams et al. 2015) to test whether student attitudes and performance in quantitative research methods 'improved' after a specific curriculum intervention. There was, on some measures, improvement in the experimental group, but on others performance/attitudes was more negative than the control group. A complex mechanism of ambivalence, self-selection and fear of number, amongst UK undergraduates, has been clearly articulated (see e.g. papers in Payne and Williams, 2011 or Platt 2012), but we only tested with one specific treatment. A further strategy would be to repeat the experiment with undergraduate students in other universities, but also to conduct additional research to test other assumptions of the mechanism. The other research may be experiments, although it may be survey or qualitative work.

Experiments in open systems need a broader theory of causality that combines statistical results with narratives, then attempts to make testable *moderatum* generalisations about mechanisms and effects, which allow us to 'close in' on an adequate causal explanation.

REFERENCES

Adair, J (1984) 'The Hawthorne effect: a reconsideration of the methodological artefact', *Journal of Applied Psychology*, 69 (2): 334–345.

Cook, T and Campbell, D (1979) *Quasi Experimentation: design and analysis issues for field settings.* Chicago, IL: Rand McNally.

Evans, R J and Crocker, H (2013) 'The Imitation Game as a method for exploring knowledge(s) of chronic illness', *Methodological Innovations Online*, 8 (1): 34–52.
Güth, W, Schmittberger, R and Schwarze, B (1982) 'An experimental analysis of ultimatum bargaining', *Journal of Economic Behavior & Organization*, 3 (4): 367–388.
Oakley, A (2000) *Experiments in Knowing: gender and method in the social sciences*. Cambridge: Polity.
Pawson, R (2013) *The Science of Evaluation*. London: Sage.
Payne, G and Williams, M (eds) (2011) *Teaching Quantitative Methods*. London: Sage.
Platt, J (2012) 'Making them count: how effective has official encouragement of quantitative methods been in British sociology?', *Current Sociology*, 60 (5): 690–704.
Williams, M, Sloan, L, Cheung. S-Y, Sutton, C, Stevens, S and Runham, L (2015) 'Can't count or won't count? Embedding quantitative methods in substantive sociology curricula: a quasi-experiment', *Sociology*, doi: 10.1177/0038038515587652.

KEY READINGS

Campbell, D and Stanley, J (1966) *Experimental and Quasi Experimental Designs for Research*. Boston, MA: Houghton Mifflin.
Cook, T and Campbell, D (1979) *Quasi Experimentation: design and analysis issues for field settings*. Chicago, IL: Rand McNally.
Oakley, A (2000) *Experiments in Knowing: gender and method in the social sciences*. Cambridge: Polity.
Pawson, R (2013) *The Science of Evaluation*. London: Sage.

KEY THINKERS

Donald Campbell; Carl Hempel; Ann Oakley; Ray Pawson

See also: *Causality; Complexity; Explanation; Generalisation and Laws; Hypothesis(es); Realism*

Explanation

An explanation is an answer to a 'why' question. In everyday life it can be informally satisfied by a good enough answer, but in science (and social research) an explanation should tell us why something happened within the context of a theory, or possibly a law. Causal explanation is central to social research, but in the form it has often taken may not exhaust what can be meant by an explanation.

Explanation is at the heart of science. This section begins from explanation as an answer to 'why questions' in everyday life and then considers their more formal role in laws, in particular, Hempel's 'deductive nominological' (DN) approach to explanation and the problems this presents. The role of causal explanation in social science is considered, alongside its realist alternative. Finally the section examines the relationship of understanding to explanation

An explanation is the answer to a 'why' question. Why is men's pay higher than women's pay? Why do people exhibit altruistic behaviour? Why are there differentials in educational achievement between ethnic groups? Why has crime fallen? The quality of our social research is ultimately reflected in the quality of our explanations.

Philosophers refer to an explanation as involving an *explanandum* (that which must be explained) and an *explanans* (a statement, or set of statements) satisfying the former. In the social sciences explanation has become all but synonymous with causal explanation, but the identification of a cause–effect relationship may not satisfy what might be considered an adequate explanation. There is a second kind of explanation in social science, that of 'understanding' or *verstehen* (see **interpretation and meaning**) that many would regard as being something quite separate to explanation, but possibly that is because the form of explanation that has dominated social science, either explicitly or implicitly, for many decades was that which emerged from logical positivism.

SCIENCE, EXPLANATION AND LAWS

Logical positivism revered natural science and its project was to bring philosophy in line with the former. Yet it projected a somewhat simplistic epistemology of science that was to be later fatally challenged by other philosophies of science from people such as Polanyi, Popper, Kuhn, Lakatos and Feyerabend (see **positivism**). A key feature of this was its concept of explanation, articulated by Carl Hempel (1965). This is referred to as the deductive nominological (DN) or 'covering law' model. In this the *explanandum* is deduced from a set of true statements, the *explanans*, of which at least one should be a law. Thus the rate of cooling of an object can be deduced from the known properties of that object, but in relation to the second law of thermodynamics. This model works very well in the relatively simple instances where reference can be made to fundamental physical laws (see **generalisation and laws**). The logical positivists were well aware that, even in the physical world, this is hard to achieve, so for them it was as much a goal as a prescription.

Even before we consider the applicability of this model to the social world, there are some general objections to the model itself (Van Bouwel and Weber 2011).

- *Accidental generalisations*: Wesley Salmon (1989: 15) illustrates this problem with two logically equivalent statements:

    - No gold sphere has a mass greater than 100,000 kg
    - No enriched uranium sphere has a mass greater than 100,000 kg

  The first statement is true by virtue of the fact that no one has yet produced such a sphere, though this would be physically possible, but the second is true because the critical mass for uranium is just a few kilos. The second is an expression of a law of nature, but the first is just a contingent fact. The problem is that it is often difficult to determine the difference in an empirical investigation.
- *Irrelevant premises*: Similarly in any explanation of an empirical phenomenon it is not always (at least initially) possible to tell which premises are relevant to the explanation. If your computer suddenly freezes, there is in principle an explanation, but the freezing may be due to a complex array of software and/or hardware problems. It is unlikely to be a simple causal explanation, but involve an interaction of several things. But in your diagnosis, how do you know which, if any of these things, was irrelevant?
- *Asymmetry*: The problem here is that the logical form of the explanation can be reversed substituting the *explanans* for the *explanadum*. Hempel was aware of this (Van Bouwel and Weber 2011: 635), but did not see it as a problem, because an empirical understanding of the explanation would show that it was symmetrical. A fair point, but nevertheless a positivist concession to the need for interpretive judgement.

These three problems together do produce difficulties for the DN model. Sandra Mitchell (2000) suggests that the key matter lies in seeing a dichotomy between laws and contingency. Rather we should see these as a continuum, with some things more contingent than others. As long as they perform an explanatory function, thus they hold under a range of conditions, then they can be called laws. This is not so very different to the practical stance that social scientists take in relation to generalisations that can be made within a particular time or place, but are not universal (see **generalisation and laws**).

EXPLANATION IN SOCIAL SCIENCE

Hempel's model was (and to some extent, through variations on Mitchell's prescription, still is) important in social science. But the elephant in the room (acknowledged by Hempel) is the difficulty in finding the law-like statements. For a long time this remained a goal for many, but it was an easy target for those social scientists persuaded by the post positivist critiques of Kuhn, Feyerabend and others (Outhwaite 1987: 8–18) and opened the door to a more thoroughgoing relativist critique of the possibility of explanation in the social world that emanated from linguistic philosophy (see **language**). To this day there remains a divide between those who cling on to a modified version of the DN model through various forms of causal analysis and those who reject explanation in favour of non-epistemologically privileged descriptions of performative or linguistic phenomena.

Historical explanation or explanation of institutions at a macro level are more complicated and there is a 'third way' in empirical social science, in realism. I will turn to these presently, but first there are two questions to address:

- *Is explanation a tenable goal in social science?* If it is agreed that a goal of science is to explain phenomena and it is also agreed that there is a science of the social, then explanation must be part of the latter as it is the former. But to explain what? Description and understanding of micro level phenomena is indispensable, but does not exhaust what society wants of social science – that is an explanation of the social: that is large or medium sized institutions or phenomena, either contemporary or historic. Its possibility rests upon its success in offering good enough explanations under given circumstances. The counterfactual being, if this was not achieved then social science would have withered for lack of success (and crucially funding!) a long time ago (see Williams 1998 for a further discussion of this claim).

- *Is causal analysis good enough?* Causal analysis is a particular (though important) activity in social science, especially in sociology, but is worth alighting on because it exposes the limits of DN type explanation. Causal analysis (see **causality**) uses variants of the generalised linear model to produce probabilistic causal models, which aim to explain a dependent variable through its relationship to a number of independent variables. One or more of the latter may be placeholders for a 'law', that is, a known regularity under given circumstances. Suppose that in location A, young Afro-Caribbean boys experience educational under achievement and this is said to be explained by variables v1, v2, v3 acting in concert. This hypothesis may be tested by repeating the research in location B, to see if v1, v2, v3 still have the same explanatory (in a statistical sense) power. The aim is to try to find out whether educational under achievement is 'caused' by one or more of these variables. Assuming that the model holds in several places, then the cause might be said to be established. So far, so good and effective enough then to formulate policy to tackle the problem.
  However, strictly speaking, all we have established is that v1, v2 and v3 are present when there is educational under achievement in Afro-Caribbean boys. In fact, most of the time the models are messier than this, partly because in different circumstances variables will explain (again statistically) differing amounts of the variance in the models and quite often there are slightly different arrays of independent variables. Certainly the first two general problems with the DN model: accidental generalisations and irrelevant premises may be present, but more fundamentally the causal explanation on offer does not get at *why* the particular array of variables are co-present (or not). Causal analysis merely describes the statistical relationship of regularities, possibly a necessary but not sufficient condition for full explanation.

It is my lot in life to be a frequent traveller on trains in the UK, where lateness is a more or less constant state of affairs. Frequently a reason given for a late train is 'earlier delays', which though probably correct is as annoying as it sounds because it does not explain very much. Suppose that (say) the earlier delays were the result of signal failure. This is better, we have a causal explanation. But signal failure, broken trains, points failure are very common everyday occurrences and between them explain the great many late trains. But... this not an explanation even so, because neighbouring countries, such as France and Germany, do not suffer from so many late trains, that need to be explained by the aforementioned circumstances. So what I am getting at is that an explanation needs to show why it is that similar phenomena behave differently under different circumstances. Causal analysis (importantly) can show you that they do, but not why.

WEBS OF MEANING AND REALISM

Two philosophers, Pierre Duhem at the beginning of the 20th century and Willard Van Ormen Quine in the middle, independently advanced a radical view of theories, and therefore explanation, that challenged the way explanation was seen. They proposed, *contra* the standard view in empiricism, that scientific statements cannot be tested in isolation in a direct confrontation with experience, but rather their meaning comes from a complex web of metaphors, models and theories in which they are located (Outhwaite 1987: 15). Thinking about my train example above (Outhwaite also deploys a late train example!), one can see that the lower level explanations for late trains makes no sense, unless it is explained within a much more complex set of socio-economic and historical circumstances. Quine's perspective led him to a view that embraced indeterminacy of any statement on its own and consequently a somewhat defeatist, or at least unworkable, model of science.

Nevertheless, it does not take much imagination to see that historical explanation, at the very least, requires a more holistic approach (Watkins 1994), but not to privilege any particular element(s) in an explanatory 'web' is to end up producing mere descriptions of events and the very least falling prey to the problem of irrelevant premises.

Realist explanation (see **realism**) begins from a metaphysical premise that there are real things in the world that act independently of our knowledge of them. That they 'act' thus implies causal processes that make a difference. One formulation, due to Roy Bhaskar (2008: 56), is that there are three separate domains:

- The real, consisting of processes, entities and mechanisms.
- The actual – events.
- The empirical – the way we experience the world.

A realist explanation aims to identify processes, entities and mechanisms by proposing theories which, if true, would show them to be real. This would count as an adequate explanation. However, realism is a fallible doctrine and such explanations are to be sought, and although possibly partially realised, will never be final or complete.

There are three things to be said about the realist model of explanation.

First, and this is becoming increasingly the case (Byrne 1998), realism has embraced complexity and contingency in the social world (see **complexity** and **probability**). A mechanism can only be identified within a changing context, which in itself changes the mechanism. Mechanisms are not fixed entities but dynamic and exhibiting only partial invariance (see **mechanisms and models**). They evolve in a non-linear way and can be subject to relatively rapid change (though some mechanisms are relatively enduring). There is, then, in realist explanation, a much greater reliance on ontology (effectively absent in the DN model).

Second (and because of the above), the realist model is a 'good enough' model of explanation. This is exemplified in Ray Pawson's (2013) view of a key goal of evaluation research, to establish what works, for whom, in what circumstances?

Third, and an anathema to positivists, realists introduce 'non observables' into explanation. That is, explanations will inevitably have a content in statements that purport to explain X, that go beyond the observational evidence of X. This is a most terrible sin in positivism, yet is both the actual and inevitable state of reasoning in science. Though it must be said that some areas of theoretical physics, evolutionary psychology and grand theory in social science are pretty much observational evidence-free zones, which in my view is the opposite but equally sinful practice as that of reifying observation!

UNDERSTANDING

The relationship between explanation and understanding is not much discussed in the social sciences. This may be partly due to the schism between scientific and humanist approaches to social knowledge, but also philosophy of science, post-Hempel (and excluding later versions of realism) relegated understanding to a subjective realm that had little place in science. This is unsatisfactory because explanation, at least in the DN form, represents a set of logical relationships that in turn stand in for the empirical characteristics of the world. Understanding goes further than this and might be thought of as a cognitive relationship to those characteristics. That is, the researcher moves beyond an assessment of formal or observed relationships to grasp underlying unobserved relationships or meanings. Thought of in this way, understanding can be seen as a subjective stage prior to explanation that allows us to consider what might constitute a good explanation of a phenomenon (Williams 2015), and once explanations are presented to us, be able to adjudicate between them. In the latter sense we might even think of understanding as a 'meta' form of explanation, but one that cannot be captured sufficiently in a formal model of explanation. This is perhaps exemplified in Harry Collins' (1985) argument that tacit forms of knowledge play a key role in the practice of science.

Something like the above was proposed by the linguistic philosopher Paul Ricoeur, who distinguished between a text as a free-standing artefact, without author or context, that may be explained in terms of its internal relations, or we can treat it as recorded speech, which may be interpreted (Blaikie 2007: 155–156). Ricoeur was not necessarily thinking of scientific explanation but of 'texts' in general, nevertheless taken as a metaphor for the relationship between formally expressed relationships (linguistic or statistical) in social research it is a useful metaphor (see **language**).

In social research practice, perhaps the relationship between explanation and understanding is a symbiotic one, where understanding clarifies explanation, but explanations call for understanding to provide adequacy? Though the relationship may be at different stages and take different forms, this would be the case in both qualitative and quantitative research. Understanding may not be a necessary nor sufficient condition for an explanation, yet understanding plays an important role in framing an explanation and adjudicating on explanations provided.

REFERENCES

Bhaskar, R (2008) *A Realist Theory of Science*, 2nd edn. London: Routledge.

Blaikie, N (2007) *Approaches to Social Enquiry*, 2nd edn. Cambridge: Polity.

Byrne, D (1998) *Complexity Theory and the Social Sciences: an introduction*. London: Routledge.

Collins, H (1985) *Changing Order: replication and induction in scientific practice*. Chicago, IL: University of Chicago Press.

Hempel, C (1965) *Aspects of Scientific Explanation and other Essays in the Philosophy of Science*. New York: Free Press.

Mitchell, S (2000) 'Dimensions of scientific law', *Philosophy of Science*, 67: 242–265.

Outhwaite, W (1987) *New Philosophies of Social Science: realism, hermeneutics and critical theory*. New York: St Martin's Press.
Pawson, R (2013) *The Science of Evaluation: a realist manifesto*. London: Sage.
Salmon, W (1989) *Causality and Explanation*. Oxford: Oxford University Press.
Van Bouwel, J and Weber, E (2011) 'Explanation in the social sciences', in Jarvie, I and Zamora-Bonilla, J (eds), *The Sage Handbook of the Philosophy of the Social Sciences*. Thousand Oaks, CA: Sage. pp. 632–646.
Watkins, J (1994) 'Historical explanation in the social sciences', in Martin, M and McIntyre, L (eds), *Readings in the Philosophy of Social Science*. Cambridge, MA: MIT Press.
Williams, M (1998) 'The social world as knowable' in May, T and Williams, M (eds) *Knowing the Social World*. Buckingham: Open University Press.
Williams, M (2015) 'Situated objectivity, values and realism', *European Journal of Social Theory*, 18 (1): 76–92.

KEY READINGS

Outhwaite, W (1987) *New Philosophies of Social Science: Realism, Hermeneutics and Critical Theory*. New York: St.Martin's Press.
Van Bouwel, J and Weber, E (2011) 'Explanation in the Social Sciences' in Jarvie, I and Zamora-Bonilla, J (eds) *The Sage Handbook of the Philosophy of the Social Sciences*. Thousand Oaks, CA: Sage. 632–646.

KEY THINKERS

Roy Bhaskar; Carl Hempel; Wesley Salmon

See also: *Causality; Generalisation and Laws; Interpretation and Meaning; Language; Realism*

Falsification

In natural and social science, theories are corroborated by empirical evidence, but this is an inductive process that can never wholly confirm the correctness of a theory. Karl Popper proposed instead that good science involves rigorous attempts to falsify theories. A good scientific theory is one that is capable of being falsified.

Karl Popper considered falsification as an answer to the problem of induction and whilst this claim had logical force, in its simplest form it was seen as naïve and unworkable. Here I begin with a brief description of Popper's falsification and then go on to discuss some key problems a simple or 'naïve' version of falsification presents. The section then goes on to examine the possibility of a more sophisticated version. However, in social science, the probabilistic nature of social data presents further challenges, but we can perhaps conclude that a principle of falsification may nevertheless be retained, despite these difficulties.

Falsification is mainly associated with Karl Popper and his followers, but was advanced by him as a methodological solution to the problem of induction, first identified by David Hume in the 18th century. 'Hume's Problem' (see **induction**) was that although we frequently make inductive assumptions about other times and other places, there are no grounds upon which this is valid. If we claim that all Xs have Y characteristics, it takes only one X not to possess Y characteristics to show such a claim to be wrong, however many prior instances of Xs that were Ys we had found before. In everyday life when we act on informal inductive reasoning ('it won't rain today, because the wind is in the wrong direction'); the consequences are mostly trivial, but can we do science on this basis?

Karl Popper thought not, and his early experiences as a student in Vienna, where Marxists and psychoanalysts each claimed to be 'scientific', led him to a critical attitude toward claims to be scientific. According to him, Marxists and psychoanalysts would marshal all the evidence they could find (sometimes contradictory) to prove their cause was right (Chalmers 1999: 64). Was there any possible evidence that could be put to them that they would agree proved them wrong? Popper believed not, their stance was an uncritical inductivism. He heard Albert Einstein speak in Vienna and was impressed with the latter's critical attitude, to seek to replace a scientific theory with a better one (Popper 1986: 38) and thus sought to devise a demarcation criterion that would divide science from non-science.

Ever since the time of Francis Bacon (1561–1626) the natural sciences had depended on corroboration through repeated observation and this, according to Popper, could not set them aside from non-science. Though by the time Popper was seeking a new approach, the logical positivists had devised the hypothetico-deductive model (see **hypothesis**) which introduced an element of deduction. I will return to this below. Popper believed science should be a critical and fallible enterprise, not a corroborative one. He believed that scientific theories could only ever be proven wrong (falsified) and never proven right (Popper 1959). Until they are falsified, all scientific theories are therefore conjectures. He advocated that scientists should propose theories that can be empirically tested and that science should use the most rigorous tests available to them to attempt to falsify the theory proposed. The more testable content a theory has, the better the theory because it has more components that can be falsified.

Popper, never falsely modest (he also claimed to have killed off logical positivism and resolved major interpretation problems in quantum physics), maintained that he had solved the problem of induction. And on the face of it, it seemed he had. He had replaced an inductive statement about the way the world is (all Xs are Ys) with a deductive one (see **logic and truth**) at least one X is not a Y). But it was not quite that simple and whilst the principle of falsification attracted many adherents, it was also very controversial – not the least because very little science, even that which had yielded the great discoveries of the 19th and early 20th century, was falsificationist. It followed, according to Popper's criterion, that very little science was therefore scientific!

In some ways Popper's work was more influential in opening a wide-ranging debate in philosophy of science (and later social science) about the status of our knowledge claims and helped to shape the epistemological agenda in science for the next 30 years. (Elements of this debate are evident in this book, but also see e.g. Couvalis 1997; Newton-Smith 1981; O'Hear 1995). However, here we must assess the value of the principle of falsification to social science.

PROBLEMS OF FALSIFICATION

The key problem of falsification (in both natural and social science) is that it depends on a single observation to refute a theory, when we cannot know a priori whether elements of the theory were specified incorrectly, or whether the observation itself was problematic: for example, a classic middle-range sociological theory, that of 'reference group theory' (Stouffer 1949). It specifies that the actual conditions experienced by a group will be less important to their feelings of well-being than a comparison with other groups. Samuel Stouffer's finding that this was the case in the US army has been confirmed in many other settings, but its value to organisation theory remains controversial because there have been clear exceptions and in most cases people belong to different groups at the same time and will use different comparators. Should one abandon what has, nevertheless, been a useful theory because it has been 'refuted', or should one attempt to modify it?

In social science practice this is precisely what has happened and has been the norm for most theoretical advances in social research and indeed in the natural sciences. Researchers do not simply abandon theories because of anomalous findings, though this does lead to issues of knowing when to quit! To what extent is it legitimate to try to 'save' a theory? Popper himself was clear on this matter. Theories should be specified as precisely as possible. For example, instances of reference group theory may specify particular organisational settings and the qualification to be a 'reference group'. Indeed in Stouffer's original research this was particular US army units, and consequently there were direct comparators. When a theory is falsified by an observation, a modification may be introduced, but this too must be testable (Chalmers 1999: 75–77). In the natural and social sciences, researches quite often do just this, but equally untestable theories are retained for long periods. A recent example exists in quantum theory, where a modification to quantum field theory predicted the existence of an elementary particle called the 'Higgs boson', which if discovered would have enormous explanatory power and has sometimes been called the 'God particle' (see e.g. Morris 2002: ch. 6). This was proposed in 1964 by Peter Higgs (and others) but remained elusive. Arguably this elusiveness has been due to scientists not having sophisticated equipment equal to the task of discovery. In July 2012, scientists at the Large Hadron Collider, near Geneva, announced that they found a particle with many of the predicted properties. The Large Hadron Collider is one of the most expensive scientific projects ever, as have been other similar ones engaged in the same search. Physicists were long convinced of the existence of such a particle, but for many years held on to this theoretical conviction in the absence of empirical evidence and the 'falsification' of many earlier attempts to find it. Yet holding on to this theory clearly offends the spirit of falsification, but equally if the particle discovered does turn out to match that predicted by Higgs, this discovery cannot be 'undone' by falsification.

RETAINING FALSIFICATION

Philosophers and historians of natural science (see e.g. Newton-Smith 1981) have attempted to account for scientific progress and discovery. Many do not rule out falsification, but see it as one element in scientific method. Falsification, as a principle, is retained but alongside corroboration. Degrees of falsifiability or corroboration can be expressed probabilistically, and some scientists use Bayesian statistics to establish the level of 'trust' we can have in a theory (Howson and Urbach 1989). Bayesian statistics depend on the modification, through further evidence, of initial 'prior' probabilities (see **probability**). Imre Lakatos (1970) proposed a sophisticated model of falsification, which he termed 'research programmes'. He proposed that theories are exposed to varying degrees of modification, but this takes place over a longer period. In this model a 'hard core' of theory is retained over long periods and is mostly not challenged, but taken as a given for the development of auxiliary theories. These latter are tested, some will be falsified, some corroborated and some modified. When a great many of these are falsified, then the hard core of theory is under threat. Research programmes are assessed on the basis of how productive they are. As long as they continue to make new predictions and these hold up under test, the programmes will be retained and are deemed progressive, but if they are not empirically successful, they will be gradually abandoned by scientists.

Research programmes may be a good historical model for social science, though unlike the natural sciences where there are numerous examples of abandoned programmes, in social science their abandonment is rarely total and rarely permanent. One could, for example, cite Marxism as being falsified in a number of respects: the absence of 'proletarianisation' in capitalist societies as a result capital concentration, revolutions occurred in peasant societies, not advanced industrial ones and where socialism had been (more or less) established, its failure to develop toward communism. Whilst Marxism is much less influential in social science and may be thought of as an 'abandoned programme', this is not wholly the case and some elements, such as its materialism, have been retained in other research programmes, for example critical realism (see **realism**).

FALSIFICATION AND PROBABILITY IN SOCIAL SCIENCE

One of the difficulties for falsification that is a particular feature of social science is that the social world is inherently complex (see **complexity**) and probabilistic, and many of the methods of social research are themselves probabilistic. The ontological problem is that most testable conditions are subject to change over time and place, made more difficult by the existence of feedback mechanisms. For example our knowledge of social class mobility or identity will be dependent upon our being able to measure social class. Yet its measurement has necessarily changed over time as a result of fundamental changes in occupational structure (Payne et al. 1996) and those structures can differ in important respects, even between neighbouring countries. That in itself does not mean that theories of class cannot be falsified, but the conditions specified must take into account such variability.

Social science methods, particularly the survey method, rely on probabilistic estimates about a population that are derived from sample data. Theoretical predictions are rarely wholly corroborated or falsified, more usually results will specify the probability or percentage agreement with the proposition. One may theorise, for example, that 'British people are in favour of legalising cannabis, but survey results may show that only 25 per cent or 1 in 4 people are in favour (and likely a proportion who have no opinion)'. Has the proposition been falsified? On the face of it, yes, because a clear majority were against its legalisation, but these things change and it is perfectly possible to imagine that the numbers in favour of legalisation could increase over time and the falsification would no longer hold. It is hard to think of an analogue of this in the physical world, except perhaps in some complex biological systems.

At this point one may wonder about the relevance or value of falsification at all, especially for social researchers. In my view it is of value in two important respects. First, any 'science' must show how over time its theories can advance and adapt, creating new knowledge. In the natural sciences this has clearly been the case (see Williams 2000: ch. 1), where whatever we may feel about scientific knowledge and its uses, we know a lot more now than we did 200 years ago. Scientific 'progress', the accretion of knowledge, requires error and somehow and somewhere theories have been falsified for this to happen. Perhaps 'progress' in social science has been less clear, more halting, but most would agree we know more now about the social world than we did in (say) the 19th century. Again, this has required that some theories have been falsified empirically, at least in so far that they are no longer in the mainstream of social research, even though they may retain a few adherents.

The second respect in which a falsification principle is valuable is as a personal (or possibly professional) principle that theories in social research should be testable, and the greater the degree of testability specified, the more scientific the theory is. Perhaps somewhat controversially, one might therefore propose that a social science demarcation criterion exists between such theories (sometimes referred to as 'middle range' theories after Merton 1968) and the 'grand' theories of Bauman, Beck, Giddens or Foucault, which claim to tell us much about social life, but nothing about how their theories could be shown to be wrong, or right (or even probably right!).

REFERENCES

Chalmers, A (1999) *What is This Thing Called Science?*, 3rd edn. Buckingham: Open University Press.

Couvalis, G (1997) *The Philosophy of Science: science and objectivity*. London: Sage.

Howson, C and Urbach, P (1989) *Scientific Reasoning: the Bayesian approach*. La Salle, IL: Open Court.

Lakatos, I (1970) 'Falsification and the methodology of scientific research programmes', in Lakatos, I and Musgrave, A (eds), *Criticism and the Growth of Knowledge*. Cambridge: Cambridge University Press.

Merton, R (1968 [1957]) *Social Theory and Social Structure*. New York: Free Press.

Morris, R (2002) *The Big Questions: probing the promise and limits of science*. New York: Henry Holt.

Newton-Smith, W (1981) *The Rationality of Science*. London: Routledge and Kegan Paul.

O'Hear, A (ed.) (1995) *Karl Popper: philosophy and problems*. Cambridge: Cambridge University Press.

Payne, G, Payne, J and Hyde, M (1996) *Refuse of All Classes? Social indicators and social deprivation*. London: Sage.

Popper, K R (1959) *The Logic of Scientific Discovery*. London: Routledge.

Popper, K R (1986) *Unended Quest: an intellectual autobiography*. London: Fontana.

Stouffer, S (1949) *The American Soldier*. Princeton, NJ: Princeton University Press.

Williams, M (2000) *Science and Social Science: an introduction*. London: Routledge.

KEY READINGS

Couvalis, G (1997) *The Philosophy of Science: science and objectivity*. London: Sage.

Popper, K. (1979) *Objective Knowledge: an evolutionary approach*, 2nd edn. Oxford: Oxford University Press.

Williams, M and May, T (1996) *Introduction to Philosophy of Social Research*. London: Routledge.

KEY THINKERS

Karl Popper; Imre Lakatos

See also: *Complexity; Hypothesis(es); Induction; Probability; Rationality; Realism*

Feminism

Feminism is a wide-ranging social movement that seeks to identify and correct gender imbalances, patriarchal practice and thinking in the political, economic, cultural and social spheres.

> *The section is principally concerned with the development of feminist philosophy in science and social science and its effects on social research. Some key principles in the analysis of patriarchy are outlined and the two main approaches to feminist epistemology, feminist empiricism and standpoint epistemology are described. The final part of the section is critical discussion of the influence of feminist philosophical thinking on social research.*

Feminism takes many forms and emphases, such as liberal feminism, radical feminism and socialist feminism (Walters 2005). Feminist thinkers have analysed the forms of social relations and philosophical assumptions that create the imbalances in these spheres of life, both empirically and philosophically. This entry is concerned with the contribution feminism has made to philosophy, especially those areas of philosophy (particularly epistemology and philosophy of science) that have a bearing upon social research. To a great extent feminist philosophies of social science are a subset of those of philosophies of science, because each depends both on an analysis of the relations of knowledge production, but also ways of knowing and being that have come about and are sustained by those relations.

SCIENCE, MASCULINITY AND WAYS OF KNOWING

From the 1970s to the present, but especially in the 1980s and early 1990s, there was a sustained and detailed feminist critique of the foundations of knowledge, in Western society, that had great relevance for the natural and social sciences. It began with fundamental questions about ways of thinking, knowing and being that had become culturally 'naturalised', that is, they were seen to be the way the world is (and should be), rather than being socially produced. Feminists showed that in society hitherto gender behaviour, social relations and outcomes were assumed to arise from biological difference and not social relations.

Feminists began to examine the lived experiences of women, and feminist philosophers sought to show how naturalised ways of thinking and being were often unknowingly masculine, in for example language. In everyday life gender-neutral roles or characteristics were masculinised (e.g. 'chairman', 'manhole', 'mankind'), or in social status that was derived from a relationship to a man (before marriage 'Miss', after marriage 'Mrs'). The patriarchal nature of language, it was argued, is much more than cosmetic, but can lead to actual oppression. For example, what we now know as sexual harassment has perhaps always existed, but it was not 'named', and only by being named could women recognise and combat it (see **language**). This critique extended to other areas of activity, including science and social science.

The traditional characterisations of women as emotional, subjective, illogical and men as rational, cultured, objective, logical were not only discriminators in the division of labour between women as 'housewives' and mothers and men as 'breadwinners' and workers, but also permeated the activities that women and men engaged in (Sydie 1987). Science, in particular, was for much of its history a male activity, that feminists argued was conducted to serve male interests (notably military technology), but also was masculine in the way it was done . Many feminists argued that the ideals or goals of science: objectivity, explanation and prediction also arose from a masculine way of conceiving the world. The term 'androcentric' was used to describe this process (Gilman 1911). The argument was not simply that science was male and was done in a male way, because by the 1980s many women had entered and been successful in science. The gendering of science was achieved through language and ways of knowing that were adopted by both men and women (Scheman 1996: 27–28). Science, it was argued by many feminists, was masculine. And because scientific thinking and method had, to a large degree, been imported into social science, this critique was equally relevant to the latter.

FEMINIST EPISTEMOLOGY

Much early feminist epistemology was not taken seriously by the philosophical community (which, of course, in a sense reinforced the original feminist critique). Indeed Norman Blaikie describes feminist epistemology as an uneasy relationship between feminism and philosophy of science (Blaikie 2007: 166). However, in recent years, much of the feminist critique of science has influenced the mainstream of philosophy of science, though arguably the earlier critiques of Kuhn and Feyerabend (see **positivism** and **social constructionism**) had prepared the way for a post-positivist reconstruction of the philosophy of science.

Although some feminist thinkers have sought to reject all science and scientific thinking as masculine, most have engaged in specific critiques and proposed alternative epistemologies for science. Two of the most influential of these are 'feminist empiricism' and 'feminist standpoint epistemology'.

Feminist empiricism, far from rejecting scientific method as irredeemably masculine, maintains that the masculine bias is a result of science not living up to its own methodological ideals. Therefore, if scientists adhered to the rules of scientific method and practice in the formulation of problems and concepts, in theory choice, methods and the interpretation of results, then the gender bias would be eliminated. Taken at face value, this presents difficulties because such an approach recognises only the internal values of science, but the feminist critique of science is that these values are themselves social values that are a product of an androcentric culture in science.

A sophisticated variant of feminist empiricism was proposed by Helen Longino (1990). Whilst she defends the role of the internal values of science, what she calls 'constitutive values', she also maintains that science is shaped by external social values, what she terms 'contextual'. Empiricism had long rejected the legitimacy of such values entering science, but Longino maintains that not only do they enter science, it is also necessary that they do. Like others before her, notably Karl Popper, she sees science as a community enterprise. What counts as objective science, in terms of priorities or methods, will be determined by that community. In examples from biology, Longino works through what this would mean in terms of theory choice (1990: 134–161). Given two theories, with equal empirical evidence, which should the scientist choose? Longino's answer is pragmatist in tone (see **pragmatism**). One should choose the theory with the best outcome for the community of interest – in her case, women. There are specific criticisms of this aspect of her work in theory choice, but these are not specifically feminist, or aimed at her feminism. However, there is a more general criticism of the community of science as an arbiter of what is good science – that it abrogates the notion of 'truth' to social process (Couvalis 1997; Williams 2006) and leaves no room for the 'deviant' voice, who may actually be the bearer of the truth of the matter.

Feminist standpoint theory, or at least standpoints, have a long history in the work of Marx and Mannheim, and before that in Hegel (Scott 2013). It has become associated with Dorothy Smith, Nancy Hartsock and particularly Sandra Harding (1986). Like so many arguments, it is complex and nuanced, but begins from the widely-held feminist position that knowledge is socially situated, that what we know and its limits, are those of our social location. It is then argued that those in positions of power in society are unable to fully understand that society because they are unable to critique the dominant beliefs. Conversely, those who are dominated or oppressed (as with Marx's proletariat) can come to have a better understanding of society and its problems. A key question is, would the problematics of science be the same if they were formulated by the dominated – in this case women? It is not hard to think of examples of what science might look like if it were shaped by the concerns of women and not men, and feminists have provided plenty of examples, particularly in healthcare and childbirth (see, e.g. the work of Barbara Katz-Rothman 2000; and Gayle Letherby 2002).

However, there are many criticisms from within and outside of feminism. First, would all of the problematics of science be different, or just some, and on what basis would they be selected? How would this impact upon scientific method? We already know that method itself is not immune from social influence (see **statistics**), but what would be the basis of methodological choice? A criticism from within feminism has been the definition and boundaries of a standpoint. Most obviously the biological category of 'woman' is insufficient, because the experience of being a women is itself socially differentiated. Possibly all women are oppressed by patriarchy, but this oppression is not the same in time and place and it would be stretching a point to a slogan to say all women are equally oppressed. The solution is perhaps to conceive of different standpoints that can reflect such differentiated experience, but how are these to be defined or known?

Harding herself has never answered these criticisms in detail and the difficulty in specifying the nature of a standpoint may be one of the reasons for this approach now being fairly moribund. Nevertheless the standpoint critique, if not the solution, holds and the idea that knowledge is socially situated, as indeed is objectivity, and has influenced and changed mainstream philosophy of science (Williams 2006). There are, for example, very few defenders of 'value freedom', as conceived by 'traditional' empiricism. Science itself has not always changed as a result of feminist critique, but feminist critique has equipped philosophy of science better to itself understand and critique the practice of science.

Nevertheless a key contradiction lies at the heart of feminist epistemology and it is implicit in the above. It has also been articulated by Susan Hekman (1997) and summarised by Norman Blaikie (2007). Feminism is a political project that maintains that particular forms of social relations produce particular forms of knowledge, hence its critique of patriarchy for producing forms of practice and knowledge that oppress women. Yet feminist epistemologies, particularly empiricist and standpoint ones, aim to produce better and truer accounts of the world. But these too must be socially situated and subject to the same scrutiny as patriarchal ones. Feminism is torn between the relativism implied by its critique of truth and method and the need for epistemological authority.

FEMINISM, SOCIAL SCIENCE AND METHOD

The influence of feminism on social science and its methods has been enormous. Indeed in most social sciences (with the possible exception of economics and political science) women are in the majority as students and faculty, and feminist approaches now often define the nature of the research question, its methods and the interpretation of results.

Feminism has influenced methods in three principal ways. The first, I would say, has been beneficial to social science, the second has had a somewhat mixed effect, but the third has been damaging both to social research and specifically feminist social research.

The culture of social science, even in qualitative methods, up until the 1960s and 1970s, was underpinned by the claim by social scientists of epistemological authority. Respondents, often called 'subjects', were seen as simply people to be studied, much as one would study a chemical reaction, and research was seen as value free – indeed objectivity and value freedom were synonymous (Williams 2006). The post-positivist revolution of the 1970s onwards, greatly influenced by feminism, brought subjectivity back in. No longer were people just objects of enquiry, but people who had views, ideas and experiences that could not simply be channelled through the narrow lens of 'value free' social science. This led to a revolution in qualitative methods and a questioning of the epistemological and ideological authority of the researcher. Feminists showed that the researcher brought her own experiences, views and knowledge to the research. A methodological acknowledgement of these and indeed more – a searching one's consciousness to acknowledge one's own subjectivity – became methodologically crucial. This, in turn, led to the widespread adoption of 'reflexivity' as methodological virtue in research (Bourdieu and Waquant, 1992).

The second influence, somewhat related to the first, has been the critique of objectivity. As I have shown, the work of those such as Longino, Harding and Hartsock has demonstrated that the ideal of value freedom is misplaced and is a performative contradiction (see **objectivity – subjectivity**). Thus any reworking of objectivity has to take into account the social context of the research. It is never 'neutral'. This had led to some fruitful debates, which although beginning in feminism have extended generally to philosophy of science and social science (see Kincaid et al. 2007; Letherby et al. 2013). However, some feminists have rejected any possibility of objectivity (particularly those influenced by postmodernism,; see Hekman 1997) *tout court* and have maintained that feminist research is grounded in the researcher's own subjectivity and it is consequently only possible to tell 'stories' of those researched through the 'story' of the researcher. Whilst bringing the subjective and the intersubjective 'back in' is surely a good and necessary thing, it is insufficient to provide epistemological authority to social research and to generate useable data that might bring about social change (Barwell 1994).

The third influence arises out of the above positions. Though several feminist methodologists have maintained and indeed carefully argued that 'feminist research' does not prescribe any particular methodological approach (see Ramazangolu and Holland 2002; Letherby 2003), nevertheless many feminists have prioritised qualitative methods and either ignored or rejected altogether the utility (or indeed morality) of using quantitative methods. A champion of this approach, and in particular the use of the in-depth interview, was Anne Oakley. In-depth interviews were seen as non-hierarchical and non-exploitative and able to get at the experiences of the interviewee in a way that provides more valid data than quantitative methods. The latter, in contrast, were seen as superficial and their problematics, instruments and analyses essentially patriarchal in character (Oakley 1981). Many feminists saw them as reflecting the 'logocentrism' of science (the fetishisation of number and logic) over experience. Feminism became part of a more general anti-positivist critique of social science that equated quantitative methods with (a somewhat caricatured version of) positivism (see **positivism**).

Many feminists now acknowledge that these critiques and the rejection of 'science' and quantitative methods were damaging to the cause of women, because qualitative methods alone could not provide data on inequalities and stratification necessary for a feminist critique of power, the position of women and minorities. Somewhat ironically Anne Oakley, in her later work (2000), was in the vanguard of feminists, arguing that quantitative methods had an important role to play in feminism, and has become an advocate for the use of experimental method in social science (see **experiments**).

REFERENCES

Barwell, I (1994) 'Toward a defence of objectivity', in Lennon, K and Whitford, M (eds), *Knowing the Difference: feminist perspectives in epistemology*. London: Routledge.

Blaikie, N (2007) *Approaches to Social Enquiry*, 2nd edn. Cambridge: Polity.

Bourdieu, P and Waquant, L (1992) *An Invitation to Reflexive Sociology*. Cambridge: Cambridge University Press.

Couvalis, G (1997) *The Philosophy of Science: science and objectivity*. London: Sage.

Gilman, C (1911) *The Man-Made World, or Our Androcentric Culture*. New York: Charlton.

Harding, S (1986) *The Science Question in Feminism*. Milton Keynes: Open University Press.

Hekman, S (1997) 'Truth and method: feminist standpoint theory revisited', *Signs: Journal of Women in Culture and Society*, 22 (2): 341–365.

Katz-Rothman, B (2000) *Recreating Motherhood*. New Brunswick: Rutgers University Press.

Kincaid, H, Dupré, J and Wylie, A (eds) (2007) *Value-Free Science? Ideals and illusions.* Oxford: Oxford University Press.

Letherby, G (2002) 'Challenging dominant discourses: identity, change and the experience of "infertility" and "involuntary childlessness"', *Journal of Gender Studies*, 11 (3): 227–288.

Letherby, G (2003) *Feminist Research in Theory and Practice*. Buckingham: Open University Press.

Letherby, G, Scott, J and Williams, M (2013) *Objectivity and Subjectivity in Social Research*. London: Sage.

Longino, H (1990) *Science as Social Knowledge: values and objectivity in scientific enquiry*. Princeton, NJ: Princeton University Press.

Oakley, A (1981) 'Interviewing women: a contradiction in terms', in Roberts, H (ed.), *Doing Feminist Research*. London: Routledge and Kegan Paul. pp. 30–61.

Oakley, A (2000) *Experiments in Knowing: gender and method in the social sciences*. Cambridge: Polity.

Ramazanoglu, C and Holland, J (2002) *Feminist Methodology: challenges and choices*. London: Sage.

Scheman, N (1996) 'Feeling our way toward moral objectivity', in May, L, Friedman, M and Clark, A (eds), *Mind and Morals: essays on ethics and cognitive science*. Boston, MA: MIT Press.

Scott, J (2013) 'Relationism and dynamic synthesis', in Letherby, G, Scott, J and Williams, M (eds), *Objectivity and Subjectivity in Social Research*. London: Sage.

Sydie, R (1987) *Natural Women, Cultured Men: a feminist perspective on sociological theory*. Milton Keynes: Open University.

Walters, M (2005) *Feminism: a very short introduction*. Oxford: Oxford University Press.

Williams, M (2006) 'Can scientists be objective?', *Social Epistemology*, 20 (2): 163–180.

KEY READINGS

Lennon, K and Whitford, M (eds) (1994) *Knowing the Difference: feminist perspectives in epistemology*. London: Routledge.

Letherby, G (2003) *Feminist Research in Theory and Practice*. Buckingham: Open University Press.

KEY THINKERS

Sandra Harding; Donna Harraway; Nancy Hartsock; Susan Hekman; Helen Longino; Dorothy Smith

See also: *Language; Objectivity – Subjectivity; Positivism; Pragmatism; Social Constructionism; Statistics*

Functionalism

Functionalism is a theoretical approach mostly associated with anthropology and sociology and is based on the claim that stable social phenomena fulfil a social function.

Functionalism first became prominent in the early 20th century, particularly in anthropology, though it can be traced back to ancient Greek philosophy. Here, its development in classical anthropology is described and particularly Malinowski's biological argument for societal reproduction. It goes on to discuss functionalism in sociology and the work of its major advocate, Talcott Parsons, who united functional explanation with a theory of action. Two key criticisms of functionalism are then explored; that it cannot explain conflict and that it is teleological form of explanation. Finally 'strong' and 'weak' functionalism and the empirical consequences of functionalism are discussed.

Functional explanations of the social world are ancient and can be traced back to Plato and in more recent centuries to an argument of Leibnitz that all the evils of the world have beneficial consequences for the larger pattern that justify and explain them. In social science, functional explanation has come in different forms and 'strengths', but in broad terms it is the argument that the parts of society work to maintain others and produce social phenomena at a higher, or macro level. Functionalism has less explicit followers than it once had and arguments for and against it are less prominent than they were in the 20th century. These were often associated with arguments for or against holism or individualism (see **individualism and holism**). Whether or not functionalist arguments are sustainable or not, they probably have renewed relevance in light of the development of complexity approaches and the empirical investigation of feedback loops in, for example, new social media such as Twitter (see **complexity**).

20TH-CENTURY FUNCTIONALISM IN ANTHROPOLOGY AND SOCIOLOGY

Anthony King (2011) identifies two main trends in functional thinking in the 20th century. The older of these was a British anthropological tradition, associated with Bronislaw Malinowski and Alfred Radcliffe-Brown. Malinowski's social functionalism arose from a fairly simple biological functionalism, in which he maintained that food, shelter and procreation are both primary and necessary for society to be reproduced. In the Western Pacific societies he studied, many of these were linked with ritual and custom. His argument then extended to claim that societies needed to fulfil certain functions in order to sustain and reproduce itself. For example, his analysis of the myths of the Trobriand islanders were not irrational fantasies, but rather they functioned as 'sociological charters, justifying the social hierarchy and therefore inducing stability' (King 2011: 430). Later work, by Meyer Fortes (1969), claimed that kinship could be seen as a collective resource to justify familial strategies, rather than a representation of real relationships. Most of these anthropological studies used relatively simple and isolated societies as 'laboratory models', for more generalising arguments about societies. These were, in the Durkheim's sense, models of mechanical solidarity and may not work so well in more complex societies based on 'organic' solidarity (Durkheim 1972).

The second and perhaps more theoretically sophisticated trend was associated with Talcott Parsons (Parsons and Shils 1951) and later, though in a much modified form, with Robert Merton (Merton 1968). Parsons was a student of Malinowski, so although there were later departures in his work, the two trends are not entirely separate. As Anthony King observes, Parsons' argument rests on a very strong logical point (King 2011: 422), that if we assume rational individuals are not themselves determined by objective factors (that would render them not independent or autonomous), then their choices and actions must be random and social order becomes inexplicable. Parsons' argument, at its core, is that individuals co-ordinate their actions because they are committed to common ends and means. This, according to Parsons, does not mean they lack autonomy, because their actions and choices are based upon understandings. Parsons, then, combines functionalist explanation with a more Weberian voluntarist approach. Agents are conscious, active participants in action, but are constrained by collective normative obligations.

Merton's work built on that of Parsons, but was also a radical departure because of his emphasis on empirical work and the operationalisation of theory (see **theory**). A key feature of his functionalism was to distinguish between manifest functions, which produce consequences, of which agents who participated in their creation are aware, and latent function, which are unintended consequences and which may not be beneficial to agents' aims or intended social outcomes. Merton's functionalism, though 'weaker' than that of Parsons, was nevertheless intended to be operationalisable at an empirical level.

AGAINST FUNCTIONALISM

The arguments against functional explanation are many and varied and I can only touch upon a few of them here; indeed functionalism itself is varied and sometimes inconsistent. The latter point is strongly made by Ernest Nagel, when he identifies six different uses of the term 'function' in everyday use, biology and the social sciences (Nagel 1979: 522–525). This inconsistency is important in identifying in a deeper and more analytic way how the term is being used in an argument. Nevertheless, the core of functionalism is that parts, specifically human action, serves to create or maintain social order or structure, and the varied use of the term is not central to arguments for and against functionalism.

Two of the more popular arguments of the 1960s or 1970s were that functionalism fails to account for conflict or deviance, or that it is teleological in its form.

The first of these can be countered by functionalists who could claim that conflict or deviance serves to reinforce normative behaviour and thus conflict or deviance can be said to serve social structure; indeed Durkheim held that the existence of criminal behaviour demonstrated the flexibility of the *conscience collective*. Such an argument is hard to prove or disprove without reference to empirical evidence, which was rarely presented. What is perhaps key, however, is how widely one should draw the societal parameters that are disrupted or reinforced (depending on your position). For example deviance, through bad pupil behaviour, can lead to a school closure. Thus, if the social structure comprised the school, then conflict or deviance won out. But in a wider social policy context, such a closure, might help to reinforce or create educational priorities. A criticism of Parsons was that his functionalism was simply a normative description of social relations in the mid-20th century US. Within such parameters, it is perhaps relatively easy to 'save' functionalism by claiming internal conflict or deviance served to uphold the social order. Rather ironically Parsonian functionalism was criticised on political grounds, in that its articulation was itself a defence of a particular social order and contributed to its existence (Gouldner 1971: 253–254).

A teleological explanation is a process that is explained by the end state to which it contributes, or the end state is itself explained by the function it performs for other parts of a society. Whilst it is considered acceptable that individuals and groups of individuals may pursue known ends, through purposive action, to claim that societies as a whole, independently of individuals, move toward such ends is considered illegitimate because it suggests a purpose to entities, which in themselves cannot have purpose, other than individual or group goal-directed behaviour. It proposes, then, a 'ghost in the machine'.

How the problem of teleology is countered depends on whether one subscribes to a 'strong' or 'weak' version of functionalism. Elster describes these variants, as in the first case the functionalism of Malinowski:

> All social phenomena have beneficial consequences (intended or unintended, recognised or unrecognised) that explain them.

And in the second case, the functionalism of Merton:

> Whenever social phenomena have consequences that are beneficial, unintended or unrecognised, they can also be explained by these consequences. (Elster 1994: 404)

Elster himself raises a simple objection to strong or weak functionalism by the analogy that the breaking of eggs does not contribute to the flavour of the omelette. This is a particularly apposite analogy because but for the breaking of the eggs the omelette would not be made. Is it that functionalists are claiming a direct relationship between phenomena and the consequences, or can the causal chain be indirect or multiple (see **causality**)? Indeed the claim is more subtle and rests on the existence of feedback in a social system. A custom or an outcome may arise accidentally, or it may have originally been intended, but then it comes to be something else for that society. Many countries have constitutional monarchs and quite a few of these monarchies arose as a result of a person (or group of people) violently seizing power. But as time goes on the monarchy takes on a different function as a guarantor of a particular set of constitutional arrangements that may be represented through rituals, such as the state opening of parliament in the UK. Such arrangements exist in a complex web of meaning and action (and indeed quite possibly feedback loops), through time, that sustains them.

This simple example and Malinowski's conclusions about Trobriand rituals suffer from what is a key problem for Elster: that the feedback mechanisms are asserted or implied, rather than empirically demonstrated. This is a fair criticism and I will return to it below.

WEAK AND WEAKER FUNCTIONALISM

Let us return to Parsons' opening argument, that something must be going on for individuals to act in concert to reproduce society, rather than just acting randomly. We can concede that individuals act purposefully and mostly rationally (see **rationality**), but not all of their actions have intended consequences and not all of those consequences contribute to what becomes manifest, though like the breaking of the eggs, there may be an indirect contribution to the outcome. The outcome we see is just one of many possible outcomes. For example, an analysis of millions of Tweets will show that a huge proportion get few, or no re-tweets. But some will not only lead to thousands of re-tweets, but potentially create, sustain or threaten social phenomena. As social scientists we mostly pay attention to what did happen, rather than what did not. Some phenomena are created and sustained by complex causal processes that depend on feedback. A weak functional explanation for these as having social utility for enough people seems perfectly legitimate, but they do not wholly explain social processes (in this case even within the domain of new social media).

A red herring in many of these discussions (and a basis of the political criticism of Parsons), is that functional explanation refers to beneficial consequences, but if we substituted beneficial for utility, then the net of functional type explanation may be drawn wider. A civil war, on most accounts, would be seen as dysfunctional for a society if stability and harmony were seen as the beneficial outcomes. Yet for a war to be sustained suggests a utility for that condition, that itself depends on complex causal and feedback mechanisms. On both sides there is usually a desire to win, but at least for a period this goal is frustrated by the outcome of the continuation of violence, a state which perhaps neither side wishes, but nevertheless produces an ugly equilibrium.

Jon Elster's criticism of the assertion of the existence of feedback mechanisms was made in 1994 and he conceded that in at least a couple of examples that function can be established, but in the 20 years since the data revolution allows us to follow naturally occurring phenomena in real times, particularly through new social media such as Twitter feeds and Facebook. Feedback loops and the consequences of these can be shown because researchers have thousands, or even millions of data points (Burnap et al. 2014). Weak forms of functional explanation seem empirically tenable, but an account of what a valid functional explanation should look like was proposed by Arthur Stinchcombe (1968) and summarised by Elster in the above mentioned paper as:

> An institution or a behavioural pattern X is explained by its function Y for a group Z if and only if:
>
> 1. Y is an effect of X.
> 2. Y is beneficial for Z (I would prefer the term 'has utility' for Z).
> 3. Y is unintended by the actors producing X.
> 4. Y – or at least the causal relationship between X and Y – is unrecognised by the actors in Z.
> 5. Y maintains X by a causal feedback loop passing through Z.

It is perhaps this weakest form of functionalism that can now be empirically demonstrated through new social media.

REFERENCES

Burnap, P, Williams, M L, Sloan, L, Rana, O, Housley, W, Edwards, A, Knight, V, Procter, R and Voss, A (2014), 'Tweeting the terror: modelling the social media reaction to the Woolwich terrorist attack', *Social Network Analysis and Mining*, 4: 1.

Durkheim, E (1972) 'Forms of Social Solidarity', in Giddens, A (ed.), *Emile Durkheim: selected writings*. Cambridge: Cambridge University Press.

Elster, J (1994) 'Functional explanation in social science', in Martin, M and McIntyre, L (eds), *Readings in the Philosophy of Social Science*. Cambridge, MA: MIT Press.

Fortes, M (1969) *Kinship and the Social Order: the legacy of Lewis Henry Morgan*. Chicago, IL: Aldine.

Gouldner, A (1971) *The Coming Crisis of Western Sociology*. London: Heinemann.

King, A (2011) 'Functionalism and structuralism', in Jarvie, I and Zamora-Bonilla, J (eds), *The Sage Handbook of the Philosophy of the Social Sciences*. Thousand Oaks, CA: Sage. pp. 429–446.

Merton, R. (1968) *Social Theory and Social Structure*. New York: Free Press.

Nagel, E (1979) *The Structure of Science: problems in the logic of scientific explanation*. Indianapolis, IN: Hackett.

Parsons, T and Shils, E A (eds) (1951) *Toward a General Theory of Action*. New York: Harper & Row.
Stinchcombe, A (1968) *Constructing Social Theories*. New York: Harcourt Brace.

KEY READINGS

Holmwood, J (2005) 'Functionalism and its critics', in Harrington, A, (ed.), *Modern Social Theory: an introduction*. Oxford: Oxford University Press. pp. 87–109.
King, A (2011) 'Functionalism and structuralism', in Jarvie, I and Zamora-Bonilla, J (eds), *The Sage Handbook of the Philosophy of the Social Sciences*. Thousand Oaks, CA: Sage. pp. 429–446.
Nagel, E (1979) *The Structure of Science: problems in the logic of scientific explanation*. Indianapolis, IN: Hackett. ch.14.

KEY THINKERS

Alfred Radciffe-Brown; Jon Elster; Bronislaw Malinowski; Robert Merton; Talcott Parsons

See also: *Causality; Complexity; Individualism and Holism; Rationality*

Generalisation and Laws

Generalisation in social research is the practice of inferring characteristics from particular instances to other places and times, whereas laws aim to make general propositions that will always hold across specified domains.

Laws play a fundamental role in natural science and here their role and limits and their relationship to theories is considered. Many have questioned whether there are laws in the social world, but nevertheless social research relies on its ability to generalise. The section, then, explores the possibility of social science laws, but also the possibility and limits of generalisation in quantitative and qualitative research.

Laws and theories have the same logical relationship of descriptions to phenomena. Both claim to describe relationships between variables that will hold under specific circumstances. It is a matter of historical accident that in the natural sciences some things are described as 'laws' (gravity, thermodynamics) and some as 'theories' (relativity, evolution) when the scope of the relationships they describe is rather similar. Laws and theories (see **theory**) are generalisations, but in the social sciences there are only a few named laws, though generalisation is all but universal. Claims to the existence of laws in the social sciences are controversial and the laws that are said to exist are rather different to what are called laws in natural science.

WHAT IS A LAW?

Many statements and phenomena are called 'laws' and they have different epistemological connotations. Some are descriptions of regularities, such as the 'law of large numbers' (see **statistics**), some express invariant relationships between things in nature, and some only statistical relationships within given domains. For our purposes (and excluding mathematical laws), there are two main kinds of empirical laws, which for shorthand I will term 'invariant' and 'variant', and two different ways of thinking about them: that they are manifestations of nature, or they are simply expressions of how we experience the world.

It has been said that there are no loopholes in the laws of nature, but like criminal laws their scope is a function of their specification. Some laws seem to brook no exceptions and are based upon deterministic properties of the world, for example gravity. Whilst wind and air pressure may change the rate of fall of an object, such as a leaf, ultimately it must fall. Similarly, the second law of thermodynamics specifies that heat cannot flow from cold regions to hot regions without external work being performed, such as that by a refrigerator. These might be termed 'invariant laws'.

All laws will allow local variation (wind, pressure, intervention etc.), but some will be based on statistical regularities. An 'ideal gas' is a hypothetical statistical description of properties, but a 'real' gas will deviate somewhat from these, and there is no such thing as an ideal gas in nature, just approximations. Other kinds of laws operate *ceteris paribus*: that is, they allow exceptions (which should be stated), or they are simply generic approximations. Most of these kinds of laws are found outside of physics, particularly in economics, such as the law of diminishing marginal utility. This states that, other things beings equal, the additional benefit which a person derives from a given increase of his or her stock of a thing diminishes with every increase in the stock that he or she already has, but this may not happen. Many exceptions are known, but we don't know if they are all known. These we might term 'variant laws', though the ways in which they vary can be very different.

In scientific method the principle of the 'covering law' – mostly associated with Carl Hempel, though initially formulated by John Stuart Mill (Hedstrom 2005: 15) – is an important principal that expresses the deductive relationship between a law and some particular phenomenon. For example, a pipe which bursts in freezing conditions can be explained by the general property of water to expand as it freezes. Similarly, if we find a new phenomena, we can say whether or not it is 'covered' by a particular law because that law will state that it should have certain properties. The covering law model works well with invariant laws and quite well with statistical laws, but it is problematic with *ceteris paribus* laws because we cannot know whether an empirical finding is a warranted exception, or evidence against the law.

Some philosophers of science are sceptical about whether laws are really manifestations of nature, or just ideal models that may approximate to nature, or are possibly chimerical and phenomena must be described by deeper descriptions. As Rom Harré (2000: 214) notes, much of what we call laws are based on the observation of messy regularities, that they describe a more perfect world than that with which we are acquainted. At first sight, then, the concept of a scientific law looks straightforward, but on closer examination it is complex and controversial.

WHAT IS A GENERALISATION?

Generalisations, on the other hand, are unavoidable inductive statements (see **induction**) that specify the continuation or existence of phenomena observed in one place or time to another place or time. In survey research it might include generalisation from samples to populations, or in social science more broadly theoretical generalisations about social trends.

Informal generalisations are ubiquitous and in everyday life have a practical utility we cannot do without. However, most of the time, in our everyday lives errors in our inductive generalisations are unimportant and can be corrected, but in science we need to put them on a firmer footing. The information content of a generalising statement will be determined by what it is possible to say and the level of certainty we require. For example, what engineers might say of tolerances in bridge construction will have huge implications and needs to be accurate, whereas in political polling we can tolerate some error (see **statistics**). Also, in the physical world statistical generalisations can be more accurate because often they are within closed, or mostly closed, systems and depend only on a finite and usually measurable number of variables. In the social world the number of variables we could potentially measure are almost infinite and when we measure only a few we are capable of only capturing a representation of a small part of reality (and of course this assumes the variables themselves have been validly operationalised). Indeed sometimes statistical measurement is neither possible nor desirable, and generalisation must depend on a more loosely specified set of initial conditions.

We can identify three main kinds of generalisation (Williams 2000: 219):

- *Total generalisations*: where situation *S´* is identical to *S* in every detail. Thus *S´* is not a copy of *S* but an instance of a general deterministic law that governs *S* also, though as we have seen even deterministic laws will encompass some local variance.
- *Statistical generalisations*: where we infer from sample to population, or from an experimental set up to a specified population. This is the commonest form of social science generalisation.
- *Moderatum generalisations*: where aspects of *S* can be seen to be instances of a broader recognisable set of features. This is the form of generalisation made in interpretive research, either knowingly or unknowingly. I will return to this below.

LAWS IN SOCIAL SCIENCE

Social science laws have been something of a holy grail for a long time, partly because the predominant model of science has been a positivist one that aimed to produce covering laws. Economists have had some success with laws that would satisfy Hempel's model (law of supply, law of costs, law of returns, law of supply and demand), but they are usually of the *ceteris paribus* kind (see **explanation**). In politics, Duverger's Law is sometimes cited. This asserts that election systems tend to favour a two-party system (termed the 'plurality rule'); however, it is very much a *ceteris paribus* law in that there are many exceptions which themselves have relatively stable characteristics (Riker 1982). The problem for social science laws is that if they are widely generalisable then their explanatory value is poor, but if we try to increase their explanatory value by applying them to varied circumstances we encounter the *ceteris paribus* problem. Nevertheless the possibility of social science laws has had its defenders outside of economics.

In the 1960s defenders of 'scientific' social science mostly believed that the discovery of laws that could have widespread explanatory power was really just a matter of improving our theorising or methods. Hans Zetterberg (1962: 13–14) cites the work of Berelson and Steiner, where they identified 1045 propositions that were candidates for laws. For example:

> Prolonged unemployment typically leads to a deterioration of personality: passivity, apathy, anomie, listlessness, dissociation, lack of interest and caring.
>
> Television viewing by children is heaviest among the duller and emotionally insecure.
>
> People prejudiced against one ethnic groups tend to be prejudiced against others.

Of the 1045, Zetterberg believed he had identified 5 to 50 of them that 'are general enough to qualify as laws, depending on how strict we make our criteria' (1962: 14).

More recently, the sociologist Harold Kincaid, drawing on the work of Jeffery Paige on agrarian political behaviour, has shown that large-scale cross-national generalisations can be made and testable hypotheses derived, even though *ceteris paribus* clauses are incorporated (Kincaid 1996: 58–100).

The problem lies in Zetterberg's qualifying statement about strictness. The examples I cite (and all that he gives), at least, are simply generalisations about behaviour in mid-20th century industrial societies – in most cases, simply the USA. It would be rather like physicists proposing 'laws' that only operate in our solar system! Moreover, in each case these are descriptive inductive statements that explain nothing.

The debate about laws in social science is less fierce than it was and most social scientists are catholic on the matter, allowing that laws may be possible, but in practice are indistinguishable from wide-ranging generalisations (see Mitchel 2000). Furthermore, the aim would be to produce better generalisations with a greater information content. Realists (see **realism**) begin from a somewhat different starting point, preferring to locate generalising claims within explanatory mechanisms. In this view laws and confirmed generalisations simply reflect observed regularities and do not tell us much about underlying causes.

GENERALISATION IN QUALITATIVE RESEARCH

Whilst there is a large literature on generalisation in quantitative research (sometimes expressed as 'generalisability'), there is little mention of generalisation in qualitative research, partly because it has followed a different agenda of inquiry based on interpretation, rather than explanation (see **interpretation and meaning**). However, generalisation inevitably takes place, often implicit and sometimes denied (Denzin 1983). Any kind of research would be pointless unless it said, however informally, that we have found X here and all things being equal, we would expect to find X under similar circumstances elsewhere. For example, we might research how manual workers deal with 'dirt' (say in a garage) (Dant and Bowles 2003), and it should be possible to hypothesise that strategies and practices in other garages or similar occupations would yield similar behaviour and meanings. Generalisation in qualitative research is certainly possible (Payne and Williams 2005), but the claims made will be relatively informal and should be testable either through quantitative methods or through other qualitative research in other places.

REFERENCES

Dant, T and Bowles, D (2003) 'Dealing with dirt: servicing and repairing cars', *Sociological Research Online*, 8 (2).

Denzin, N (1983) 'Interpretive interactionism', in Morgan, G (ed.), *Beyond Method: strategies for social research*. Bevereley Hills, CA: Sage.

Harré, R (2000) 'Laws of Nature', in Newton-Smith, W (ed.), *A Companion to the Philosophy of Science*. Oxford: Blackwell.

Hedstrom, P (2005) *Dissecting the Social: on the principles of analytic sociology*. Cambridge: Cambridge University Press.

Kincaid, H (1996) *Philosophical Foundations of the Social Sciences: analyzing controversies in social research*. Cambridge: Cambridge University Press.

Mitchell, S (2000) 'Dimensions of scientific law', *Philosophy of Science*, 67: 242–265.

Payne, G and Williams, M (2005) 'Generalisation in qualitative research', *Sociology*, 39 (2): 295–314.

Riker, W (1982) 'The two-party system and Duverger's law: an essay on the history of political science', *American Political Science Review*, 76: 753–766.
Williams, M (2000) 'Interpretivism and generalisation', *Sociology*, 34 (2): 209–224.
Zetterberg, H (1962) *On Theory and Verification in Sociology*, 3rd edn. New York: Bedminister Press.

KEY READINGS

Beed, C and Beed, C (2000) 'Is the case for social science laws strengthening?', *Journal for the Theory of Social Behaviour*, 30 (2): 131–153.
Payne, G and Williams, M (2005) 'Generalisation in qualitative research', *Sociology*, 39 (2): 295–314.
Turner, R (1953) 'The quest for universals in sociological research', *American Sociological Review*, 18 (6): 604–11.

KEY THINKERS

Carl Hempel; Rom Harré; Peter Hedstrom; Harold Kincaid

See also: *Idealism; Induction; Interpretation and Meaning; Realism; Statistics; Theory*

Hypothesis(es)

The term 'hypothesis' is used in two main ways in social research. First, as a propositional statement, that if a set of conditions P hold, then Q will come about. Second, though following the same logical form, it is used to test for the statistical significance of data.

Theories and hypotheses are closely related in science. The section begins by describing the relationship of hypotheses to theories through the hypothetico deductive model and their role in explanation more generally. The role of hypotheses in social science is discussed and how we might 'infer to bet explanation'. Finally I discuss statistical hypotheses and their limitations.

Hypotheses are a concept that lies at the heart of scientific method and (in this book) connect with many other concepts.

An hypothesis is a deductive statement, of much the same kind as a theory (see **theory**), though usually it is much more specific and testable. Despite the insistence of Karl Popper that theories should be capable of being falsified (see **falsification**), rarely is whole body of theory overturned by a particular finding. Such an occurrence is rare in the natural sciences and more so in social science. However, an individual research hypothesis (sometimes referred to as the 'research question(s)') is capable of being overturned by evidence, and a statistical hypothesis actually sets a specific criterion (the 'null hypothesis') for falsification.

A natural science model of the hypothesis is one in which the specific statement embodied in the hypothesis H is, if confirmed, an instance of a covering law (Hempel 1965). Covering laws are found mostly in physics and chemistry, for example gravity or thermodynamics (see **explanation**). These laws hold in all known circumstances and their local exceptions are known to the scientist. A proposed hypothesis, when tested, must produce results that are consistent with its covering law. If, when tested through experiment, it produces findings that strictly contradict a hypothesis, then it is rejected. However, in most cases findings are less categorical. This is the case in much of modern physics and chemistry and certainly in biology, or the social sciences, such categorical results are rare. Indeed in the social sciences laws of any kind are few and some say non-existent (see **generalisation and laws**), so when a statistical hypothesis is tested its finding (confirmed or falsified) is in relation to a more local explanation of a phenomenon.

The 'covering law' model is an idealisation, mostly honoured in its breach, but nevertheless common as an explanatory framework (see **explanation**). Likewise, another related concept is that of the hypothetico-deductive (HD) model of science. The model represents the course of discovery and justification and may have its starting point in any of its phases. First, it is an acceptance that hypotheses cannot be simply derived from observation (because observation is contextual – see **observation**) and must arise out of an existing theory. Second, the hypothesis must be conjoined with the initial conditions that exist at the time. By this it is meant all of those things in the environment that may have an effect on the hypothesis, or subsequent observations. Third, from the hypothesis and initial conditions a prediction is made which can be tested by observation. Whether, or to what extent, an empirical result will confirm or falsify a theory is very controversial (see **falsification**), but as a rough guide as to how scientific investigation proceeds – at least over the longer term it has some merit. In some sciences the HD model of science is not at all a regulatory ideal because crucial experiments are not possible. Sciences such as cosmology or geology instead search for consistency and patterns which are not simply random, and from this deduce explanations. The increasing importance of 'big data' to social science is likely to signal a shift to this mode of reasoning, previously criticised as abstracted empiricism or 'data dredging'.

HYPOTHESES IN SOCIAL RESEARCH

The term 'hypothesis' is sometimes used very loosely in social research in, for example the Sapir–Whorf hypothesis, which is a claim that language determines or affects the way in which speakers understand or construct their world (see **language**). Though it (and other examples) are propositional statements, their terms are very loosely conceived, such that they would be all but impossible to falsify. So, even in social research, we usually expect a hypothesis to do more specific work. Nevertheless, and despite the attempts of philosophers of science to legislate on what a hypothesis is, or can do, in practice its specification and testing are usually informal and relate to quite local circumstances. Take for example the theory of migratory elites (Musgrove 1983). Broadly speaking, this theory suggests that those persons who do migrate are those in the originating society that will have the economic or social capital to permit migration. In other words, the migrants will not be the 'poorest' in the originating society. A hypothesis may be formulated in respect of a group in a destination migration that they had greater means to migrate than others in their originating society. There are plenty of instances where this hypothesis is verified, thus further confirming the theory. The theory does not operate as a covering law (see **generalisation and laws**) because there are exceptions, which may be expressed as *ceteris paribus* clauses, allowing the theory to be 'saved' (e.g. forced migration). But there are other issues.

First, what counts as an 'elite' in the originating society could never be specified in exactly the same way because the societies will differ greatly. Compare, for example, skilled migrants from newer European Union countries to Western Europe with migrants from sub-Saharan Africa, who pay for illegal transportation into European countries. Both are 'elites', in the broadest sense, because they had forms of capital to permit migration. But the resemblance stops there.

Second, by definition, those able to migrate had the wherewithal to do so and to falsify the hypothesis, there would have to be considerable numbers – at least more than those who migrated – who had the same or greater means in the originating country.

Third, and this would nearly always be the case, that not everyone specified within the scope of the hypothesis definition will conform to the behaviour or characteristics specified, even if a majority do. In this case, what proportion of the migratory elite actually migrated?

None of this is to suggest that testing of theories (yet alone my exemplar) through hypotheses is not a worthwhile activity, and indeed propositional statements of the form if P then Q are unavoidable in any investigation. The social world is an 'open system' (see **contingency and necessity**), both spatially and temporally and precise hypotheses (unless they are trivial) are rarely confirmed and broader ones rarely falsified. In practice, rigorous social research will try to specify the terms of H as precisely as possible. Furthermore such a specification within an analysis is rarely a singular action, but may be re-specified within the process of analyses (Salkind 2015: 125). These analyses are often in the form of regression models (see **mechanisms and models**), or at the very least bivariate or multivariate elaborations that require an interpretation of likelihood and significance and may incorporate several interrelated hypotheses.

INFERENCE TO THE BEST EXPLANATION

In both the natural and the social sciences it is quite common for data to be logically compatible with a number of different hypotheses. This may be because the theory that they are testing is specified in broad terms, or they may be derived from quite different theories. Specific examples of economic stagnation will be hypothesised quite differently from a Keynesian or Monetarist perspective and the data may support both. How social and natural scientists choose one theory over another has long been a topic of interest to philosophers (see e.g. Giere 2000). However, one approach that relates specifically to a hypothesis(es) is that of 'inference to the best explanation'.

This is a form of inductive reasoning, whereby a researcher faced with alternative hypotheses that will explain the data will choose the one that provides the 'best explanation' on the basis of what is already known. Suppose that migration from country A to country B can be explained by two alternative hypotheses. The first (H1) is that country

B has more a more generous welfare regime and this attracts migrants from country A. The second (H2) is that country B has a sectorial skills shortage. There is empirical evidence for both H1 and H2. Which should the researcher prefer? Neither, it should be stressed, can be either wholly confirmed or falsified. The researcher, using the technique of inference to the best explanation, may compare such things as the relative gain available to the skilled migrant or welfare seeker. In other words, would the decision to migrate be equally rational for both? She may count the number of recipients of welfare in B who came from A and she may count the number of skilled jobs in B, taken by migrants from B. If her conclusion is that a) the skilled worker will proportionally gain more from migration than the 'welfare seeker', b) the proportion of migrants from A to B receiving welfare is smaller than those in jobs, and c) there is a high proportion (however defined) of migrants from A to B in areas of skill shortage, for the inference to the best explanation she should prefer H2. She is reasoning that H2 is more likely to be correct than H1, not that it necessarily is. Actually H3, not yet formulated, may be a still better preference.

Inference to the best explanation is a form of informal reasoning that depends on what we know already. There are plenty of criticisms about its lack of precision in each element 'inference', 'best' and 'explanation' (Lipton 2004), yet its defenders (and I think I am one of them) will say it is practically useful and also incorporates a good scientific principle, that of parsimony. That is, an explanation should not contain any more terms than is necessary and, all things being equal, we should prefer the more parsimonious explanation over a more elaborated one. Inference to the best explanation is not dissimilar to Bayesian reasoning (though less formal), the latter setting initial subjective estimates on the likelihood of confirmation of a proposition (see **statistics**).

STATISTICAL HYPOTHESES

Statistical hypotheses incorporate probability into an expression that allows the researcher to accept or reject a hypothesis, thus emulating the laboratory procedure of the natural sciences whereby a hypothesis is either confirmed or falsified. Indeed hypothesis testing has long been in favour in psychology, which is mostly laboratory based, but is used in social research, especially in experimental methods (see **experiments**).

Research hypotheses are posed positively of the form if P then Q, but a statistical hypothesis is initially posed negatively and is called the 'null hypothesis' (its opposite is usually called the 'alternative hypothesis'). If something is found to be statistically significant, then the researcher *rejects* the null hypothesis and *accepts* the alternative one. Statistical hypotheses may be derived from research hypotheses, but that does not necessarily give them fidelity to the phenomenon and many of the issues above still obtain.

However, in the case of statistical hypotheses there are two other issues. The first is that significance (or the lack thereof) may just be a function of sample size (see **statistics**), and the second, which has gained increasing attention in recent years, is the status of the null hypothesis.

Gigerenzer et al. (2004) have questioned the rigour and efficacy of hypothesis testing and suggest the following parody of procedure followed:

1. Set up a statistical null hypothesis of 'no mean difference' or 'zero correlation'. Don't specify the predictions of your research hypothesis or of any alternative substantive hypotheses.
2. Use 5 per cent as a convention for rejecting the null. If significant, accept your research hypothesis.
3. Always perform this procedure. (2004: 392)

There are two objections here: a) the arbitrariness of the significance level, which wrongly often then becomes associated with substantive significance (see **statistics**); and b) the tendency to accept the alternative hypothesis on the grounds that the null one was falsified. In other words, the test says nothing about the confirmatory level of the alternative or research hypothesis.

Hypotheses are, then, either propositional linguistic constructs that aim to accurately explain the world, or they are linguistic constructs operationalised into statistical expressions. Either way they are tools, albeit imperfect but useful in social research. Rarely do they provide definitive confirmation, or falsification, but over longer periods they may amend or gradually erode a theory, or lead to new theories.

REFERENCES

Giere, R (2000) 'Theories', in Newton Smith, W (ed.), *A Companion to the Philosophy of Science*. Oxford: Blackwell.

Gigerenzer, K, Krauss, S and Vitouch, O (2004) 'The null ritual: what you always wanted to know about significance testing but were afraid to ask', in Kaplan, D (ed.), *The Sage Handbook of Quantitative Methodology for the Social Sciences*. Thousand Oaks, CA: Sage.

Hempel, C (1965) *Aspects of Scientific Explanation and other Essays in the Philosophy of Science*. New York: Free Press.
Lipton, P (2004) *Inference to the Best Explanation*. 2nd edn. London: Routledge.
Musgrove, F (1983) *The Migratory Elite*. London: Heinemann.
Salkind, N (2015) *100 Questions (and answers) about Statistics*. Thousand Oaks, CA: Sage.

KEY READINGS

Hoover, K and Donovan, T (1995) *The Elements of Social Scientific Thinking*. New York: St Martin's Press.

KEY THINKERS

Ronald Fisher; Carl Hempel; Karl Popper

See also: *Contingency and Necessity; Experiments; Explanation; Falsification; Generalisation and Laws; Language; Mechanisms and Models; Theory*

Idealism

Idealism incorporates a wide range of doctrines in philosophy and the social sciences. They have in common the view that the external world is a creation of mind. It does not mean that idealists necessarily deny the existence of a 'real' world, but rather that we can never directly perceive it.

In the first part of this section Idealism is described as opposing materialism and as a broader philosophy which prioritises 'ideas'. The work of key idealist thinkers in social science: Weber, Husserl, Schutz and Dilthey are introduced. The Kantian influence on social science is discussed. In the second part of the section I talk about the relationship of idealism to interpretation and meaning and in turn their influence on hermeneutics, and phenomenology. Finally I assess the way idealism has shaped social research.

We can think of idealism in two ways. First, as an opposing **ontology** to **materialism**, a monist belief that the world consists only of 'ideas' (mental monism, associated with philosophy of George Berkeley), and second, a broad range of philosophical positions that prioritise ideas to one extent or another.

Most idealists are therefore not guilty of what Ortega y Gasset called 'ontophobia' – an antipathy to reality. Rather, idealists will usually hold to a position that the knowable properties of physical existence are mediated through sensory perception to create ideas in minds. Turn it around the other way, only minds are capable of knowing the world, only what we think is real, is real.

Those often described as idealist philosophers, who we can think of influencing the social sciences (Hegel, Kant, Wittegenstein) are not straightforwardly idealist. Yet somewhat ironically, later thinkers such as the social constructionist Kenneth Gergen, and postmodernists such as Jean Francois Lyotard and Jean Baudrillard, come close to ontophobia (see **postmodernism**), but their positions are slippery and somewhat agnostically they neither assert nor deny the existence of an external reality.

IDEALISM AND SOCIAL SCIENCE

Idealism has entered the social sciences in many guises, most importantly through the Kantian-influenced work of Max Weber, the linguistic philosophy of Wittgenstein (see **language**), the phenomenology of Husserl and Schutz and hermeneutics through Schleiermacher and Dilthey. Each of these combines other influences, but in each of these philosophies ideas play a central role.

Whatever their attitude to 'reality' or the physical world, idealist social scientists will distinguish mind inert nature from human culture, who are capable of meaningful social action, rather than just behaviour. Social reality is the sum total of the interpretations of meanings by agents and the creation of new meanings through action. Methodologically idealism favours interpretive methods (see **interpretation and meaning**), either exclusively or primarily. The argument for only using the methods of interpretation amounts to an ontological claim about the social world. Norman Denzin (1983: 133) maintains that every instance of human interaction represents a 'slice from the lifeworld', carrying layered meanings, which come in multiples and are often contradictory. Denzin's argument can be summarised as 'individual consciousnesses are free to attach different meanings to the same actions or circumstances'. Conversely, different actions can arise out of similarly expressed meanings. Similarly the ontophobic or agnostic positions, such as the **social constructionism** of Gergen and Jonathan Potter, effectively rule out a macro-level science of the social world because they refuse to move beyond a study of how people socially construct meanings through talk, writing and images, and concepts such as social structure are seen simply as the social constructions of social scientists. Though presumably these constructions themselves would be of interest to thinkers of this persuasion!

A great deal of poststructuralist-, postmodernist- or feminist- inspired studies that condemn **positivism** do so on the basis of such a social ontology, though it should be said that often this is combined with epistemological **relativism**. This combination then constituted one side in the 'science wars' of the 1980s (Baringer 2001) and by extension the rather crude dichotomisation of social science into 'interpretivism v. positivism', or 'science v. humanism' (see **social constructionism**). Yet not all idealist positions in social science are 'anti-science' or humanist, and these are often influenced by a very different kind of idealism, that of Immanuel Kant.

Though Kant still emphasised the characteristic of humans as mind-endowed beings, this must be done in the context of existing in a world of space and time (Körner 1955: ch. 4), thus he admits of things that are beyond mind. Nevertheless, he also held that we can only know phenomena through mind dependent perception of it, we cannot ever know the thing in itself and what he called 'noumena' is ever beyond our perception. Kant's 'transcendental idealism' was particularly influential in the work of Max Weber. In the social world (as in the world in general) we can never grasp the essence of something, 'the thing in itself', but we can hold in our minds a representation of something in the social world that may not exist in such form in reality. Weber coined the term 'ideal type' to describe such representation. Ideal types are not averages or the most desirable form of social phenomena, but a way in which an individual can reason from a shared rational faculty (see **rationality**) to a model or pure conceptual type that would exist if all agents acted perfectly rationally. Weber's methodology therefore crucially depends on rationality as the product of minds (Albrow 1990).

Weber's idealist social science, unlike those versions which deny anything beyond the local construction of meaning, is consistent with **realism** or **positivism** because it does not deny the possibility of causal explanation, and indeed ideal types are consistent with the 'transitive objects' in science of the former philosophy and inference in the latter. Idealism has influenced a wide range of ontological positions in social science from those that either embrace, or imply, a monist ontology, to those which simply admit of the centrality of ideas and their interpretation. However, idealism also gave rise to two other approaches to social science, that are not straightforwardly idealist but are nevertheless methodologically important: phenomenology and hermeneutics.

PHENOMENOLOGY

Phenomenology came to the social sciences principally through the theoretical work of Alfred Schutz, though the work of others, such as Husserl, Merleau-Ponty, Dilthey and Heidegger are often cited as directly influenced some approaches. Phenomenology was also an important contributing influence on ethnomethodology (see **language**).

Phenomenology was created by the German philosopher Edmund Husserl. Its aim was a new beginning in thinking about consciousness that bypassed the presuppositions of psychology and philosophy. The starting question can be summed up as asking 'what is it that shows up in lived experience prior to reflection', thus (in the second sense above) it is a thoroughgoing idealist concept. A key feature and something social scientists take for granted now is that a key feature of consciousness is intentionality – that we direct our consciousness toward things. Consciousness is always about something. Husserl distinguished between the 'natural attitude', our everyday stance in the 'lifeworld' in regard to dealing with the objects of the world, whether these are physical things, actions, events or persons and the phenomenological attitude. The latter is an attempt to 'bracket off' our presuppositions and focus on the objects of pure consciousness. If this can be achieved then the essence, the true meaning of something can be grasped.

Alfred Schutz was influenced both by Husserl's work and that of Weber. He grasped a fundamental philosophical problem in social science: 'how can we form objective concepts and verifiable theory from agents' subjective meanings?' (Blaikie 2007: 128). It is the emphasis on the 'reality' of such objects that moves Schutz a little way from idealism, and indeed his adoption of a reductive strategy in order to discover these objects of consciousness can be interpreted as consistent with realism (Williams 2014).

Schutz was also influenced by Weber and particularly the concept of the ideal type, but the latter's strategy of reduction required a distinction between agent's own first order constructs and the second order constructs of the social scientist. Thus, social science constructs must arise from the agents themselves (Schutz 1967).

Few social scientists are straightforward followers of Schutz nowadays, but the idea of prioritising agent constructs and 'bracketing off' one's own prior constructs influences much contemporary interpretive social science, especially through reflexive approaches (May 2011) and to the point of reification in ethnomethodology.

HERMENEUTICS

The origins of hermeneutics pre-date most of the philosophers mentioned above. The strategy of hermeneutics is all but interchangeable with that of interpretivism, but hermeneutic philosophers and social scientists will follow through the epistemological implications of the approach, to the exclusion of any other. Hermeneutics had its origins in 17th-century biblical study. The Bible and other religious texts were written in different historical times, and it was the job of these scholars to interpret the meanings of the texts for a contemporary audience. At the risk of over simplifying then, hermeneutics is the philosophical and research strategy to make clear that which is obscure to a culture. One can see the purchase of this idea for anthropology, in both its traditional form in non-Western societies, but also to understand the culture of sub-groups in modern Western society.

Hermeneutic philosophy was proposed as an alternative approach to the scientific study of society by the German philosopher Schleiermacher. He moved from the narrower concern with understanding linguistic texts, to a historical focus on understanding past societies, in the present. His approach might be seen as the beginning of the differential foci, in social science, on either causal explanation or interpretation. This was made more explicit in the work, later, of Wilhelm Dilthey, who advocated an approach which emphasised the understanding of agent subjectivity in the social world (*verstehen*) and causal explanation (*erklaren*) in the study of natural phenomena. Dilthey placed almost passionate emphasis on the lived experience, which could only be understood 'through its expression – gestures, facial expressions, informal rules of behaviour, works of art, buildings, tools, literature, poetry, drama, laws, social institutions (such as religion and cultural systems) – which come to possess an independent existence of their own' (Blaikie 2007: 119). Though both (almost) contemporaries, one can immediately see the difference between Dilthey's approach and the Kantian-influenced Weber, who retained *erklaren* as a component in the study of the social and indeed insisted on the need of an explanation to be adequate at the level of cause (*erklaren*) and meaning (*verstehen*).

Unlike phenomenology, hermeneutics has a wide contemporary methodological influence on social research. A key more recent thinker, in this regard, is Hans-Georg Gadamer, who died only in 2002. Central to his thinking is the idea of the 'hermeneutic circle'. Like Schleiermacher, he places great emphasis on an understanding of historical context. To understand a historical process, we must situate ourselves in that process. Similarly, to understand persons from a different culture, there has to be a 'merging' of perspectives. The 'circle' is the almost paradoxical problem of needing to know a part of something in order to know the whole, but to know the whole we must come to know the part. This is a similar issue to that identified by Peter Winch (see **rationality**) in coming to know an 'alien' society. Where do you start? For Gadamer and contemporary hermeneutisists, this is not an insurmountable problem and can be achieved somewhat dialectically by moving from the part to the whole, and back again until an understanding is achieved. Some would say that this is an example of social science stating the obvious, but nevertheless sometimes the obvious is worth stating!

An epistemological corollary of hermeneutics is relativism. Whilst the cultural relativism implied by the emphasis on difference between historical periods and societies is an important insight, what can follow is an epistemological relativism which gives equal weight to any perspective and this direction in hermeneutic thinking merges into and is a component of **postmodernism**.

IDEALISM AND SOCIAL RESEARCH

It would be too simplistic to wholly associate idealistic approaches to social science with an idiographic approach to social knowledge, because some idealist-influenced social scientists, especially those in the Weberian tradition, are influenced by Kantian philosophy, which though 'idealist' in its emphasis on 'ideas' leads often to methodological approaches consistent with realism and will embrace both nomothetic and idiographic approaches to knowledge (see **epistemology**). However, constructionist, phenomenological and hermeneutic approaches count mostly for an idiographic approach to researching the social world and will almost exclusively adopt interpretive methods. The extent to which these are 'ontophobic' or epistemologically relativist is quite broad and in empirical research often remains implicit.

Yet it would be a very militant empiricist (perhaps a behaviourist, or positivist) that would deny the importance of the insights the idealist tradition in social science and research has provided. The notion of interpretation permeates not just qualitative research, but also much quantitative research (Byrne 2002), where the need to remember that measurable constructs are just that, and that they and their contexts must be interpreted, is now commonplace. In this regard, Weber's equal emphasis on both meaning and cause can be seen as the philosophical and methodological centre of gravity in social research.

REFERENCES

Albrow, M (1990) *Max Weber's Construction of Social Theory*. London: Macmillan.

Baringer, P (2001) 'The science wars', in Ashman, K and Baringer, P (eds), *After the Science Wars*. London: Routledge.

Blaikie, N (2007) *Approaches to Social Enquiry*, 2nd edn. Cambridge: Polity.

Byrne, D (2002) *Interpreting Quantitative Data*. London: Sage.

Denzin, N (1983) 'Interpretive interactionism', in Morgan, G (ed.), *Beyond Method: strategies for social research*. Bevereley Hills, CA: Sage.

Körner, S (1955) *Kant*. Harmondsworth: Penguin.

May, T with Perry, B (2011) *Social Research and Reflexivity*. London: Sage.

Schutz, A (1967 [1932]) *The Phenomenology of the Social World*. Chicago, IL: North Western University Press.

Williams, M (2014) 'Situated objectivity, values and realism', *European Journal of Social Theory*, 18 (1): 76–92.

KEY READINGS

Ayer, A (1984) *Philosophy in the 20th Century*. London: Unwin-Hyman.

Blaikie, N (2007) *Approaches to Social Enquiry*, 2nd edn. Cambridge: Polity.

Körner, S (1955) *Kant*. Harmondsworth: Penguin.

Manicas, P (1987) *A History and Philosophy of the Social Sciences*. Oxford: Blackwell. especially ch. 7.

KEY THINKERS

Wilhelm Dilthey; Hans-George Gadamar; Immanuel Kant; Georg Fredrich Hegelm; Alfred Schutz; Peter Winch; Max Weber

See also: *Epistemology; Interpretation and Meaning; Ontology; Positivism; Postmodernism; Rationality; Realism; Social Constructionism; Time*

Individualism and Holism

Individualism and holism are opposite perspectives in social explanation. Individualists maintain that all social phenomena are reducible to individual characteristics, whereas holists maintain that social phenomena are not reducible to individual characteristics, beliefs, actions or desires.

The holist – individualist debate is an old, but important one in social science. Here I first assess the present state of the holist–individualist debate. I then describe the origins of holism and its advocacy in Spencer and Durkheim. The critique of holism is then made through the argument for individualism, namely that the social world is brought into being and maintained through individual actions and beliefs. Finally I describe the retreat from the holism–individualism debate into versions of structuration theory.

Often referred to as 'methodological individualism' and 'methodological holism', these concepts are philosophical and often methodological opposites, and for much of the history of social science they have been at the heart of a debate about the nature of society. In more recent years, some of the heat has gone out of the debate as new theories, often referred to as 'structuration theories' and advanced by thinkers such as Anthony Giddens (1984) and Roy Bhaskar (1998), have gained in popularity. Nevertheless they are important concepts, for to understand what is at stake assists our understanding of the ontology of the social world (see **ontology**).

Individualists claim that social phenomena must derive from the characteristics and dispositions of individual agents, whilst holists maintain that social wholes are more than the sum of individual attitudes, beliefs and actions and that the whole can often determine the characteristics of individuals. As can be seen from the preceding term, in each case 'methodological', these positions are starting points for thinking about how we should conceptualise and indeed research society. It is this aspect I shall concentrate on here, because there is a second aspect to the philosophical antinomy and that is the normative political position associated with each (Lukes 1994). The philosopher Karl Popper maintained that 'collective' (holist) explanation blinded us to the truth of the matter that the functioning of all social institutions result from the attitudes, decisions and actions of individuals. Moreover, he claimed, collectivist views about what *is* lead to collectivist views about what *should be* and ultimately the totalitarianism of fascism and communism (Popper 1986). His political critics, however, argued that methodological individualism led also to free-market liberalism and the undermining of collectivist civic values.

Whatever the merits or demerits of this political argument, it is widely acknowledged to be a non-sequitur from the methodological argument, which has been associated with thinkers of both the right and left (Phillips 1976). For example, a prominent advocate of rational choice theory (see **rationality**), John Elster (1985), is also sympathetic to Marxism.

HOLISM

Holist thinking was popular amongst 19th-century biologists influenced by Darwin's evolutionary theories. It entered the social sciences, particularly in the work of Herbert Spencer who saw society evolving through the adaptation of structures, in much the same way as biological structures evolved. A more sophisticated version of organic thinking was advanced by Talcott Parsons (1968) in which, like the organs of the human body, the constituent parts of society function to maintain each other (see **functionalism**). Parsons' holism was explicitly functionalist, but critics of holism and functionalism have maintained that the latter is necessarily at least implicit in the former.

These arguments were theoretically driven and evidence for and against them has been advanced, but an early empirical exception came from Emile Durkheim. An analysis of suicide statistics across several European countries indicated that whilst suicide rates rose and fell, the proportions attributed to individual causes by coroners remained constant, suggesting that even such an individual act as suicide was shaped by social forces. Hitherto suicide had been considered an entirely individual matter and whilst Durkheim did not dismiss mediating individual psychological factors, that the patterns of suicide and its attribution, between countries, over time indicates some pattern of social causation.

By modern standards, Durkheim's analyses were unsophisticated and could be subjected to methodological critique, but over a century later researchers are highly skilled at administering cross-national surveys, such as the European Social Attitudes Survey, which are able to show consistent patterns of behaviour and attitudes (and indeed differences) across countries. See Newton and Montero (2007) for an example of how cross-national research can contrast political and social participation across many countries and identify not only fragmentation but also common patterns explained by supranational characteristics.

INDIVIDUALISM

The existence of what Durkheim (1952) called 'social facts' are adequately revealed by the social survey, but critics argue that this is little more than description. The methodological critique of holism has centred on the incompleteness of explanations that do not make ultimate reference to individual beliefs, desires and actions. For example, longitudinal analyses of how individuals answer questions about their ethnicity in surveys indicates a high level of consistency over time, nevertheless (even when the measurement remains the same) a significant minority change their affiliation, indicating that whilst ethnicity is indeed a social phenomenon, it is mediated through individual beliefs and desires.

Individualists reject the holist's claim that there can be social wholes existing beyond or separate to individuals, not by saying these the social does not exist but rather claiming that the social world is brought into existence by individuals acting according to the 'logic of the situation' (Popper 1986). That is, individuals create social situations by directing their actions according to the expected behaviour of other individuals in particular situations. Complex social situations, for example economic systems, are said to result from particular alignments of individual dispositions, beliefs and physical resources or characteristics. In explaining a given economic system, reference to constituent parts such as the behaviour of the stock market can only be seen as partial explanation, though they may be constructed as heuristic models. A full explanation must, at rock bottom, refer to actual, or possibly 'ideal' (statistical) agents.

An important argument against individualism is that it leads to the conclusion that social characteristics can only be described in terms of individual psychologies, yet most individual characteristics (such as being a banker, a teacher or a police officer) can only be explained in terms of social institutions. A second 'realist' objection concerns the ontological status of social practices or objects. Methodological individualists maintain that, unlike physical objects which have real properties, social phenomena are simply collective mental constructions. The response to this is that many things in the physical world can only be known by their observed effects (e.g. gravity), and much the same is true of social phenomena such as a foreign policy, or a body of law, but they are none the less real for this.

AGENCY, STRUCTURE AND STRUCTURATION

The individualism–holism debate is an analogue of the old debate amongst physicists as to whether light consisted of waves or particles (Wheaton 2009). Both sides were both right and wrong and much depends on measurement. Indeed we now know that light has dual aspect, referred to as 'quanta'. The social science debate has not been so conclusively resolved, but more interactive theories that stress how agents create structures, which then constrain or enable their future attitudes and actions, are now more dominant. These 'structuration theories' (e.g. those of Giddens and Bhaskar) emphasise either agency or structure, dependent on context.

Giddens' version of structuration theory begins with the individual agent able to reflexively monitor their actions and by doing so produce those which are rational in the circumstances. However, he acknowledges that many of the motivations and actions depend on unconscious motives (Blaikie 2007: 163). Whilst agents may act rationally, their actions will have unintended consequences. This active relationship between the individual and society creates, maintains and modifies that society. Thus, unlike the physical world where local conditions can be explained in relation to some immutable laws, in the social world only relatively local regularities can be established (see **generalisation and laws**).

Though other versions of structuration place, different emphases, the notion of an active interplay between partially knowing and creative agents, with social structure is common to all of them.

Methodologically structuration approaches have advantages for mixed methods approaches to social research because they require both structural explanation as well as a more hermeneutic understanding of individual actions and beliefs.

REFERENCES

Bhaskar, R (1998) *The Possibility of Naturalism*, 3rd edn. London: Routledge.
Blaikie, N (2007) *Approaches to Social Enquiry*, 2nd edn. Cambridge: Polity.
Durkheim, E (1952 [1896]) *Suicide*. London: Routledge and Kegan Paul.
Elster, J (1985) *Making Sense of Marx*. Cambridge: Cambridge University Press.
Giddens, A (1984) *The Constitution of Society*. Cambridge: Polity.
Lukes, S (1994) 'Methodological individualism reconsidered', in Martin, M and McIntyre, L (eds), *Readings in the Philosophy of Social Science*. Cambridge, MA: MIT Press.
Newton, K and Montero, J (2007) 'Patterns of political and social participation in Europe', in Jowell, R, Roberts, C, Fitzgerald, R and Eva, G (eds), *Measuring Attitudes Cross Nationally*. London: Sage.
Parsons, T (1968) *The Structure of Social Action*, 3rd edn. New York: Free Press.
Phillips, D (1976) *Holistic Thought in Social Science*. Stanford, CA: Stanford University Press.
Popper, K (1986) *The Poverty of Historicism*. London: ARK.
Wheaton, B (2009) 'Wave-particle duality: some history', in Greenberger, D, Hentschel, K and Weinert, F (eds), *Compendium of Quantum Physics*. Heidelberg: Springer. pp. 830–835.

KEY READINGS

Lukes, S (1994) 'Methodological individualism reconsidered', in Martin, M and McIntyre, L (eds), *Readings in the Philosophy of Social Science*. Cambridge, MA: MIT Press.

KEY THINKERS

Emile Durkheim; Jon Elster; Anthony Giddens; Karl Popper; Steven Lukes

See also: *Functionalism; Generalisation and Laws; Rationality*

Induction

Induction is a form of reasoning that is based on the assumption that the world remains the same in important respects. Much of social research depends on informal inductive reasoning through our theorising that our findings are a good enough representation and on more formal reasoning through probability.

The section discusses the philosophical problem of induction and how it relates to reasoning in social research. The section illustrates how social researchers use informal and formal inductive reasoning and whilst understanding the logical problem identified by philosophers, concludes that such reasoning is both inevitable and advantageous to researchers.

Bernard Russell (1995) tells us the story of the chicken who got fed every day by the farmer, until one day when instead of being fed the farmer killed him for Christmas. The chicken's reasoning (assuming chickens could reason) was inductive and although unfortunate in this case, a reasonable way to think about the world. It is often said that the weather tomorrow is most likely to be like the weather today than anything else. Now we know the weather changes, as we know other things change in the world, but we also know that many things remain much the same – at least in important features. Social research depends on inductive reasoning, not the least to generalise (see **generalisation and laws**) from one time or place to another. It does this in a number of ways to establish typicality. For example, the classic community research of Robert and Helen Lynd in the 1920s concentrated on one particular town, 'Middletown' (actually Muncie in Indiana), providing a detailed picture of the lives and the organisations of the community in a 'typical' American city (Lynd and Lynd 1929). A key finding of their study was the lack of radicalism or solidarity amongst workers during the Great Depression, the prior sociological reasoning being that such solidarity might be expected to exist. The Lynd's study was the first of its type and the findings provided the basis for reasoning about other communities that were deemed to have similarities, for example Vidich and Bensman's *Small Town in Mass Society*, based on 'Springdale' in New York state in the 1950s (Vidich and Bensman 1960). The rural class structure and its relationship to external processes was a key focus, and in this study and others, research themes to be explored have their origins in the work of the Lynds.

In these kinds of community studies reasoning was inductive at two levels. First in the specifics of the research, say about divisions of labour that rely on general descriptions of roles (e.g. teachers, fire fighters, shopkeepers) that are assumed to be rather the same in key features as elsewhere (see **generalisation and laws**). What becomes interesting then is how they might differ in the specifics from elsewhere, for example Middletown was much larger with more complex divisions of labour than Springdale, a small town with one main street and located in a relatively rural area. The second level at which such research made inductive assumptions was that in the most general respects the communities were typical of the US in that period: Middletown as a manufacturing town in transition during the Great Depression, and Springdale a small town in a period of relative wealth and growing suburbanisation.

These examples are drawn from classic sociological studies of community, but one could pick almost any other area of social research where one begins from informal inferences about what is already known, to what we might expect to find in our prospective study. Indeed one might say that the role of the literature review in research is to establish just these things.

More formerly, social research uses probability (see **probability**) to make inferences from one set of circumstances to another, quite often on the basis of samples to populations. A sample of teachers across an education authority might be assumed to have the characteristics of the teachers in that authority more generally. The way informal and probabilistic inductive reasoning differs is that the first claims only to say that other situations will resemble the researched one in key but indefinite ways, whereas probabilistic induction from sample to population will specify the specific nature and extent of a characteristic that might be found and it will do so with a given degree of certainty.

This kind of induction, with the kind of caveats I discuss in the section on probability, has been very successful. For example, pollsters are very good at predicting election outcomes and market research companies are very successful at predicting the demand for goods and services. Though there are exceptions, such as the UK General Election of 2015, or the Ford Edsel respectively.[8] But back to Russell's hapless chicken!

Philosophers maintain there is no rational foundation to induction, that our assumptions about the world are constantly challenged, just as the chicken's was. A recent book by Nasim Nicholas Taleb, *The Black Swan,* has as its central argument that the world has in fact been shaped by random and unexpected events rather than by safe prediction (Taleb 2007). The black swan in question refers to the assumption by Europeans that all swans were white until they went to Australia and encountered black swans. However many instances of X with Y characteristics we might observe (see **observation**), it only takes one X with no Y characteristics to refute the argument that all Xs are Ys. This argument is at the basis of **falsification**, and I discuss it in more detail in that section.

What I have just outlined is sometimes called 'Hume's problem'. Hume maintained that there was nothing in any object, considered in itself, that would allow us to draw conclusions beyond it. We have no experience of those things we have not seen, things that are elsewhere or in the future, so we have no rational grounds for making inferences about them (Howson 2000: 181). That we do constantly make such assumptions is, strictly speaking, not rational because at some point, somewhere, that assumption will be wrong. Hume, however, was a very pragmatic philosopher and maintained it was a characteristic of humans that we base our decisions about the future on our experiences of the past, when perhaps we ought to be sceptical about claims or beliefs that the future will resemble the past (or things in one place will resemble

[8] The Ford Edsel was launched by the Ford Motor Company in 1958 and despite market intelligence indicating it would successfully compete with Chrysler or GM models, it was a massive commercial failure and not the finest hour for market research. The pollsters did not predict the outcome of the 2015 UK General Election, but their predictions are quite often within a ±3 per cent margin of error.

things in another). Taleb' s problem is a good one, though in my view his answer (we need to get smarter) is less convincing; after all, Taleb himself in writing *The Black Swan* must have assumed that people will read it and he himself will profit financially from this inductive assumption!

There is a very good reason to be an inductivist as a social scientist: the social world exhibits a great deal of stability and if it didn't, it would cease to exist in any meaningful way. This informal rule is 'proven' by its exceptions. In the 2000s there was much talk in international relations of 'failed states', such as Somalia, where internecine warfare had made governance and stability impossible. Inductive assumptions in Mogadishu are much shakier than in Manchester! Yet, looking at TV pictures or reading accounts of people's lives, one is struck by the desire to find stability, to do those normal things one has always done. To say that inductive reasoning has no philosophically rational basis is not the same as to say that it is irrational to make assumptions based upon experience to guide decisions. Most everyday assumptions that are based upon past experience turn out to be justified. Social science itself is founded on the assumptions that there are repeatable and observable patterns of social behaviour, that is, humans are natural inductivists, and this fact is a rational basis for social researchers to theorise about the social world inductively and researchers to test these theories.

However, to end on a note of caution. Inductive assumptions are (or should be!) testable. Social research is not in the business of simply gathering those data that support what we think or believe is the case, but rather to begin from such assumptions and to test them. The Lynd's findings about the relatively weak mobilisation of social class was relatively unexpected. (See **hypothesis(es)** and **falsification** for further discussion of where induction fits in the wider reasoning process.)

REFERENCES

Howson, C (2000) 'Induction and the uniformity of nature', in Newton-Smith, W H (ed.), *A Companion to the Philosophy of Science*. Oxford: Blackwell.

Lynd, R S and Lynd, H M (1929) *Middletown: a study in contemporary American culture*. New York: Harcourt Brace.

Russell, R (1995 [1914]) *Our Knowledge of the External World*. London: Routledge.

Taleb, N (2007) *The Black Swan: the impact of the highly improbable*. London: Penguin.

Vidich, A and Bensman, J (1960) *Small Town in Mass Society: class, power and religion in a rural community*. New York: Anchor.

KEY READINGS

Russell, B (1967) [1912] 'Induction' (Chapter 6) in Russel, B, *The Problems of Philosophy*. Oxford: Oxford University Press.
Medawar, P (1969) *Induction and Intuition in Scientific Thought*. London: Methuen.

KEY THINKERS

David Hume; Karl Popper; Bertrand Russell

See also: *Empiricism; Falsification; Generalisation and Laws; Hypothesis(es); Logic and Truth; Probability*

Interpretation and Meaning

The interpretation of phenomena is inevitable in everything we do. Even the simplest sense data requires some kind of evaluation or decoding, but in social science, interpretation is closely linked to meaning and gives its name to a whole way of doing social science: interpretivism.

The section first describes the philosophical underpinnings of interpretivism and how this has been translated into both a research strategy, but also a way of doing social science that is opposed to scientific or naturalistic approaches. Meaning is central to this approach, and the second part of the section sets out some of its key features and limitations. In the third part the apparent antinomy between interpretivism and causal explanation is discussed in relation to commonly used methods.

INTERPRETIVISM: STRATEGY AND PHILOSOPHY

Throughout much of the history of social investigation, there have been two diverse views of the social world and how we can know it.

Interpretivism, or at least its methods, are not necessarily inconsistent with a naturalistic (or scientific) philosophical position, but many interpretivists – and in this I include postmodernists and poststructuralists – believe that the naturalistic goal of causal explanation is untenable in social investigation.

To interpret something is to make sense of it in context. It is to search for the meaning of something. A chemist interpreting a chemical reaction seeks to understand it in relation to other features of the experiment, and therefore to understand its meaning to those features or underlying theory, and in this way it can be thought of as a special form of explanation. But the interpretation of meaning in the social world is the act of trying to understand the actions, beliefs and desires of other agents (see **rationality**). Philosophers often describe these as intentional; that is, they are meaningful for those agents and directed toward other agents, objects or situations. Social life requires its participants to be interpreters in order to act successfully as social agents. Interpretation in social research is, then, a version – possibly more formalised and skilled – of what we do every day.

Historically the most important social science interpretivist was Max Weber. He maintained that not only could an understanding of meaning provide an explanation, but that an adequate explanation of the social world must be one that can be adequate in explaining meaning and cause (Weber 1978: 15). It is his version of interpretivism and the claim that it is consistent with causal explanation that is defended by modern naturalistically inclined social scientists (Kincaid 1996: ch. 6). I will return to this below.

The position I outline is underpinned by the philosophy of idealism (see **idealism**), which in social science can be characterised as claiming that the social world is ultimately 'mind dependent' and that there is nothing we can know except that which we know through mind. The most extreme form of this is 'solipsism', the view that all we can ever know is what we perceive in our own minds. Few people explicitly hold this view because philosophically it is a dead-end and closes down any further debate about phenomena. Nevertheless, if we remove external referents as guarantors of knowledge, for example observed phenomena in empiricism, or an underlying causally efficacious reality in realism, then mind-dependent accounts of the world have no other arbiter than one's own mind. Not all idealist interpretivists go that far (Weber certainly didn't), but those that do will claim that there can be no privileged account of the social world over any other because each of us is able to interpret that world independently from all others. For some thinkers, this accords social science accounts the same epistemological status as travellers' tales or fiction, in that they can all generate insights equally valuable in knowing the social world (Clifford and Marcus 1986).

However, there are those who reject the possibility of causal explanation that do not embrace such overt epistemological relativism (see **relativism**). Their argument against causal explanation and in favour of interpretation has an ontological claim about the social world at its heart.

In this view, what we call 'social reality' is the outcome of the interpretations of individual actors in the social world. We create the social world by interpreting the actions and beliefs of others and then on the basis of this we take our own actions, which in turn are interpreted by others. Ontologically 'education', 'parenting', 'sexuality', 'work' are of different categories to chemical compounds or physical structures, for they are free to vary in their characteristics as a result of how they are interpreted and then recreated by their participants. Individuals can attribute different meanings to the same action or circumstances, and conversely different actions can arise out of similarly expressed meanings. This, interpretivists argue, leads to a quite different way of knowing the social world, and whilst few social scientists would deny the importance of interpretations, some maintain that this is the sole basis of social knowledge and consequently deny the possibility of causal explanation (see **causality**). In this view, it is said that though people will commonly talk as if their behaviour was 'caused', the causes are said to be underdetermined. That is, ten different people performing the same action could give ten different reasons (or causes) for their doing it (Denzin 1983: 133). And of course ten different actions could be motivated by the same reason (or 'cause'). Knowledge of the social world becomes a conjectural, or uncertain, web of meanings and alternative interpretations of meanings.

If this philosophical position is correct, then causal explanations are not viable and indeed descriptions that go beyond those at the micro level must be grounded in meaning (if indeed any descriptions can go beyond the micro level). On the other hand, those who maintain that there is no antinomy between meaning and explanation must show how an explanation can be valid beyond individual meaning, if there is such variability in meaning (see **explanation**). I will return to these problems below, but first I will look a little more closely at 'meaning'.

MEANING

Meaning is at the core of interpretation and its possibilities and limits of the former are those of what we can know, or infer, from meaning. The interpretation of meaning predates social science and has its origins in medieval hermeneutics. Hermeneutics was originally employed by biblical scholars to search for and interpret meaning in scriptures. The translation of biblical texts was made complex by the tendency for them to have been already translated several times previously. In order to discover their original meaning, the biblical scholar had then to attempt to understand the wider social context within which they were produced (see Bauman 1978; Hughes 1990). An extension of this method to an understanding of history, though advocated by Vico in the 17th century, was first adopted by Frederich Schleiermacher in the 19th century (see **idealism**), but its use as a strategy in contemporary social investigation was not widely applied until well into the 20th century.

Meaning and language are inextricably linked. Some philosophers have argued that meaning is bounded by the possibilities of language (see **language**). Certainly to understand meaning it is necessary to understand the form and nature of the communication used – at least to some extent (this is also controversial). Language might be natural language (such as English, Punjabi or Arabic), or it might be other forms of communication. For example, in many cultures, a scratching of the head indicates puzzlement, or the tapping of the nose indicates a privileged knowledge of a matter. A few gestures are pretty much universal – the ubiquity of the wink, for example. But ultimately the goal of verbal and non-verbal language is communication through meaning, and the role of the interpreter is to understand that meaning. Similarly, actions are to be understood for their meaning to the person taking the action. Action itself can be performance for an intended audience. Erving Goffman (Ytreberg 2009) and symbolic interactionism take this as the key aspect of social life. Goffman, for example, in his PhD research studied the crofters of the Shetland Isles (Goffman 1959: 111–21). The external appearance of their homes was one of poverty and that their homes appeared like this was intended as a sign, to their landlords, that they were poor (and thus, it was hoped, the landlords would not raise the rents), whereas Goffman found that internally the crofters were nowhere near as poor as the appearance of their homes would suggest.

Meaning is, however, not straightforward and though all meaning is intentional, it comes in different forms and purposes. In everyday life we may talk of the 'meaning of life', 'what Denzil meant', 'the barometer falling means rain' and so on. We know what we mean and our audience (usually) knows what we mean, but these different uses of the concept provide a puzzle for the researcher. Harold Kincaid has noted six different uses of the term by sociologists or anthropologists:

- *Perceptual meaning*: how a subject perceives the world, including the actions of others and him- or herself.
- *Doxastic meaning*: what a subject believes.
- *Intentional meaning:* what a subject intends, desires etc., to bring it about.
- *Linguistic meaning*: how the verbal behaviour of the subject is to be translated.
- *Symbolic meaning*: what the behaviour of the subject – verbal or non-verbal – symbolizes.
- *Normative meaning*: what norms the behaviour of the individual reflects or embodies. (Kincaid 1996: 192)

In interpretivist research, these different uses of 'meaning' are rarely differentiated, and indeed it is questionable whether such differentiation would always be possible.

Apparent meaning can disguise a complex pattern of beliefs and desires, not all discernible to the agent expressing them. To venture into this territory is to make psychological assumptions about the underlying motivations for actions or utterances, though some have argued that is precisely what we should do (Jones 1998).

EXPLANATION AND UNDERSTANDING IN SOCIAL RESEARCH

The criticism of infinite variability rests upon both the misunderstanding of social life and what can be meant by a 'cause'. In the first case, whilst social life may contain huge variability, some stability must be present for social life to be possible at all (Williams 2000). Indeed the intelligibility of meaning rests on some kinds of assumptions about social settings and characteristics. It follows from this that, at the very least, explanations of social actions or settings should be possible. In the second case, a greater specificity of what is meant by a 'cause' is required (see **causality**) and cannot be narrowly construed as a simple cause–effect relationship.

Other problems with interpretation can be summarised:

- Meaning must be approached with a theory or conceptual schema (which may be changed or falsified). Pre-theoretical access to meaning, as advocated by Jack Douglas (1976: 7), reduces interpretations to abstracted empiricism (Mills 1959: 50–76) (see **observation**).
- As implied above, agents may misunderstand or misinterpret situations themselves and the researcher is simply accessing those misunderstandings or misinterpretations. Moreover intentionality does not necessarily imply reflection, and mostly agents do not monitor their actions or utterances.
- Agents do not necessarily have a privileged access to the social world they inhabit (or are willing/able to recount this to researchers). Theirs is just one perspective, and the 'quality' of that perspective as an account of that social world may not be apparent. They cannot know, for example, the extent of their institutional embeddedness and may be only partially, or completely unaware of the power relationships that shape their social situation.
- The problem of 'other minds' is ever present. Much is made of the need to understand a social situation (and the agents themselves) at least partly as an 'insider', but to know other minds as others know them requires the researcher to be one of them, and to be 'one of them' properly requires an abandonment of the researcher role. One 'goes native'. This is entertainingly illustrated in Alison Lurie's novel *Imaginary Friends* (Lunie 1995).

These are a brief overview of some key problems that interpretivism faces. In practice the antinomies of causal explanation v. interpretation, naturalism v. humanism (or anti-naturalism) are largely overcome in social research. Interpretivist research uses a range of non-statistical methods, such as documentary/media analysis of existing texts (rather like biblical scholars), participant observation, interviews and focus groups. Each of these are capable of producing data which are descriptive or explanatory. Interviews and focus groups, for example, are often used to provide relatively modest descriptions, explanations of the actions or beliefs of agents, which can be fairly straightforwardly mapped onto the types of meaning Kincaid describes.

For the anthropologist or sociologist, greater depth is often required, but the interpretations of meanings, in actions or expressed beliefs and desires, does not exist in an epistemological vacuum. Classic studies, such as William Foote Whyte's *Street Corner Society* (1955), will begin from at least a fallible knowledge base of a society (in this case an immigrant Italian community in a 1940s urban America). Documentary analysis likewise depends on a fallible knowledge of the social context in which the documents (or other media) were produced and (likely) their relationship to other documents. In other words, the interpretation of meaning in actual research is grounded in social context, which in turn means that hypothetical generalisations to other contexts may be attempted (Payne and Williams 2005, Williams 2000). Weber's call for explanations adequate at the level of cause and meaning, though never closely specified by him, can be actualised because the presence of an explanation provides at least the possibility of formulating it in causal terms.

REFERENCES

Bauman, Z (1978) *Hermeneutics and Social Science*. London: Hutchinson.

Clifford, J and Marcus, G E (1986) *Writing Culture: the poetics and politics of ethnography*. Berkeley, CA: University of California Press.

Denzin, N (1983) 'Interpretive interactionism', in Morgan, G (ed.), *Beyond Method: strategies for social research*. Bevereley Hills, CA: Sage.

Douglas, J (1976) *Investigative Social Research*. Beverley Hills, CA: Sage.

Goffman, E (1959) *The Presentation of Self in Everyday Life*. Garden City, NY: Doubleday.

Hughes, J (1990) *The Philosophy of Social Research*. Harlow: Longman.

Jones, T (1998) 'Interpretive social science and the "native's" point of view', *Philosophy of the Social Sciences*, 28 (1): 32–68.

Kincaid, H (1996) *Philosophical Foundations of the Social Sciences: analyzing controversies in social research*. Cambridge: Cambridge University Press.

Lurie, A (1995) *Imaginary Friends*. London: Minerva.

Mills, C Wright (1959) *The Sociological Imagination*. New York: Oxford University Press.

Payne, G and Williams, M (2005) 'Generalisation in qualitative research', *Sociology*, 39 (2): 295–314.

Weber, M (1978) 'The nature of social action', in Runciman, W (ed.), *Weber: selections in translation*. Cambridge: Cambridge University Press.

Whyte, W F (1955 [1943]) *Street Corner Society*, 2nd edn. Chicago, IL: University of Chicago Press.

Williams, M (2000) 'Interpretivism and generalisation', *Sociology*, 34 (2): 209–224.

Ytreberg, E (2009) 'The question of calculation: Erving Goffman and the pervasive planning of communication', in Jacobsen, M (ed.), *The Contemporary Goffman*. London: Routledge. pp. 199–231.

KEY READINGS

Hammersley, M (1998) *Reading Ethnographic Research*, 2nd edn. London: Longman.
O'Reilly, K (2009) *Key Concepts in Ethnography*. London: Sage.
Seale, C (1999) *The Quality of Qualitative Research*. London: Sage.

KEY THINKERS

Franz Boas; Norman Denzin; Erving Goffman; Martyn Hammersley; Max Weber; William Foote Whyte

See also: *Causality; Explanation; Idealism; Language; Relativism*

Language

Language might be said to be the 'glue' of social life. Taken broadly as communication, which expresses intentionality (see **interpretation and meaning**), it is a necessary condition of social life. Yet despite its centrality, or maybe because of it, the extent and ways in which it creates the social and how we can come to know the social through language has often been controversial. This section summarises a debate between those who see language as constructing reality and those who see it as representing reality.

> *The place of language in philosophy is initially discussed firstly in relation to positivism and then in the work of Wittgenstein. His claim of the impossibility of a 'private language' is discussed and the subsequent influence on the work of Peter Winch and* The Idea of a Social Science. *The incommensurability problem and the Sapir Whorf hypothesis. Language in the possibility and limitations of social research.*

LANGUAGE AND PHILOSOPHY

Language has concerned philosophers from Plato onwards. Plato asks us to consider whether it would be just to return weapons to a madman and in doing so wishes us to consider the concept of justice contained in the word 'just'. Immediately one can see how the contestation of a word makes the concept itself contentious. The great philosophical problem of language is its relationship to concepts. By 'concepts' I mean things in the world and our thoughts about those things (never mind for the moment that this dichotomy is itself contentious!). Once there was a view, amongst some philosophers, that language not only shaped thought (and therefore social life), but that it was prior to thought. This view is not much held these days because it is relatively easily refuted through examples, such as music or art, which require no verbalisation (Webb 1995: 49). Nevertheless, 'deconstructivists' such as Derrida (see **postmodernism**) come close to this by according language both priority and autonomy – famously in the view that the 'text' takes on a meaning autonomous of its author's intention.

Two oppositional views on language, in philosophy, continue to influence social science. The first is attributable to empiricism (specifically logical positivism) and particularly A J Ayer (2001). In this view a precision about language is essential for good philosophy, as it is in science. Linguistically carefully specified theories can be tested through observation, which themselves should be specified linguistically. This gave rise to the idea of a 'theoretical language' and an 'observational language' and the consequent difficulties of their overlap or distinction (see **positivism** and **empiricism**). In positivism language is naming, and there are only observations and their naming. The more extreme version of this philosophy has few followers in social science now, but a concern with 'naming' or representation continues in science, though far less simplistically than the positivists would allow. Realists, for example, will credit a great deal of autonomy to language, but also stress the complexity of its relationship to underlying phenomena (see e.g. Sayer 2000: 36–37).

A quite opposite view is represented in the work of Wittgenstein. Wittgenstein treated language as primarily social and asks us to consider the philosophical impossibility of a 'private language'. The rules of such a language could only be known to (and therefore infinitely changeable) by the owner of such language and would therefore not be a language, because there would be no intelligibility for others. Wittgenstein extends this social, rules-based approach to the analogy of the language game. The rules of a social setting can be treated like the rules of a game, that they have their own internal logical relationships, that do not extend beyond the game (though these can be learnt by outsiders of the game). Like all games, in the language game of social life we need to know the rules to play successfully.

Wittgenstein was an important influence on the work of Peter Winch, who maintained that the task of social investigation is to make intelligible the 'forms of life' of a particular society (Winch 1990: 42). The forms of life are embodied in rules which are expressed and known through language. Therefore to understand a form of life one must understand the language. If a social 'reality' is created by the rules of its language, then the different rules in a different society create different realities, and it follows from this that the reality of an investigator is just another reality and there can be no privileging of an investigator account from that of the society investigated.

If stated in linguistic terms, this presents a major problem: can the speakers of language A ever come to know language B? Indeed the question itself, for some, makes no sense because it requires us to have an agreed specification of the expression 'to know'. This leads to what is sometimes termed the 'incommensurability problem', that is because the language of culture A contains concepts not intelligible in culture B, and this has important implications for science and social science. Its most radical form predated Winch and can be found in the Sapir Whorf hypothesis (Whorf 1956), which maintains that language does not simply reproduce ideas but actually shapes the ideas themselves (see **relativism**). In this view Newtonian space and time are not intuitions about reality, but instead are the product of linguistically produced culture (Whorf 1956: 153).

If this view is upheld, the methodological implications for social science would be very great and would even call into question any form of interpretive research that did not involve the researcher as a full participant.

LANGUAGE AND SOCIAL RESEARCH

Winch's influence was not always direct in social science, indeed it virtually amounts to a denial of its possibility! Ethnomethodology was directly influenced by him in the way it challenged the taken-for-granted ways in which we use words or combinations of words. Less directly the ideas of Winch (and indeed Wittgenstein) played a part in the linguistic relativism of postmodernism (see **postmodernism**).

Winch's ideas appeared at the time when there was the beginning of a questioning of the key tenets of positivism and also that of the 'classical anthropology' of people such as Boas, Malinowski and Radcliffe-Brown (see **functionalism**). Though anthropologists such as these were seen as theoretically and methodologically innovative in their time, language was not a central consideration to them. Malinowski, (1937) for example, pioneered participant observation in his work in the Trobriand Islands, but he did this with little knowledge of the local languages. Clifford Geertz (1979) conducted extensive observational research in Bali in the late 1950s, again with little or no knowledge of the language spoken in Bali. One does not need to embrace the radical position of Winch to see the difficulties anthropologists must have in interpreting meaning when this must be understood through translation.

Most philosophers and social scientists would say that the problem of linguistic incommensurability is overstated. Wittgenstein's concept of a language game is a useful heuristic and helps us to understand how rules are embodied in language and how language sets its limits. But if we pursue incommensurability too far, we end up with a *reductio ad absurdum*,[9] whereby to know a social group, however narrowly defined, we must become part of that social group. To research gay groups, we must be gay, to research Welsh groups we must be Welsh and consequently to research Welsh gay groups, we must be both Welsh and gay!

In everyday social life we are capable of learning through language, and although we will encounter variable amounts of difficulty (depending on both the difficulty of the linguistic expression or the concept), we can come to know the language (and the social rules) of other groups. Indeed Wittgenstein himself acknowledged this. Much depends on how socially different the groups researched are to the social experience of the researcher: the greater the difference, the greater the challenge of interpretation. Furthermore language and cultural form are not coterminous. Arguably there is as much, if not more, cultural similarity between the many linguistic groups of Western Europe, where there is no language in common, than there is across the whole of Russia where there is (that is not to imply that Russian is the only language).

[9] A term used in philosophy whereby an argument pursued to its limits leads to absurd consequences, as in the example.

So if, in everyday life, there is not a radical incommensurability created by language, then there is no reason to suppose this is a barrier for ethnography – though logically because we have no 'meta language' to adjudicate, some level of assumption of validity will always be necessary. Whilst cultural difference may possibly provide grounds for moral or epistemological relativism, the claim that this is demonstrated through linguistic relativity can be readily challenged. That this doctrine of linguistic despair is not upheld is good news for the anthropologist or ethnographer, but it does not exhaust the methodological problem of language for social research, and even for the survey researcher language can be problematic. The problem of precision, identified by the positivists, remains.

In every respect positivism isn't what it was and many maintain it is dead (Phillips 1987)! It has evolved into post-positivism, realism and pragmatism. Some of the critique of the linguistic turn that began with Sapir, Whorf and Winch has been incorporated into method, and language is central to reflexivity. Yet although possibly dead, it lives on as a powerful ghost in our methods (if not as much in methodology). For example, a key debate in survey research is in how we can validly operationalise theories into measurements?

Philosophically the problem is an old one (I began this section with Plato's challenge on what we consider to be 'just'), and as many of our theoretical concepts in social science originate in philosophy, for example democracy, alienation, morality, the dilemma of their variable stipulation persists in social research. Some terms, say 'alienation', defy operationalisation, though in everyday discourse we are often able to make our meanings clear, or at least through clarification clear enough. But is this good enough in social research?

In survey research precision to preserve validity and reliability is crucial, but often elusive. Social class is an excellent example. There are a number of clear measurable definitions of social class, but historically they have suffered from problems of reliability and validity. In the first case standardisation over societies (or time) is difficult when social class is differently operationalised. The problem of validity is found at both macro and micro levels. At the macro level, however defined and then measured, social class is quite a different concept. Compare, for example, social class in the UK with France (very similar), with Brazil (some similarities, but important differences), with Iran (completely different) (Williams 2003). At a micro level, the class people would ascribe themselves to is not necessarily the class to which the sociologist would allocate them.

The example of social class measurement goes to the core of the problem of language. Is this simply a matter of the concept is what is described in language and the issue is one of language commensurability or incommensurability? Is it that what one measures in Iran (and calls it class) is a quite different thing to that which is measured in the UK or Australia (and calls it class)?

Finally, for the researcher, there is the problem that language is not static, it evolves. This is an obvious problem for the ethnographer, who will often find that communities use a word in quite different ways. In the 2000s, young black urban cultures in the US and other Anglophone cultures inverted terms such as 'bad' and 'wicked' to mean the opposite of their former use. Young North Africans, in urban France, have transposed French word endings and beginnings to create new words and mixed them with Arabic expressions and words. This is a species of the commensurability problem, but additionally communities will take social science linguistic categories, for example 'homelessness', re-work and often politicise them, leading to whole new definitional problems for the researcher. An entirely satisfactory philosophical or methodological solution is probably elusive and we have to do what we can at a 'technical' level. Cross-national/cross-cultural (and linguistic) measurement is possible (see Jowell et al. 2007). In cross-national social surveys it has been possible to standardise concepts and measurements, even though the questions are not always exact linguistic translations. And finally, yes, it must be conceded that not all social settings can be researched through standardised instruments and indeed it is possible that some cannot be researched at all with any reasonable claims to validity, yet alone reliability.

REFERENCES

Ayer, A J (2001 [1946]) *Language, Truth and Logic*, 2nd edn. London: Penguin.

Geertz, C (1979) 'Deep play: notes on the Balinese cockfight', in Rabinow, P and Sullivan, M (eds), *Interpretive Social Science – A Reader.* Berkeley, CA: University of California Press.

Jowell, R, Roberts, C, Fitzgerald, R and Eva, G (eds) (2007) *Measuring Attitudes Cross Nationally*. London: Sage.

Malinowski, B (1937) *Sex and Repression in Savage Society.* London: Routledge and Kegan Paul.

Philips, D (1987) *Philosophy, Science and Social Inquiry: contemporary methodological controversies in social science and related applied fields of research*. Oxford: Pergamon.

Sayer, A (2000) *Realism and Social Science*. London: Sage.

Webb, K (1995) *An Introduction to Problems in the Philosophy of Social Science*. London: Continuum.
Whorf, B (1956) *Language, Thought and Reality* (edited by J Carroll). New York: Wiley.
Williams, M (2003) 'The problem of representation: realism and operationalism in survey research', *Sociological Research On Line*, 8: 1.
Winch, P (1990 [1958]) *The Idea of a Social Science and its Relation to Philosophy*. London: Routledge.

KEY READINGS

Gellner, E (1959) *Words and Things: a critical account of linguistic philosophy and a study in ideology*. London: Gollancz.
Hacking, I (2002 [1983]) 'Making up people', in Hacking, I (ed.), *Historical Ontology*. Cambridge, MA: Harvard University Press.
Hollis, M and Lukes, S (eds) (1982) *Rationality and Relativism*. Cambridge, MA: MIT Press.
Wilson, B (ed.) (1991) *Rationality*. Oxford: Blackwell.

KEY THINKERS

A J Ayer; Jaques Derrida; Ernest Gellner; Peter Winch, Ludwig Wittgenstein

See also: *Explanation; Idealism; Postmodernism; Rationality; Relativism*

Logic and Truth

Deductive logic is the basis of reasoning and is a foundation of science. It is an abstract concept which requires a symmetry between premises and a conclusion in an argument. The search for truth is an attempt to provide the content for that argument, but truth unlike logic is an elusive concept.

The section begins with an overview of the difference between logical statements and statements of truth. It goes on to describe some key properties of a logical statement and the importance of this form of reasoning to science. Theories of truth and their relationship to logic are then discussed.

Deductive logic and truth underpin science, though philosophically they are contested concepts, particularly that of truth. An epistemological rejection of scientific reasoning leaves one free to reject logic and truth, but once it is allowed that there should be a systematic pursuit of knowledge (call it science, or something else), then concepts become necessary (Williams 2000: ch. 1). Some philosophers, for example Nietzsche, maintained that all knowledge is situated in historical periods, there is no view from nowhere and consequently no abiding truths. This relativist view was much promoted by postmodernist in the second half of the 20th century and is discussed in the section on **relativism**. However, even relativist arguments rely on logical reasoning, even if they reject that there can be any universal truths. Indeed even in our everyday reasoning we must employ notions of logic and truth. If I say that 'there is no point arriving on time because Denzil is always late', then I have stated a premise, which I believe to be true concerning Denzil's habits, and my conclusion leads me to advocate acting upon this. Almost every action we take is based on this form of reasoning, however informal.

In science, just as in this kind of everyday example, we seek a convergence between logic and truth, but they are actually quite different concepts. We can have truths without logic and logic without truths. Moreover, here I am talking about deductive forms of logic, and there are (or many claim) inductive forms of logic.

Consider these three statements:

- The capital of Canada is Ottawa. English and French are spoken in Ottawa. Therefore, my friend Paul, who lives in Ottawa, speaks English and French.
- All cats have nine lives. Calico is a cat, so Calico has nine lives.
- Water expands when it is frozen. Last night my pipes froze and this morning one was burst. The burst pipe was caused by the water expanding.

The first statement contained three true sentences, yet the conclusion from the first two, that Paul speaks both English and French, does not follow. The first sentences, though true, do not imply the third. The third is a non sequitur.

The second statement is not true (well at least there is absolutely no empirical evidence that cats have nine lives, even if cat lovers would like to believe it!), though it is entirely logical. If all cats have nine lives and indeed Calico is a cat, then Calico must have nine lives. This example illustrates a key characteristic of deductive logic: that of abstraction. Deductive logic does not rely on empirical evidence, but rather on the linguistic structure of a sentence. Indeed we do not even need linguistic structure to express an argument, but may use symbols instead to stand in for the premises and conclusion.

The third statement is both logical and true (see **generalisation and laws**). The cause of the burst pipe can be deduced from the prior known characteristics of water and that the pipe froze last night. But there is a slight sting in the tail. Whilst this is a reasonable piece of empirical deduction, it may have been the case that the pipe burst for different reasons (say as a result of a weakness that had nothing to do with the freezing).

In social research we aim to produce statements that are both logical and true, though like the burst pipe example our deduction might be based on the best possible empirical evidence. Consider two more statements:

- House building has declined by 50 per cent during the recession of the last two years. Meanwhile housing officers report an increase of 10 per cent in those recorded as homeless. It is perfectly clear that the reduction in house building has had consequences for those seeking housing and increased homelessness is the result.
- Last year the median household income was £21,000 and the mean house price in the lowest quartile was £150,000. Banks will mostly only lend up to three times annual income and require 5 per cent deposit. Consequently those earning less than £50,000 will have difficulty in buying property.

Both statements have been adapted from real examples, the first from a local newspaper editorial, the second from a research report. The first sounds logical and true and is persuasive. The first two premises may indeed be true, but there are two conclusions in the final sentence. The first one is rather vague and may or may not be true, but the second was almost certainly not true because the housing supply for the past ten years or more in the area the newspaper covered had been predominantly unaffordable for local people and most certainly for those who were homeless. In this case the increase in homelessness was due to a number of complex factors, including a reduction in the numbers of available cheap rented properties and a dramatic rise in unemployment that put even cheap rented accommodation beyond the affordability of many.

The second statement is a fairly modest, yet persuasive, conclusion. Based on income and price data, it does not say that no one earning £21,000 or less would be able to buy, but is fairly typical research finding that policy makers would be prepared to act upon.

In logic we aim to produce valid arguments. A valid argument is where the conclusion must follow from the premises, which do not have to be true but must be in agreement with the conclusion. To challenge the logic of an argument, as opposed to its truth, it is necessary to challenge the validity of its structure. However, if the premises are themselves true statements about the world, then logic is 'truth preserving', that is, the conclusion that follows must be true.

I have laboured this final point for two reasons. First, as you can see from the 'pipe' and the 'homelessness' example above, premises are rarely this 'tidy' and their truth seems likely, though not guaranteed. Indeed in the pipe example a logician would question (for the reason I gave) whether the conclusion was valid. Yet much of the time we must settle for a syllogism that is not quite perfect and the conclusion is an inference to the best explanation (see Lipton 1991) (see **hypothesis(es)**). Second, and related to this point, much of our knowledge is inductive (see **induction**). Inductive logic uses forms of probability (see **probability**) to analyse 'risky' arguments. Thus, the greater the probability of X, then the greater the probability of any outcome statement. In practice a hypothesis will predict an outcome in the form of a deductive claim, which is empirically testable, thus it aims to move from induction to deduction and in so doing shows something is true.

DEDUCTION V. INDUCTION

In social research both deductive and inductive reasoning are used. Though it is sometimes said that qualitative research uses inductive reasoning, because it often begins from observations and builds theory, whilst quantitative research uses deductive reasoning, because it tests theories for their logical and empirical validity. However, in practice it is more complicated. All research begins from at least informal theory assumptions/hunches and so on, and qualitative research is no exception. Even grounded theory (see **pragmatism**) will develop a deductive structure as it progresses. Quantitative research does indeed deductively test theories, but most quantitative research is based on sample data and the inferences to populations are inductive (see **induction** and **probability**).

FUZZY LOGIC

Some would claim that 'fuzzy logic' is an oxymoron, yet it has value in describing complex concepts (see **complexity**). In the above bivalent logic statements must ultimately be reducible to P or not P, but in fuzzy logic adjectives do not have specifically defined boundaries, such as 'large', 'many', 'heavy' which might be used to specify characteristics. In some applications or methods, for example 'fuzzy set qualitative comparative analysis' (fQCA), they stand in as imprecisely defined logical relationships (QCA depends specifically on logical relationships) (Glaesser and Cooper 2014). However, in most social science, traditional forms of logical reasoning cannot be replaced with 'fuzzy logic', even if the concepts described are themselves subject to flux in time and space.

TRUTH

Sometimes philosophers will use the expression 'true in all possible worlds', meaning that there could be no circumstances under which a statement could be false. An exemplar of this is mathematics, though even mathematical claims are sometimes contested. Matters of empirical truth that satisfy this criterion are rare, even non-existent. In the last few decades cosmologists have demonstrated that even the fundamental laws of nature will break down in a 'black hole singularity' (Davies 1994: 88–91). More mundanely, there are many things that were once held to be true, but this is no longer the case. In this I exclude moral truths (though that moral truths change through time and place is itself an important feature of social science) and am thinking solely of scientific truths, say in medicine, biology or physics. The latter, the bedrock of science, has experienced numerous refutations of what it held to be true. Even when a theory or law (such as Newton's Laws) is not shown to be wholly wrong, it becomes incorporated into a new theory or law as a limiting case. Newton's law of gravity is not wrong, but just part of the 'truth' and is incorporated into relativity, which in its turn looks like being only a part of the truth.

Given the historical legacy of refutation, can we really talk of 'truth', especially in the social world? Relativists (see **relativism**) dispute whether there are any truths, whether they are based on observation, cognition, knowledge or moral judgement, and relativism has been an influence on much social 'science' in the last quarter of a century. The belief that we can say anything about the world without making truth claims of some kind is disputed and philosophers have attempted to get over the kind of problems I outline by proposing alternative theories of truth.

THEORIES OF TRUTH

The common-sense theory of truth is also that employed by most scientists and is called the 'correspondence theory of truth'. In this something is true if there is agreement with the facts, which sounds rather like the structure of a logical argument because it requires an agreement between premises and conclusion. But there are two important difficulties. First, there is the logical problem of sentences such as 'this statement is false'. If the sentence is true, then what it says must be true – that it is false, but if it is false then what it says must be false, so it must be true! The logician Alfred Tarski attempted to solve this problem by saying that the truth of a sentence can only be established in a further sentence(s) (Popper 1989: 116). Nevertheless, this requirement for a 'meta-language' appears counter intuitive and complex. Second, most of the really important questions are matters of dispute about the constitution of the facts. It is all very well saying that truth is agreement with the facts when we can agree what the facts are! This is especially problematic in social research where a decision as to what and how to measure something will shape the conclusion. Note that the housing example above measured mean house prices within price quartiles, which (in my view) provides a more accurate picture of affordability. But the researchers could have used the mean of all house prices which would have made affordability seem a worse problem, or the median that might make it seem less of a problem.

Some philosophers abandon correspondence for coherence, which retains the logical structure of a statement but seeks intersubjective agreement about what is true. This can work in arbitrary, but nevertheless agreed matters such as measurement. Statisticians (or at least those involved in social measurement), for example, agree that we should use confidence intervals of 3 per cent or 5 per cent, but these numbers are a product only of historic agreement. However, intersubjective agreement on empirical matters works until there is disagreement with observations (not uncommon in science), leaving the supporter of this theory of truth to deny the coherence, or the fact of the matter.

A version of truth that has underwritten a great deal of social science, particularly in the US, is the pragmatic theory of truth (see **pragmatism**). This version requires us to make a decision about utility. Suppose we have two theories, A and B. The empirical evidence for both is the same. How do we choose? The pragmatist says we choose the one with the greater utility. This might be the one that offers greater predictive value, will benefit one group more than another, or is perhaps simpler. The point is one must decide on utility, and in some circumstances this may mean assigning degrees of belief to a particular theory. This, of course, is the way Baysian statistics proceeds (see **statistics**). More than any other theory of truth, this one has implicitly moral connotations. To choose A over B on the grounds of its benefit to a community is a moral decision which must be defended on grounds outside of those underlying a truth claim. Similarly when odds are equal and A is chosen over B, the reasoning requires reference to other external criteria.

It should be apparent that whichever theory of truth one adopts it is not without consequences. I, as most scientists, prefer to stay with the correspondence theory of truth, despite its shortcomings. This is for three reasons. First, that deductive logic is truth preserving only if the premises match the facts. This may be hard to achieve with inductive statements, but is possible with deductive ones. For example, '82 per cent of the sample of residents opposed the building of the incinerator, so we can conclude from our sample that there is a majority opposition to its construction'. Second, if we regard truth seeking as a value, not an outcome that can necessarily be achieved, it provides us with an important 'value' in social research, in much the same way as 'validity' or 'reflexivity'. Third, it seems inescapable that other theories of truth must make reference to the fact of the matter at some point and consequently 'collapse' into correspondence.

REFERENCES

Davies, P (1994) *The Edge of Infinity*. Harmondsworth: Penguin.

Glaesser, J and Cooper, B (2014) 'Exploring the consequences of a recalibration of causal conditions when assessing sufficiency with fuzzy set QCA', *International Journal of Social Research Methodology*, 17 (4): 387–401.

Lipton, P (1991) *Inference to the Best Explanation*. London: Routledge.

Popper, K (1989) *Conjectures and Refutations*. London: Routledge.

Williams, M (2000) *Science and Social Science: an introduction*. London: Routledge.

KEY READINGS

Hacking, I (2001) *An Introduction to Probability and Inductive Logic*. Cambridge: Cambridge University Press.
Phelan, P and Reynolds, P (1996) *Argument and Evidence: critical analysis for the social sciences*. London: Routledge.

KEY THINKERS

Bertrand Russell; Charles Sanders Peirce; Alfred Tarski, Ian Hacking

See also: *Generalisation and Laws; Hypothesis(es); Induction; Pragmatism; Probability; Relativism; Statistics*

Materialism

Materialism should be contrasted with **idealism** and is a foundational idea in metaphysics that holds that the world is material in composition, rather than mental. It is important in the social sciences (and social research) because some social scientists maintain that the material world fundamentally shapes and limits the social world.

The materialist–idealist divide in philosophy and its relationship to realism, idealism and empiricism. Materialism and study of the social world. What we understand by the 'material' and the 'mental'. Non-human agents, consciousness and the social world. Accommodating the material world in the social.

Throughout the history of philosophy there has been a debate about what the world consists of. Famously, Descartes separated existing and thinking and ever since, the mind–body problem has troubled philosophers, psychologists and biologists. There has been a divide between dualists, those who believe there is a physical and mental phenomena (dualists), monists, who believe there is only one kind of thing in the world – or at least that we can know of, be it mental or physical – and pluralists, those who believe there are many different kinds of things in the world. Although we will talk of philosophical positions, such as **idealism**, **empiricism** or **realism**, there is a more fundamental divide between materialists who say the world is material and idealists who say it consists of the mental (ideas). Realists will tend toward either materialist or pluralist explanation. Similarly, empiricists may be materialists, but often they avoid the question by avoiding reference to anything beyond sense data, but in logical positivism (see **empiricism**) and particularly the writings of Ernst Mach, there is a strong tendency to anti-materialism (Cohen and Seeger 1975).

The more radical form of materialism is exemplified by the eliminative materialism of Paul and Patricia Churchland (see McCauley 1996 for an account and criticism), which holds that all mental concepts, such as beliefs and desires (see **rationality**), are 'folk psychology'. This leads to a strong form of behaviourism and would make what is usually understood as a social science impossible because mental concepts are central to it, but would not be admissible in this radical from of materialism.

In its more moderate form, materialism emphasises the importance of the physical world to social science claiming that mental properties must always be explained by physical ones, that they are at least in principle reducible. Even more moderately, some forms of non-reductionist social science aim to bring the 'material back in', that is to say the ways in which the material world enable and constrain the social world must be part of any adequate social explanation. An example of the latter is Marx's historical materialism, which holds that changes in the material conditions of existence, such as production and technology, will greatly determine economy and society (Giddens 1995).

WHAT IS THE MATERIAL AND THE MENTAL?

One of the paradoxes of materialism is that we require mental concepts to describe the material world and to argue for its existence, or indeed that only it exists, so whether or not the mental (and by implication, of course, the social) is reducible to the material, there is something that perhaps masquerades as the mental to be explained (Margolis 2006: 208). It is possible to trace mental phenomena to physical processes and sensations – precisely what biological psychologists do. Though the brain itself is complex (in the mathematical sense) (see **complexity**), progress has been made in linking particular mental processes to areas of the brain. Mental processes are in the brain and only in the brain and cannot exist without the complex material existence of the brain. However, beyond the description of a thought as information transmitted as an electro-chemical signal, what thoughts 'are' remains elusive. That is not to say that thoughts cannot be stored and are accessible to other brains, what Karl Popper called the 'third world' (the first world consists of things, physical objects, and the second world is that of subjective experiences, or thought processes) (Popper 1994); indeed the ability of civilisation to do this through books, music, electronically (in analogue and digital form) is perhaps a requirement for the possibility of a debate about the material and mental! However, the higher mental processes that make the third world possible are relatively new to humans and are a product of evolution. Other higher mammals possess mental capacity in varying degrees (consider the 'intelligence' difference between a chimpanzee and a rabbit). The 'mental', whatever it is and if it exists, is something that appears to differ between species and evolves, at least in humans.

Even if we do not know what the mental is, we do know that it has physical origins and moreover in itself, apart from electro-chemical stimulus in the brain, it is incapable of operationalisation without the physical. My words on the screen may have originated as thoughts, but are mediated through my own complex physiology and electro-mechanical and digital workings of a computer. However, the picture I have painted of no mental concepts without physical ones only works to an extent.

What we can mean by 'material' is in itself not straightforward. In the 19th century the material was solid matter, forms of energy such as light and sound were excluded. But nowadays the picture is very much more complicated and there is no universal definition of matter. At a sub-atomic level, matter and energy can display characteristics of both waves and particles, so we must talk of 'states' rather than 'matter' as before.

An analogous problem afflicts definitions of the 'mental', which is a summary term for many things, such as thoughts, beliefs, memories, experiences, emotions, dreams, hallucinations, motives and so on. Moreover, it is almost certainly the case, as Freud believed, that not all mental states are accessible to us and certainly not all are immediately accessible.

NON-HUMAN AGENTS AND THE SOCIAL WORLD

There is a further argument for the evolution of the mental from the physical, though this is even more contentious, and it is that humans have been able to build machines that have intelligence and the most advanced ones are capable of faster and more complex thought processes than humans. Famously, the computer 'Deep Blue' beat the World Chess Champion, Garry Kasparov, in 1997.

In less than a century we have moved from machines that can react to simple stimuli and perform a task, to those which appear to emulate human thinking and behaviour and are capable of performing complex mental tasks very much more quickly and in more sophisticated ways than humans. In a sense the argument that the computational ability of machines is traceable to hardware and software components is correct, but the crucial thing about even the most sophisticated computer is that it only simulates mental conditions. We cannot answer whether or not future computers are able to develop mental conditions directly attributable to them, but such conditions would require them to have sensations, moods, dreams and, most importantly, reflection. Not just first-order reflection, which may simply be an awareness of existing, or states of existing, but to be aware of such awarenesses.

Of course, computers can do a good job in tricking us into thinking they are human, as in the Turing Test where the aim is for a computer to successfully mimic a human being, and this will present methodological challenges both for survey and interpretivist social researchers, when it may be increasingly difficult to detect a human agent from an avatar, through digital media. Even more speculatively, the increasing use of digitally proxemic technologies will turn humans into cyborgs (as indeed predicted by the feminist philosopher Donna Haraway in 1991). A cyborg was originally understood as a human–machine system, in which regulatory or stimulatory devices enhance human environmental adaptation. However, even without thinking in science fiction terms, one can imagine the existing and future possibilities of amalgamating machine and human mental processes. Even more fascinating is what should count as the boundary between human and machine, particularly when the machine itself is imbued with many human characteristics? In a world consisting of human, machine and human-machine agents, what will count as 'social research' in some (maybe not so) distant future?

An interesting development in this direction, in the last few decades, has been that of actor network theory (ANT) (Latour 2005). ANT sees humans as existing in networks with non-human objects, but it also treats those objects as actors in those networks. ANT originated in the sociology of science, particularly in the work of Bruno Latour, whose studies of the work of scientists in the laboratory led him to theorise that the 'objects' of study, chemicals, micro-organisms, instruments and so on were as much part of laboratory interactions as the scientists themselves, and indeed could have a social existence beyond the laboratory (Benton and Craib 2001: 69). ANT blurs the ontological distinction between the material and the mental, although again paradoxically a theorisation of this process is itself exclusively a mental event.

MENTAL MONISM AND IDEALIST SOCIAL SCIENCE

The truism noted above, that whatever the fact of the matter the material world can only be known through mental processes, is emphasised by idealists who will assert either that a material world beyond mental processes is unknowable or that there is only the mental. In 'idealist' social science, the distinction is not particularly important, but the primacy of the mental is. **idealism** is underwriting philosophy of approaches to knowing the social that emphasise interpretation of discourse and action as reducible to a knowledge of mental processes or 'ideas'. Such an argument can be made not only in respect of temporal knowledge, but also historical knowledge and even natural science. To know an event or process in nature is really to know how humans mentally (and socially) construct that process.

Most idealist-inspired social science is not in denial in any kind of simplistic way of the existence of a material world, but a more sceptical stance about whether we can ever know anything beyond ideas. What we call 'social reality' is constructed through meaningful shared interpretations. Many idealist social scientists will separate out the world of 'nature' from the social world and many will allow that the former can enable and constrain. This does not necessarily make them dualists because they still see the physical world as 'constructed' through the ideas of the social.

A strict adherence to mental monism has its methodological limitations in social science. First, causal explanation must be ultimately attributable to mental properties, so a causal explanation of educational under-achievement must be traceable to accounts of how individuals interpret the world, leading to a radical methodological individualism (see **individualism and holism**). In practice, most interpretivist social scientists eschew causal explanation, more on the grounds of an ontological claim about the variability of human consciousness and the consequent constant interpreting and reinterpreting of the social world.

ACCOMMODATING THE PHILOSOPHICAL CONTRADICTION

The foregoing indicates some of the philosophical problems for materialism and its denial. Dualists, likewise, must show the causal relations between the mental and material and whilst pluralism seems philosophically attractive, particularly now that it is hard to provide a clear distinction between the mental and material, it too suffers from the need to provide causal or relational explanation between plural phenomena.

In practice, for the social researcher, a moderate interactionism is practically possible. Few support radical materialist positions, such as those of Paul and Patricia Churchlands, though there are still plenty of 'idealist' or 'constructionist' researchers who ignore, deny or downplay the role of the material world in creating (and indeed being created by) the social world. Yet we are almost certainly on the brink of a revolution in computing that will both change how we think about the material–mental and how we do (or indeed what is) social research.

However, at the present time the concerns of the social researcher, in respect of the material world, are more mundane. Consider an account, say through interview, of a respondent in a qualitative study. Her accounts will often be replete with reference to the material world, to objects or 'forces' in that world. Of course she constructs these, but they are nevertheless enabling and constraining. In everyday conversation we attribute anthropomorphic qualities to objects and it is almost impossible to think without reference to the material world. An observation of a public space will equally show how that space is socially constructed, but the freedom to do so is a function of the physical environment. We can't just make it up.

Finally, even more mundanely, most surveys will contain questions that are first- or second-order reference to physical characteristics. Obvious ones such as age, sex, but also things like earnings, which will enable and constrain and produce material outcomes.

REFERENCES

Benton, T and Craib, I (2001) *Philosophy of Social Science: the philosophical foundations of social thought*. Basingstoke: Palgrave.
Cohen, R and Seeger, R (1975). *Ernst Mach, Physicist and Philosopher*. Berlin: Springer.
Giddens, A (1995) *A Contemporary Critique of Historical Materialism*, 2nd edn. London: Palgrave Macmillan.
Haraway, D (1991) *Simians, Cyborgs and Women: the reinvention of nature*. London: Routledge.
Latour, B (2005) *Reassembling the Social – an introduction to actor-network-theory*. Oxford: Oxford University Press.
Margolis, J (2006) *Introduction to Philosophical Problems*. London: Bloomsbury.
McCauley, R (1996) *The Churchlands and their Critics (Philosophers and their Critics)*. Oxford: Oxford University Press.
Popper, K (1994) *Knowledge and the Body-Mind Problem: in defence of interactionism* (edited by M A Notturno). London: Routledge.

KEY READINGS

Margolis, J (2005) *Introduction to Philosophical Problems*. London: Bloomsbury. ch. 8.
McCauley, R (1996) *The Churchlands and their Critics (Philosophers and their Critics)*. Oxford: Oxford University Press.
Philips, M (2015) 'What is Materialism?', *Philosophy Now*, April/May.

KEY THINKERS

Paul Churchland; Patricia Churchland; Daniel Dennett; Donald Davidson; Jerry Fodor

See also: *Complexity; Empiricism; Idealism; Individualism and Holism; Rationality; Realism*

Mechanisms and Models

Mechanisms are systems of cohering parts working together, analogously like machines, though in the social world they are much less determinate. Models are a representative simplification of the world that either abstract data from a reality, otherwise too complex to grasp, or used simulated data to construct hypothetical representations of it.

In this section the difference between mechanisms and models is shown. Models are representations, but can come in different forms, here I examine the three main forms in social science: theoretical, statistical and simulation. Mechanisms are then contrasted with models and their relationship to explanation is described. Finally I examine what we might mean by the reality of mechanisms.

Though mechanisms and models are each explanatory devices, they are not the same thing. A mechanism is a concrete system, 'real things held together by some bonds, or forces behaving as a unit in some respects and embedded in some environment' (Bunge 1997: 415). Models are heuristic devices that may seek to represent empirical phenomena, such as mechanisms. However, what social scientists sometimes describe as a 'mechanism' is a *model* of a mechanism, which if it were correct would accurately describe the mechanism itself. Put very simply, mechanisms are ontological characteristics of the world, whilst models are an epistemological device to help us know it.

Models, then, are conceptual systems, yet they are a key feature of science and social science. They may be theoretical models, methodological models or statistical models. They may have different degrees of formality: they may specify their terms statistically, or in logical form (Boudon 1974), or they may be informal and expressed discursively. What they all have in common is that they are similes or images of a part of the world and they aim to represent its most important aspects. A statistical model, for example, will summarise aggregate characteristics (e.g. test scores, pupil characteristics, school type etc.) and then produce a statistical explanation of relationships. Importantly, models are not the real world but aim to capture enough information about it to produce explanations and predictions.

A description of a mechanism, however, goes further than a model and aims to capture the real processes that underlie observed patterns. Though it is at the heart of realist philosophy of science and social science, it is not exclusive to realists. It is tempting to think of mechanisms in a kind of clockwork way, which is not a bad starting point, but in the social and biological world, at least, this under-describes dynamic and complex processes (see **complexity**).

MODELS

A key problem for natural and social scientists is representation. This is particularly difficult in measurement in the social survey. Things like age, sex, educational attainment may present varying technical difficulties and can be represented, but it is a different matter with more 'sociological' variables, such as ethnicity, discrimination and so on (Blalock 1961). Some form of abstraction from theory to measurement is required. Analogously, if you were building a scale model of a jumbo jet, your materials would be quite different to the real thing, it would be smaller, have much less detail and of course not capable of carrying passengers several thousand miles. Each sociological variable in a model is like each component in the model jumbo jet: they resemble it but they are not it, nor are they copies of it. Indeed some of the model components may not look anything like their scaled-up version of the real thing. However, with some skill your jumbo jet model, once built, should be recognisable to a person who has seen a real jumbo jet. Likewise a model in social science should resemble social reality.

Engineers build models all of the time; they build models of bridges, wave tanks and so on, and test these under laboratory conditions, from which they can extrapolate how it might function in the real world. Social scientists do exactly the same thing, but with theories, statistics or sometimes simulations.

THEORETICAL MODELS

The distinction between a social theory and a theoretical model is a fine one, though it might be that social theory simply describes and explains social features or change at a relatively broad and abstract level. Such an example might be Anthony Giddens' 'structuration theory' (Giddens 1984), whereas a theoretical model will closely specify outcomes if certain conditions are met, or offer explanations for particular features of the social world. Robert Merton's 'theories of the middle range' (Merton 1968), whilst strictly speaking not models themselves, nevertheless provide concepts which are testable empirically (e.g. opportunity structures, reference groups, role sets etc.) in theoretical models. John Skvoretz (1998: 238–239) and Raymond Boudon (1974) each provide examples of theoretical models that may be tested empirically. As Skvoretz shows, the testing of these models might be with statistical data, so that a theoretical model is operationalised through a set of methodological procedures and tested through a statistical model.

STATISTICAL MODELS

Statistical models are the commonest in social science and these are generated from data gathered through surveys and experiments. Usually they will be described as causal models (see **causality**) and purport to model why something happened. Commonly these are regression models which test hypotheses about cause–effect relationships and to test the strength of those effects.

Notwithstanding the measurement issue I described above, there are two other key philosophical issues.

First, they under-describe the world. Now, this is not the same thing as saying they lack detail, it's rather that sometimes we cannot know whether important components that are vital to a model representation of an aspect of the social world are present. That is, how good are the data that went into the model? Suppose we wished to provide a statistical explanation of housing need. We may have data on house prices, income, class, age, occupation and so on. We fit a regression model to our data (see **statistics**) and we find that income explains much of the variance in the model, followed by house prices. This sounds intuitively right, but perhaps we had not measured household composition and household composition might have explained more of the variance. Certainly, in most instances, it is an important explanatory variable. This is a problem of induction (see **induction**), that we can't know what we didn't know! It is as if we set out to build a model of a wooden house when we have previously only seen those of brick and stone.

The second problem is related to the complexity of the world. Statistical models assume linearity, that is, relationships between two or more variables are calculated by the 'best fit' along a straight line, but the social world in particular is far from linear and is complex, with some elements that appear to be completely stochastic (see **complexity**).

SIMULATION MODELS

The second kind of model, though not usually seen as a 'rival' to statistical models, nevertheless approaches the problem of non-linearity in the social world in a novel way. Simulation models use computer codes to simulate social theories and can be compared to computer gaming scenarios (see **complexity**). Simulation models are usually quite simple models, but nevertheless can capture non-linear emergence by programming the initial interactions of just a few variables and watch them develop over time (see Gilbert and Troitzsch 2005).

MECHANISMS

Much of social science seeks to explain sequences of events (often in causal models of the type described above). Though rarely are those explanations of a simple X → Y type, they are usually provided in the context of a relationship between a dependent variable and several independent variables. What is absent in such explanations is how the independent variables came to be associated in their explanation of a phenomenon. Such models, in their most fundamental empiricist guise, are merely descriptive and any explanation that moves beyond them to 'unobservables' is deemed metaphysical and illegitimate by those that take such a puritan stance. However, in practice, researchers will move beyond such statistical models to provide a narrative contextualisation (see **causality**).

Mechanisms have been central to economic explanation for many decades, but despite the use of the term in an informal way, their explicit specification in sociology (and its analogous disciplines) can be traced to the work of Robert Merton (Hedstrom and Swedberg 1998: 5). Merton rejected grand abstract theory in favour of middle range theory (see **theory**) that should seek to identify social mechanisms in order to explain specific phenomena. This is summed up by Hedstrom and Swedberg as

> social processes having designated consequences for designated parts of the social structure and [he, Merton] argues that it constitutes the main task of sociology to identify mechanisms and to establish under which conditions they 'come into being' or 'fail to operate'. (Merton, cited in Hedstrom and Swedberg 1998: 6)

Mechanisms can be said to begin where descriptions of relationships between variables finish. Analogously, we know that if we turn the ignition of a car, the engine (usually) starts, but between the ignition and the engine is an electro-mechanical mechanism. Extend the analogy. Suppose we made a list of the components involved in this causal process, and further suppose that we know the order in which the components were active: well, we have something that is a bit like a statistical model in which we know most (though likely not all) of the components, how 'close' they are to each other, in terms of the strength of relationship, and we will know the causal direction. But that would not tell us what the mechanism was. A mechanism moves from description to the explanation of why the X causes Y. Thus a mechanism may be proposed as a theoretical entity, comprising other 'objects' that relate to each other in particular ways and with differing strength or importance. The statistical model becomes the tool of the proposed set of logical relationships that constitute the mechanism. The proposed mechanism is more than an abstract theory, it is a set of empirically testable propositions. In practice it will be modified and sometimes abandoned.

Mechanisms and 'mechanistic thinking' have become central to realism, particularly in the work of Ray Pawson and his followers (Pawson 2000, 2013; Williams 2014). Almost by definition mechanisms are realist because they (if they are shown to exist) are Bhaskar's 'intransitive objects' (see **realism**), they are what makes things in the social world what they are. Moreover they are not merely appearances, but underlie appearances (which of course may be deceptive). But, as I said above, the term 'mechanism' brings to mind literally mechanical processes, as in the engine example, but social mechanisms are non-linear, fluid and changing; nevertheless have enabling and constraining causal powers (see **causality**). Pawson captures this in his CMO formulation. Outcomes (O) are explained by mechanisms (M) which operate (or fail to operate) in contexts (C) (Pawson 2000).

ARE MECHANISMS REAL OR ARE THEY JUST MODELS?

It is at this point that my initial definition of mechanisms as 'ontological' and models as 'epistemological' becomes strained. Though we can find empirical evidence for the existence of mechanisms, to fully describe a mechanism is difficult on two grounds: first, we can never know whether we have ever fully captured its essentials; and second, social mechanisms (unlike, say, those of an engine) are never simple or even relatively static. They change their characteristics as a result of agent interaction and they overlap with other mechanisms. So even though we might describe a mechanism in context, the context will change and this will likely change the mechanism and so on. Therefore it may be helpful to think of *Mechanism 1* as ontological, that which exists in the social world. Thus, when something happens it is the result of the complex interplay of many antecedent factors. Now, we might be able to identify some of these, but putting them together into *Mechanism 2*, which is epistemological, is both a philosophical and methodological issue. It is philosophical because even if we claim to have identified a mechanism and its operating context, we cannot know that we know and the best we can hope for is the logical validation of our proposed mechanism and enough empirical adequacy (what realists call 'closure') for it to be an adequate representation of the world. Arguably, one might say that *Mechanism 2* is actually logically equivalent to a model, but one that will combine testable defined theoretical propositions with statistical models.

REFERENCES

Blalock, H (1961) *Causal Inference in Nonexperimental Research*. Chapel Hill, NC: University of North Carolina Press.

Boudon, R (1974) *The Logic of Sociological Explanation*. Harmondsworth: Penguin.

Bunge, M (1997) 'Mechanisms and explanation', *Philosophy of the Social Sciences*, 27 (4): 410–465.

Giddens, A (1984) *The Constitution of Society*. Cambridge: Polity.

Gilbert, N and Troitzsch, K (2005) *Simulation for the Social Scientist*, 2nd edn. Maidenhead: Open University Press.

Hedstrom, P and Swedborg, R (1998) 'Social mechanisms: an introductory essay', in Hedstrom, P and Swedborg, R (eds), *Social Mechanisms: an analytical approach to social theory*. Cambridge: Cambridge University Press. pp. 1–31.

Merton, R. (1968) *Social Theory and Social Structure.* New York: Free Press.

Pawson, R (2000) 'Middle-range realism', *Archive Européenes de Sociologie*, XLI: 283–325.

Pawson, R (2013) *The Science of Evaluation*. London: Sage.

Skvoretz, J (1998) 'Theoretical models: sociology's missing links', in Sica, A (ed.), *What is Social Theory: the philosophical debates*. Malden, MA: Blackwell.

Williams, M (2014) 'Probability and models', in Edwards, P, O'Mahoney, J and Vincent, S (eds), *Studying Organisations Using Critical Realism*. Oxford: Oxford University Press.

KEY READINGS

Hedstrom, P and Swedborg, R (eds) (1998) *Social Mechanisms: an analytical approach to social theory*. Cambridge: Cambridge University Press.

Pawson, R (1989) *A Measure for Measures: a manifesto for empirical sociology*. London: Routledge.
Skvoretz, J (1998) 'Theoretical models: sociology's missing links', in Sica, A (ed.), *What is Social Theory: the philosophical debates*. Malden, MA: Blackwell.

KEY THINKERS

Mario Bunge; Jon Elster; Peter Hedstrom; Ray Pawson; Richard Swedberg

See also: *Causality; Complexity; Induction; Realism; Statistics*

Objectivity – Subjectivity

Objectivity is contested in the social sciences. It has many definitions and emphases, but all concern the ability of the researcher to conduct investigations that transcend his or her subjective views or preferences.

> *The objectivity–subjectivity dichotomy is important in social science. This section, whilst describing the opposed positions of positivism and humanism on the matter, will then examine attempts to transcend the dichotomy. I will maintain that objectivity and value freedom are not the same thing and that a 'situated' form of objectivity is compatable with subjectivity.*

In the literature of social science, objectivity and subjectivity are often either dichotomised or the former is described as being more or less available to us, depending on the kind of social science we do. Objectivity and value freedom are also conflated, or used interchangeably. Some deny the possibility of objectivity *tout court* and some deny it because they see it as a claim to value freedom. These positions are somewhat simplistic, and one might say that the social sciences have not kept up with the debates in the philosophy of the natural sciences. In social science one can discern two philosophically opposed positions, roughly characterised as follows:

- Objectivity is freedom from moral or cultural values and it is the job of science to transcend these in its investigations and conclusions. It follows that social science should similarly do so and should be ever watchful against bias entering investigation. This position owes much to **positivism**, though can also trace its origin to the *methodenstreit* dispute in German philosophy as to whether social science should take a scientific or humanistic approach to investigation (Manicas 1987: 124–126). Although positivism has fallen out of favour with most social scientists, the position on values has persisted, particularly in quantitative research.
- Its opposite, which might be characterised as the humanist position, is the belief that investigations of the social cannot transcend the complex mesh of individual and collective values, that we can only know our own subjectivity and perhaps come to understand the subjectivities of others. This view is close to that of epistemological **relativism**, though it may also arise from a strong moral imperative that the whole point of studying the social is to bring about social change.

For many social scientists, engaged in their quotidian labours, the extremes of these debates hold little attraction and social research methods texts often rather simplistically equate subjectivity with qualitative research and objectivity with quantitative research. This truce, or philosophical fudge, worked to an extent when the two methodological camps got on with their own business, but in these days of mixed methods and 'methodological pluralism' (Payne and Payne 2004: 148–149), we probably need to do better.

VALUES

For the subjectivist (i.e. someone who rejects the possibility of objectivity in social science), values do not pose a major philosophical problem. There are certainly methodological issues but values are subjectively (or intersubjectively) held and these values include those embodied in investigation, so no privileging can take place. Or if it does, this should be on the basis of prior ideological commitment, often to an emancipatory ideal. Positivists and neo-positivists have not been insensitive to the question of values because if one wants to rule them out of investigation, it is necessary to know what they are. A key feature of positivist (and empiricist) philosophies of science is to separate out knowledge of what is the case in the world from our views of what should be the case (commonly referred to as 'is' and 'ought' statements). In this position, it is claimed, one cannot derive an 'ought' statement from an 'is' statement. One of the more sophisticated statements came from Ernest Nagel (1979: 492–494).

Nagel offers a defence of the distinction, in social science, by attempting to separate 'describing ideas' (what he terms 'appraising value judgements') from evaluative ideas ('characterising value judgements'). In order to show that this is a problem also for natural scientists, he illustrates it with an example from physiology, that of anaemia. Its diagnosis is derived from a series of characterising judgements based on observable evidence. However, because this condition leads to diminished powers of maintenance of the animal, it may be characterised as a bad thing. Perhaps an initially persuasive contrast, but would this work in a factory or a university? The characterising judgements themselves would almost certainly be contested and we could only move from characterising to appraising if there could be agreement about what constituted the equivalent of anaemia in a factory or university. Nagel's schema can only work when there is agreement about characterising judgments. That is not to say there *cannot* be, but rather there often isn't.

In the early part of the 20th century, Max Weber also tried to distinguish between motivating values and investigation. Weber maintained that if it is the case that the concepts of the social world were subjectively constructed by agents, then it must follow that the moral and political views and regimes will differ between times and places (1974: 64). He appears to begin from a subjectivist position: that all concepts are known through human subjectivities and because then there were no concepts to discover that are free of human subjectivities, social laws have no 'scientific justification in the cultural sciences'. However, Weber did not embrace the epistemological relativism this appears to entail (1974: 110) and wanted to show how, under these circumstances, a 'value free' scientific sociology was possible. His starting point can be summarised as saying that in matters of policy there will be always be a debate about 'ends', about what should be achieved and therefore what investigation should be pursued. Investigation is value driven and in sociology the subject matter of investigation *is* values. However, he claimed that it does not follow from this that the moral and political values of commitment should bias investigation.

The social scientist should not be indifferent to policy issues, indeed the desire and need to investigate arises directly from commitment. However, in investigating the issues that arise from such commitment, the social scientist should examine his or her value positions for their logical coherence and their relationship to other concepts and principles. Weber proposes two levels of analysis (1974: 77): first, that of the cultural significance of a phenomenon; and the second, an investigation of the causal factors that lead to the mass significance of such a phenomenon. The existence of (his example) the money economy is a concrete historical fact, thus (he implies) existing outside of any given subjectivity, but nevertheless a product of subjectivities.

What is often described as Weber's 'value free sociology' was not a sociology without values, but rather a sociology that began with values, yet was neutral in the conduct and means of its subsequent investigation. The Weberian view provided a consensual view, particularly for the burgeoning US social policy in the mid-20th century. But it was criticised by Alvin Gouldner (1973). He argued that Weber's 'value free sociology' had produced a group myth that sociology was value free. The myth had become an excuse for complacency amongst US sociologists, a self-serving complacent professionalism that did not contribute to the public interest (Gouldner 1968: 109). His alternative to this, of 'objective partisanship', is that objectivity should be directed to particular goals, some of which are universal, for example the alleviation of suffering.

Most influential in sociology and its cognate disciplines, in recent decades, has been the work of Howard Becker (1967). He posed the question 'whose side are we (the sociologists) on? Becker's position has been differently interpreted (see e.g. Hammersley 2000), but the core of his argument is simple. Should sociologists be value neutral or should they express a commitment to a particular cause?

> For it [value freedom] to exist, one would have to assume, as some apparently do, that it is indeed possible to do research that is uncontaminated by personal and political sympathies ... the question is not whether we should take sides, since we inevitably will, but rather whose side we are on. (Becker 1967: 239)

Becker goes on to say that whatever perspective one takes in sociological investigation, it will always be one that is from the standpoint of 'superordinates' or 'subordinates'. The 'complacent' US sociology Gouldner complained of is in the first category. He maintained that if the sociologist adopts the standpoint of the 'superordinate', this will be the normative position and not criticised by those in power, yet if the position of the 'subordinate' is taken, the sociologist will be accused of bias. Becker's conclusion from this is that 'there is no position from which sociological research can be done that is not biased in one way or another' (1967: 245). His conclusion was that sociologists should challenge the normative and advocated that they should take the side of the underdog.

In Becker there is a recognition of the value laden nature of enquiry and the role of power and rhetoric, but there is also some justification in Gouldner's criticism of this position as replacing the myth of value free social science by a 'new but no less glib rejection of it' (Gouldner 1968: 103).

THE VALUE CONTINUUM AND SITUATED OBJECTIVITY

The feminist philosopher of science, Helen Longino (1990 (see **feminism**) has argued that not only do values enter our scientific endeavours, indeed they should. Whilst she divides values into constitutive (those of science itself) and contextual (the social values surrounding science), she maintains that the latter do and should enter science. One might go further and say that values exist along a continuum from numeric to moral values. Whilst these obviously are different, they shade into each other (Williams 2006). Temperature readings measure the physical environment, but different measures are used (Celsius, Fahrenheit, Kelvin). They are socially constructed, as are the values of scientific method and what it is that science investigates, though each of these measures are convertible into the other.

A different way of looking at the objectivity and values question is to begin from the position that science and social science are value laden enterprises. Indeed historically, science itself was born of a set of values. However, it does not follow that beginning from such a position cannot produce knowledge of the world that transcends subjectivity (or even intersubjectively held views). The values of science might be seen as philosophical tools to help us transcend the subjective. Objectivity is such a value. Examine it more closely and it too comprises values, the search for truth (see **logic and truth**), a willingness to entertain the notion that there are identifiable 'things' in the world, and that our investigation is for a purpose. That this purpose may differ from time to time and place to place does not detract either from our ability to test propositions, discover new and novel things, and indeed to show ourselves to be wrong (see **falsification**). Objectivity is socially situated and is not at all the same thing as value freedom.

THEORISING SUBJECTIVITY

Much of this section, so far, has been concerned with objectivity and values, but this is not to devalue the importance of subjectivity. Indeed subjectivity, in the form of values at least, is unavoidable in science. However, subjectivities are an important focus of social science investigation, and moreover if one is to investigate these from an acceptance of beginning from values, then it must follow that objectivity must have its roots in subjectivity (Letherby 2012; Williams 2015). Subjectivity is closely entwined with meaning and interpretation (see **interpretation and meaning**). Our psychological dispositions are undoubtedly unique to us and we are rarely aware of all of them, but equally these dispositions have developed as a result of our interaction with the external world and this is why their manifestation as subjective meaning is of interest to the social scientist, but equally the social scientist is a subjective creature.

The subjectivist will give equal epistemological weighting to all subjectivities, including her or his own, and indeed in postmodernism these become 'stories' indistinguishable from fiction (Jones 1998), but as I have suggested above and in the section on **relativism**, this precludes the possibility of social science. How, then, can we take account of our own subjectivity as social scientists and move toward objectivity? One recent suggestion comes from Gayle Letherby (2003), who argues that our starting point on this journey is to theorise our subjective experience in its social context – what she terms 'theorised subjectivity'. Just as objectivity must be situated in its social and historical context, so must our understanding of our own subjectivity.

REFERENCES

Becker, H (1967) 'Whose side are we on?', *Social Problems*, 14 (3): 239–247.

Gouldner, A (1968) 'The sociologist as partisan: sociology and the welfare state', *American Sociologist*, 3 (2): 103–116.

Gouldner, A (1973) *For Sociology: renewal and critique in sociology today*. Harmondsworth: Penguin.

Hammersley, M (2000) *Taking Sides in Social Research: essays in partisanship and bias.* London: Routledge.
Jones, T (1998) 'Interpretive social science and the "native's" point of view', *Philosophy of the Social Sciences*, 28 (1): 32–68.
Letherby, G (2003) *Feminist Research in Theory and Practice*. Buckingham: Open University Press.
Letherby, G (2012) 'Theorised subjectivity', in Letherby, G, Scott, J and Williams, M (eds), *Objectivity and Subjectivity in Social Research*. London: Sage.
Longino, H (1990) *Science as Social Knowledge: values and objectivity in scientific enquiry*. Princeton, NJ: Princeton University Press.
Manicas, P (1987) *A History and Philosophy of the Social Sciences*. Oxford: Blackwell.
Nagel, E (1979) *The Structure of Science: problems in the logic of scientific explanation*. Indianapolis, IN: Hackett.
Payne, G and Payne, J (2004) *Key Concepts in Social Research*. London: Sage.
Weber, M (1974) '"Objectivity" in social science and social policy', in Riley, G (ed.), *Values, Objectivity and the Social Sciences.* Reading, MA: Adison-Wesley.
Williams, M (2006) 'Can scientists be objective?', *Social Epistemology*, 20 (2): 163–180.
Williams, M (2015) 'Situated objectivity, values and realism', *European Journal of Social Theory*, 18 (1): 76–92.

KEY READINGS

Kincaid, H, Dupré, J and Wylie, A (eds) (2007) *Value-Free Science? Ideals and illusions.* Oxford: Oxford University Press.
Letherby, G, Scott, J and Williams, M (2012) *Objectivity and Subjectivity in Social Research*. London: Sage.

KEY THINKERS

Howard Becker; Martyn Hammersley; Helen Longino; Ernest Nagel; Max Weber

See also: *Falsification; Feminism; Interpretation and Meaning; Positivism; Relativism*

Observation

Observation is the act of experiencing the world through the senses, or through the proxy of measurement.

The section begins with the issue of observation as a basis for science? This question is examined through the centrality of impressions in Hume's philosophy and the challenge to this illustrated by Popper's observational 'experiment'? It goes on to consider the role of observation in the social sciences, particularly the controversial approach of operationalism in the social survey. The role of observation more generally in social research is discussed and the interelationship between theory and observation

Observation was historically seen as the foundation of natural scientific knowledge, and this was held to be equally true by social scientists who were influenced by empiricism. Originally observation was regarded quite literally as arising from sense data, but as time went on it came to mean both sensory data and that which might be obtained via our instruments, as 'experience of the world'. In the social sciences observation can be through direct or participant observation in a natural setting, or it may be, for example, through the questions asked in a social survey or measurements in an experiment. The question acts as an observational proxy – indeed questionnaires are sometimes referred to as 'instruments'. In the survey an 'observation' is a question asked of an individual, for example the age of a respondent. This works well for things like 'age', 'sex', 'country of birth' and so on, because whilst mistakes can be made by the respondent, or the 'observer' (in this case the interviewer) or in the subsequent analysis, there is little ambiguity around the veracity of what has been observed. However, things get more difficult when we want to measure sociological variables, such as ethnicity, class and so on, attitudes or beliefs (Williams 2003). Consider, for example, how we would measure (i.e. 'observe') alienation? As an everyday concept, to be 'alienated' from something or someone is relatively unproblematic, but think how difficult it would be for social scientists to agree on a definition of alienation that would hold good as a measurable concept across societies and through time?

This is not so different to the issues facing natural scientists who often disagree what an observation means, or indeed what they should be looking for in the first place (Chalmers 1999). Observing the behaviour of sub-atomic particles is very different to everyday observations of the world where agreement is mostly straightforward.

So where did the idea come from that observation is primary?

Of all the philosophers of the Enlightenment, David Hume was the most down to earth. He wanted to cut away at the tangled metaphysical undergrowth that had grown in philosophy in the late Middle Ages and get to its roots. For him observation was the root of all knowledge. He believed that all knowledge has its origins in experience, derived from the senses. But can we know anything that does not arise from observation? It's worth just pondering this before moving on.

Hume divided 'experience' into impressions and ideas. The first of these, he maintained, influence us more, they are our direct observations. But the second, he allowed, can be complex and may not resemble the observations. Nevertheless complex ideas are still derived from impressions. No one has seen a unicorn, but by joining together our impressions of white horses and horns we can easily imagine one. Once we have experienced simple impressions, we can 'join' these together and make more complicated ideas. Philosophers since, particularly Immanuel Kant, have challenged this, arguing that there must be some prior basis for being able to make the observation, or when made to make sense of it. Kant, for example, pointed out that concepts of time and space are presupposed by the very possibility of experience of them (see **idealism**).

Without doubt, all observations are made on the basis of some kind of a priori conditions obtaining for the observer. One of the best 'experiments' to demonstrate such necessity is that conducted by Karl Popper on his students (1989: 46), and indeed one I have conducted myself many times. It goes like this: 'When I say "start" I want you to observe for two minutes and write down what you observe'. The rule of the experiment is that the students may not ask any questions of the instruction they have been given. Now, whilst some observations will be in common ('the lecturer is wearing a blue shirt', 'it's raining outside' etc.), not all students will observe the same range of things, and virtually all students will have an observation particular to them. Why is the latter the case when they have been observing in the same environment? Popper maintained that when something is observed it depends on an individual selection criteria, itself based on past experience, reasoning, ability to observe and so on. No observation is 'neutral'. Observation is more than a physical act, it is an epistemic act. In science (and it follows social science) observation is either 'theory driven' – that is, what it is decided to measure (observe) is derived from a prior question rooted in how we theorise the world – or it simply arises from common-sense reasoning. Alienation, for example, could be theorised in a Marxist way, though Marx's concept of alienation is itself rather abstract, or it may derive from psychological theories. Yet however we think about it, 'alienation' is a concept we invented to describe particular conditions or situations. The same is true of most things we want to 'observe' in the social world – they come with prior labels!

Jack Douglas, a qualitative researcher of deviance, once said 'We begin with direct experience and all else builds on that' (cited in Bryman 1988: 119). Well, no, we don't, we begin with a theorisation, or the very least a crude common-sense 'theory' about that which we want to observe. Most social research, both quantitative and qualitative, is, then, an interplay between theory and research.

In some ways the observation problem in survey research is more difficult because one must design the observation instrument beforehand (the questionnaire) and there is less possibility to observe, interpret and re-observe in a time-specific situation than there would be in qualitative research. There is a second and related problem: even if we can theorise (say) alienation, how can we then measure it? In survey design we learn that we must 'descend the ladder of abstraction' to operationalise our variables, that is, we move from concept to indicator (de Vaus 1996: ch. 6), but George Lundberg argued in the 1940s (Lundberg 1968) that sociologists are wrong in believing measurement can only be carried out after things have been appropriately defined: for example, the idea that we must have a workable definition of alienation before we can measure it

His solution was 'operationalism' (Williams 2003), which broadly speaking is the view that a concept is that which is capable of measurement. Alienation becomes that which we can measure. But operationalism never gets us to that 'naked' observation, it is really based on a convenient contemporary theorisation that might change as a result of better technique and indeed may not be universal. Researcher X operationalises alienation in one way and researcher Y in another. Have they 'observed' the same thing? Well, probably not.

So was Hume wrong? Is observation 'impossible'? No, Hume's insight was correct, if partial. Any kind of systematic derivation of knowledge about the world will be derived from observation, but that observation will itself be grounded in prior circumstances, particularly theories. It is theory laden (Hanson 1958). But what if these theories or even common-sense constructs are all different, will this lead to a plethora of quite different observations? Does one's prior theories (or indeed whims or prejudices) determine what is to be observed? To some extent, the answer is 'yes', but there are two good reasons why this is not wholly the case.

First, observation and theory do not operate in isolation of other observations and theories. Contrary observations by other researchers may challenge, amend or even refute a theory. The world itself is not always amenable to prior theorisations of it.

Second, observations of the world will yield a lot of commonality between observers. In any given social setting there will be conventions, norms, tacit knowledge and indeed the actual manifestation of the world which will lead to commonalities of observation. Popper's informal experiment demonstrates both the a priori conceptual nature of observation, and that we observe many of the same things in similar ways.

Our theories might guide our observations and our observations may help us develop our theories, and this is an epistemological issue. For empiricists this is sufficient: our observations require theoretical interpretation and modern empiricists (see van Frassen 1980) accept the necessity of prior epistemological assumptions. But there is another matter, that of the ontological status of that which we observe. Realists maintain that we can only make sense of the social and the physical world by accepting that what we observe is merely evidence for an underlying reality that comprises complex and dynamic mechanisms and that there is a real world, with real consequences beyond sense impressions. For realists observation is not primary, but just one tool of many that scientists and social scientists use.

REFERENCES

Bryman, A (1988) *Quantity and Quality in Social Research*. London: Routledge.

Chalmers, A (1999) *What is This Thing Called Science?*, 3rd edn. Buckingham: Open University Press.

de Vaus, D (1996) *Surveys in Social Research*, 2nd edn. London: UCL Press.

Hanson, N (1958) *Patterns of Discovery*. Cambridge: Cambridge University Press.

Lundberg, G (1968) *Social Research: A Study in Methods of Gathering Data*. Longmans, Green and Co, 2nd edn, Westport, CT: Greenwood Press.

Popper, K (1989) *Conjectures and Refutations*: London: Routledge.

van Frassen, B (1980) *The Scientific Image*. Oxford: Oxford University Press.

Williams, M (2003) 'The problem of representation: realism and operationalism in survey research', *Sociological Research On Line*, 8: 1.

KEY READINGS

Chalmers, A (1999) *What is This Thing Called Science?*, 3rd edn. Buckingham: Open University Press. ch. 1.

Sayer, A (1992) *Method in Social Science: a realist approach*, 2nd edn. London: Routledge. ch. 2.

Williams, M (2003) 'The problem of representation: realism and operationalism in survey research', *Sociological Research On Line*, 8: 1.

KEY THINKERS

David Hume; Immanuel Kant; Karl Popper; Norwood Russell Hanson; Andrew Sayer

See also: *Empiricism; Epistemology; Ontology; Realism; Theory*

Ontology

Ontology is the branch of philosophy concerned with existence and the nature of things that exist. (This entry should be read in conjunction with that of epistemology.)

> *This section begins with the Kantian problem of what exists. It compares ontology with epistemology and then goes on to discuss the role of ontology in the key philosophical positions of realism, idealism and empiricism. The relationship of ontology to representation and classification is considered.*

KANT, PHENOMENA AND NOUMENA

In social research epistemological assumptions have usually been more explicit than ontological ones, and this may well be a feature of a post-Enlightenment emphasis on knowing, rather than existence. Epistemology is about *how* we know, whereas ontology is about *what* we know.

A secondary question is, then, how do we group or classify these things we claim to know?

Philosophies and their attendant methodologies make two kinds of ontological assumption: those of appearance and those about what might underlie appearances. Kant conceived of the world as phenomena and noumena (Scruton 1982: 42–46) (see also **idealism**). The former are those properties of the world that we can know, whilst noumena are the external sources of our experience, but according to Kant we can never come to know these. Noumena is the 'thing in itself', which is unknowable. A simple thought experiment will show this to be the case. If you think of yourself, how you would describe yourself – what is the 'essence of you'? You can only ever do this in terms of properties that relate to other properties and the 'essence' of you, the noumenal is ever elusive. This, of course, also applies to other people and more so, because you can only ever capture your perspective of them, never their's (expect what they tell you, or you can find out about them) and your perspective may be different to that of another person.

Whilst much of social research is not 'Kantian' influenced, the issue of phenomena and what may be underneath shapes the way we do social research. No philosophy of social research will explicitly deny the existence of an underlying reality and for realism assumptions of its existence are fundamental. However, for some approaches, that we cannot 'know' what such a reality might be like, means that their methodologies do not refer to anything that cannot be known empirically, these are sometimes called 'unobservables'.

In effect there are three general positions on ontology, though these very much subdivide (see Blaikie 2007: 12–18) into more nuanced ones.

First there are realists, for whom there is an assumption that there is an underlying reality, that is not necessarily observable but in principle at least partially knowable (see **realism**). Second, this contrasts with idealism, for whom the world consists only of representations which are created by individual minds (see **idealism**). Thus what we call 'reality' is a creation of minds and is shared socially. Because that is all we can know, nothing can be surmised beyond this. Philosophy, until around the 17th century, was divided between realists and idealists, and the third position of empiricism emerged primarily in the work of Locke (see **empiricism, positivism**). Idealism and empiricism both maintain that there is only 'sensation', but for the idealists sensation is internal, it is mind, whereas for empiricists sensation is external, it is stimuli. In the work of Hume these stimuli are not the analogues of actual things, but a manifestation of our psychology to process those stimuli.

ONTOLOGY, IDEALISM, POSITIVISM AND REALISM

A few idealists, in the tradition of the solipsism of George Berkeley, will deny the existence of anything beyond mind: in effect, 'the world is my dream', but most (at least in social science) are prepared to agree that there is something we create that we call 'reality', and that reality can enable and constrain us. This view remains in the realm of ideas, but acknowledges that these are not simply equal perspectives (a view held by postmodernists) and thus allows them to research and account for differences, say of power in society. This kind of idealism, because it admits of (at least) mind-created realities that can make a difference, begins to edge closer to some forms of realism.

Positivism does not claim that there is no underlying 'reality' that we cannot see, but rather science has no business talking about it because its character would be wholly speculative. Positivism, therefore, claims to just deal in observables. In social research this is usually manifested in some form of operationalism. What 'mobility' or 'alienation' is, can be measured, though there is no denial that the concepts may have properties beyond what can be measured. There are methodological problems with operationalism, but there is a more fundamental issue of 'kinds' in positivism. If we stick strictly to describing only observables, what is it that links these together, or provides common features, and which features should we pick out as more important than others? For example, there are plenty of 'green' things in the world, but their greenness may only be a resemblance and a different kind of classification may be more important, for example 'green *plants*', 'green *vehicles*', 'green *crayons*', if one is interested in botany, vehicle manufacture or sales, or writing instruments.

A positivist sociologist of work may measure numbers of strike days in an industry and find that these correlate with forms of production. Strikes may be more prevalent in more traditional forms of mass production than in, say, areas of distributed production, but without offering some form of theoretical explanation linked to, For example, globalisation, unionisation and so on, then explanations will be inevitably superficial. In practice, most positivist social researchers do propose theories about unobservable phenomena, and thus an underlying reality (Porpora 2008), though their defence would be that once proposed, such things should be measurable.

Realists, on the other hand (see **realism**), fundamentally depend on an ontology that admits of unobservables. An ontological starting point for most forms of realism is to ask what would need to be the case for something to exist as it does? In other words, phenomena does not simply appear fully formed, but will appear as a result of the presently unseen operation of 'forces' or 'mechanisms'. In Marxism, for example, the forces of production are an abstract concept that will take different forms and produce different relations of production in different societies, and though the forces of production are capable of being identified and analysed, they are not immediately apparent to those who experience or research them.

Realists are not saying that 'noumena' can be identified. The total extent and nature of the underlying reality would not be capable of being known, at least partly because it is dynamic through time and space. However, what was previously not known at time T1 can be known at time T2. Analogously, it is rather like endless Russian dolls (though they don't get smaller!): open one to reveal another, previously unknown, but there are always more to open.

This contrast of positivism and realism is a rather simplified one and in practice, most social ontology is more nuanced and does not assert one or other position so starkly. There is, for example, very little ontological distance between the method of causal modelling, usually attributed to positivism (see **models and mechanisms**) and realist approaches to causal mechanisms (Williams 2014).

NATURALISM

Both positivism and realism are what is termed 'naturalistic' philosophies. Naturalism in philosophy can have other meanings, but in philosophy of science it is taken to mean, first, that there is nothing outside of 'nature'; in other words, what is studied in the natural and social sciences, is all there is. Even for realists in science, this rules out reference to entities that are incapable of definition or knowing, though may be captured in the subjectivity of art. Somewhat confusingly, a stronger version of naturalism is supported by positivists, who maintain that the methodology of the natural sciences can be almost wholly replicated in the social sciences, though their argument for this depends wholly on the argument that only empirical phenomena can be measured, and if they can be measured, they are capable of scientific study.

IS AND OUGHT

A long-standing ontological problem for social science has been whether the characteristics of the social world we learn from our research are able to tell us how to act. This has long been a problem for philosophers and ethicists (see **ethics and morality**). Following Hume, philosophers, in the 'analytic' tradition, have mostly maintained that it was logically impossible to derive 'ought' statements from 'is' statements, that all statements of knowledge are based on logic or observation. Some moral philosophers, notably Alisdair MacIntyre (1967), have argued that terms like 'good' or 'bad' should not be seen within a particular set of moral judgements, but in a wider historical context where 'good' or 'bad' can be seen as overall moral goals. Certainly 'good' or 'bad' can be applied to specific things, in relation to more local measures. Ernest Nagel (1979: 492–494), for example, maintains that we can use characterising judgements, say 'efficiency', because what counts as efficient can be comparatively known and appraising judgements as to whether this is a good or a bad thing (see **objectivity – subjectivity**).

Critical realists, to an extent following Marxism, have argued that knowledge is able to produce emancipation because once we know what is 'real', then judgements about how to act follow from it (Bhaskar 1986). The is/ought problem is a particular one for social science because the way people act is based upon moral judgements, and these acts and their consequences become ontological characteristics of the social world, as researchers find it and subsequently make decisions about what and how to research (see **objectivity – subjectivity**).

CLASSIFICATION

All philosophical positions on ontology must face the problem of classification. In social research this is both a philosophical and a methodological problem. In biology it is possible to define the characteristics of a species and revise these, exclude or include members, as new knowledge comes to light, but in social research what is classified as belonging to X is not simply a taxonomic problem. The social world is dynamic in a self-referential way, but that is not the case in the physical world. Take the example of social class. Social class, as conceived by sociologists, is applicable only to industrialised Western societies. 'Social class' is not a particularly good way of measuring social stratification in developing societies, but as these societies 'develop' something like social class may emerge, though its characteristics may in some respects resemble those in 'advanced' societies, but in others not. Meanwhile processes, such as globalisation and de-industrialisation, change what can be understood by 'social class', even in the industrialised societies (Payne 1987). What counts as social class is dynamic and what can be measured by social class is a subset of this.

A practical method of classification is 'cluster analysis'. Cluster analyses are taxonomic and originally developed in biology to 'gather all possible data on organisms of interest, estimate the degree of similarity among these organisms, and use a clustering method to place relatively similar organisms into the same groups' (Aldenderfer and Blashfield 1984: 8). One begins from grouping characteristics, or events, into clusters, which are then aggregated according to similarity. Although a powerful explanatory and predictive tool, nevertheless, the classification into clusters is an idealisation of a multi-faceted dynamic reality and is a methodological illustration of the antinomy between what 'is' and what we can 'know'.

REFERENCES

Aldenderfer, M and Blashfield, R (1984) *Cluster Analysis: Sage University Paper 44*. Newbury Park, CA: Sage.

Bhaskar, R (1986) *Scientific Realism and Human Emancipation*. London: Verso.

Blaikie, N (2007) *Approaches to Social Enquiry*, 2nd edn. Cambridge: Polity.

MacIntyre, A (1967) *A Short History of Ethics*. London: Routledge and Kegan Paul.

Nagel, E (1979) *The Structure of Science: problems in the logic of scientific explanation*. Indianapolis, IN: Hackett.

Payne, G (1987) 'Social mobility', in Burges, R (ed.), *Investigating Society*. Harlow: Longman.

Porpora, D (2008) 'Sociology's causal confusion', in Groff, R (ed.), *Revitalizing Causality*. London: Routledge.

Scruton, R (1982) *Kant*. Oxford: Oxford University Press.

Williams, M (2014) 'Probability and models', in Edwards, P, O'Mahoney, J and Vincent, S (eds), *Studying Organisations using Critical Realism*. Oxford: Oxford University Press.

KEY READINGS

Hacking, I (2002) *Historical Ontology*. Cambridge, MA: Harvard University Press.
Russell, R (1995 [1914]) *Our Knowledge of the External World*. London: Routledge. especially ch. 3.

KEY THINKERS

Roy Bhaskar; Mario Bunge; René Descartes; Immanuel Kant; Bertrand Russell; John Searle

See also: *Empiricism; Idealism; Mechanisms and Models; Objectivity – Subjectivity; Realism*

Positivism

Positivism is a philosophy of social science that emphasises the scientific credentials of social enquiry, laying particular emphasis upon the primacy of observation and value freedom.

There are three main versions of positivism in Comte, Durkheim and Logical Positivism. These are first described and their influence on social science considered. The section describes the key features of positivism as a scientific philosophy of social science: the primacy of observation in its epistemology, the role of theory, causality, laws and value freedom. Finally I briefly discuss some key objections to positivism and its later evolution.

Positivism is one of the most used and misused terms in the social sciences. Frequently and wrongly it is used to indicate a scientific or quantitative approach to social enquiry, but it is a particular philosophy of science. In fact we can identify three versions of it that have, to some extent, influenced social science. The third of these was and remains the most important.

First, the term 'positivism' was coined by the 19th-century French philosopher and theorist Auguste Comte, who intended the term to indicate a more positive approach to theorising the social world. Although his 'law of the three stages' was a prototypical sociological theory, his philosophy had little or nothing to do with the form of positivism which was eventually so influential in the natural and social sciences (Ritzer 2000: 87–101).

The second version of positivism is associated with another French thinker, Emile Durkheim. Durkheim's positivism did stress the importance of empirical enquiry along scientific lines and demonstrated its feasibility in *Suicide* (Durkheim 1952), but positivism in social science was much more the product of the third version, the more general influence of empiricism on natural science and society in the early and mid-20th century.

The third version of positivism is usually associated with the Vienna Circle and its followers in the UK and US (many of the Vienna Circle fled Austria for the US after the Nazi Anschluss of 1938). Logical positivism (sometimes called 'logical empiricism') was a rigorous philosophy of science that advocated a scientific practice based on observation. Its principle Vienna Circle thinkers were Rudolph Carnap, Maurice Schlick and Carl Hempel. A later important contributor was the English philosopher, A J Ayer. Although the key features of logical positivism were present in much of early and mid-20th century social science, there was little evidence of a direct influence, at least in US social science where 'positivism' was dominant (Platt 1996: 67–105). Rather, its principles had contributed to a scientific culture that influenced the social sciences, which in turn gained legitimacy from their scientific credentials.

So, whilst science and positivism are not synonymous, there was a period in the 20th century when science was positivistic. In the natural sciences this period ended in the 1960s, partly as a result of critiques from Russell Hanson, Karl Popper, Thomas Kuhn and Imre Lakatos, but also as a result of a growth of more sophisticated philosophies of science and indeed the growing sophistication of scientific methods. In the social sciences, positivism lasted longer and was heavily criticised in the 1960s and 1970s, though much of this criticism was more generally pro-humanist and anti-scientific. Indeed it lives on in a more moderate, even sophisticated form in quantitative social science, especially causal analysis (Porpora 2008).

Positivism in social science had a few key features. Not all were present all of the time, some were exaggerated in form (e.g. operationalism) whilst others were implicitly or even unknowingly practiced.

KEY FEATURES OF POSITIVISM IN SOCIAL SCIENCE

- *Science*: It is first and foremost a naturalistic philosophy, maintaining that there is no disjuncture between the natural and social worlds, that they are not separate kinds of things. It follows from this that there are no in principle differences in the logic or methodology of the natural, or social sciences. There are, however, important differences of method between disciplines, so that economics will differ from biology, just as geology differs from chemistry. Historically this has meant that the methodological model for the social sciences was taken from natural science, rather than the other way around.
- *Observation*: For positivism observational evidence is paramount. This idea, originating with the empiricist philosopher David Hume, was based on the primacy of sense data in knowing the world. In social science this may be actual observation, with the senses, but also may be data from survey questionnaires and so on. The important thing, for positivists, is that theories, or any knowledge claim about the social world, must be verified by the data. For a further discussion, see **observation**.
- *Epistemology*: Positivists emphasise epistemology over ontology. Because our knowledge must always be grounded in observables, claims about unobservables are not scientific. For example, realism is based on the ontological claim that an underlying social reality exists and can only be known through secondary or proxy evidence (Byrne 2002: 20–21), whilst positivism does not deny the existence of such a reality, but is agnostic about its existence.
- *Theory*: Positivists do not reject theory, but hypotheses, or 'observation statements', must be deduced from theory: that is, theories should 'predict' particular things and 'explain' those predicts. In its most sophisticated form it becomes the hypothetico-deductive (HD) model, an iterative process of deduction, which has the form: theory → hypothesis → observation → new theory, though the process may begin at any of these points (see **hypothesis(es)** and **explanation**.

- *Causality and probability*: As with observation, positivist causality is traceable to Hume. Hume famously held that when one observable event follows another, we are not entitled to deduce from that, that the first caused the second. That we do is simply a psychological habit. It follows from this that the most we can say is that, when observed, Y always follows X. In the social sciences strict positivists such as Dodd or Lazarsfeld (see Platt 1996: 67–106) maintained there could be no causal reasoning, but rather we can only rely on the probabilistic association of measured variables. We cannot say that unemployment causes crime, but only that in x number of cases (usually expressed as percentages) crime increased after an increase in unemployment. Only a few positivists were so strict and in practice probabilistic causal inferences have been the norm. However, such inferences crucially require three or more variables because when two are present we cannot know if there is a causal connection, or if they are each being caused by a third variable, or indeed that there is multiple causation. For a further discussion, see **causality**.
- *Laws*: Related to this is the belief that the goal of science (and social science) is to produce factual and axiomatic statements about the world that will be generalisable. Though it is accepted that in the social world, the domain of generalisation will be culturally or time restricted, it is nevertheless the aim to produce law-like statements, such as those produced by the natural sciences (Kincaid 1996) (see **explanation** and **generalisation and laws**).
- *Value freedom*: Positivists believe that facts and values must be separated and that the latter have no place in science, because values cannot be deduced from facts. An investigation of social practices, which may have a moral or political dimension, must restrict itself to a description or explanation of these and is not entitled to rule on their correctness or otherwise. This is quite the opposite of Marx's dictum that 'The philosophers have merely described the world in various ways. The point, however, is to change it.'

CRITIQUES OF POSITIVISM

Many critiques of positivism were in fact critiques of science in the social sciences more generally, but specific criticisms, usually from philosophers of science, have found their mark. Most importantly the critique from Hanson (1958) and Popper (1959) that observation is always driven by prior knowledge, expectation or commitment undermined positivism. Our decision to measure particular variables (e.g. class, ethnicity, ill health, unemployment etc.) and the way we operationalise these variables will at least partially affect the results we get.

By extension, observation decisions are inevitably value laden. That is, what we decide to observe/measure is the product of earlier commitments. These are not necessarily political, though they might be, but may be long-held conventions.

Nowadays few people rigidly adhere to all of the above principles of positivism, or at least in their strong form. 'Positivism' has evolved into a more sophisticated and permissive philosophy of science. For example, very few people defend a view that values do not enter social science, though many will defend versions of value freedom that attempt to separate methodological values from ideological ones (Hammersley 2000[10]). Likewise causal analysis is often theoretically driven in versions of the hypothetico-deductive model (Blalock 1961).

Notwithstanding anti-scientific criticisms, other philosophies of social science, particularly realism, diverge from positivism on the question of non-observables and the nature of causality.

REFERENCES

Blalock, H (1961) *Causal Inference in Nonexperimental Research*. Chapel Hill, NC: University of North Carolina Press.

Byrne, D (2002) *Interpreting Quantitative Data*. London: Sage.

Durkheim, E (1952 [1896]) *Suicide*. London: Routledge and Kegan Paul.

Hammersley, M (2000) *Taking Sides in Social Research: essays in partisanship and bias*. London: Routledge.

Hanson, R (1958) *Patterns of Discovery: an inquiry into the conceptual foundations of science*. New York: Cambridge University Press.

Kincaid, H (1996) *Philosophical Foundations of the Social Sciences: analyzing controversies in social research*. Cambridge: Cambridge University Press.

Platt, J (1996) *A History of Sociological Research Methods in America 1920–1960*. Cambridge: Cambridge University Press.

Popper, K R (1959) *The Logic of Scientific Discovery*. London: Routledge.

Porpora, D (2008) 'Sociology's causal confusion', in Groff, R (ed.), *Revitalizing Causality*. London: Routledge.

Ritzer, G (2000) *Classical Social Theory*, 3rd edn. Boston, MA: McGraw-Hill.

[10] Hammersley's position is sophisticated and is actually closer to realism than positivism (see Hammersley 2000).

KEY READINGS

Cohen, P (1980) 'Is positivism dead?', *Sociological Review*, 28 (1): 141–146.
Pawson, R (1989) *A Measure for Measures: a manifesto for empirical sociology*. London: Routledge.

KEY THINKERS

Aaron Cicourel; Paul Lazarsfeld; George Lundberg; George Homans; Harold Kincaid; Ray Pawson; Andrew Sayer

See also: *Causality; Empiricism; Falsification; Generalisation and Laws; Hypothesis(es); Induction; Objectivity – Subjectivity; Observation; Probability; Realism*

Postmodernism

Postmodernism is a movement in the arts, humanities and social sciences that rejects the certainty of scientific, or objective, efforts to explain reality and instead focuses on the relative truths or experiences of individuals or groups.

The origins of postmodernism in literature, and the arts are described and its subsequent influence upon the social sciences is then considered. It is shown as a rejection of modernism and a critique of science. Its key characteristics: denial of truth, individualism, deconstruction and rejection of 'meta narratives' are considered and its challenge to social science is evaluated.

'Postmodernism haunts social science today' was the phrase with which Pauline Marie Rosenau began her influential book on postmodernism and the social sciences in 1991 (Rosenau 1991). To some extent the haunting has been self-exorcised through the ghosts themselves, for as a philosophy postmodernism is contradictory and epistemologically self-consuming. To a further extent, there has been an accommodation with the ghosts, and some insights of postmodernism have been benign influences or even inspirations in social science.

ORIGINS

Postmodernism can be seen as a cultural–historical movement in art, literature, music and food, but also as an approach to knowledge and existence. Thus it is possible to embrace some aspects of postmodernism (in my own case, music and food) but to reject other aspects of it. Philosophically it can be both moderate or extreme. Its latter form is militantly relativistic (culturally, morally and epistemologically) (see **relativism**) and indeed nihilistic. In social research it can be 'sceptical' or 'affirmative' (Blaikie 2007: 50). The sceptical postmodernist rejects the possibility of establishing any truth. Meanings are imposed and arbitrary, the consequence of which is the impossibility of empirical social research as we know it. More 'affirmative' approaches, whilst embracing relativism, do not rule out research that describes or interprets, and indeed sometimes celebrates, the merging of interpretation with fiction (Clifford and Marcus 2010).

Postmodernism does not have a straightforward historical or philosophical pedigree. One can detect a plethora of influences, for example: the politics of the late 60s, specifically the Paris 'commune' of May 1968, the existential philosophy of Heidegger, the nihilism of Nietzsche, romanticism, literary criticism, anti-scientism, post-Marxism and hermeneutics. The term 'postmodernism' was first used in the 19th century to describe some art that succeeded impressionism, but as a philosophical movement it is a post-Second World War phenomenon.

Philosophical postmodernism emerged from the collapse of many of the pre-Second World War ideals of modernism (Rosenau 1991: 5). Modernism was (and many would say still 'is') a progressive force, a belief in democracy, human rights, the pursuit of truth and the liberation from ignorance and irrationality. Socially, it was the belief in a rational society, exemplified through scientific and technical progress, and a pursuit of perfection in architecture and planning. But the ideals of modernism were undermined, first by the societal collapse into barbarism in Nazi Germany, the horrors of the Second World War and Hiroshima and Nagasaki, then in the anti-war protests and student risings of the late 1960s. Though incoherent, these risings were a rejection of the post-war settlement that had led to nuclear weapons,

Vietnam and the inequalities of capitalism (Williams 2000: ch. 4). But this rejection was not just political, but also a rejection of science (because of its complicity in the military industrial complex) and even rationality itself.

Though not often attributed to influencing postmodernism, around this time there was a revolution in the philosophy of science that nevertheless influenced many of those who became 'post-modern' critics of science and social science. This revolution began as a debate between the critical rationalism of Karl Popper, which was seen as philosophically and political conservative (see **falsification**) and the ideas of Thomas Kuhn and Paul Feyerabend (Lakatos and Musgrave 1970). Kuhn was interpreted as rejecting the idea of scientific progress, claiming that science was punctuated by social and epistemological revolutions and that the knowledge, methods and culture pre- and post 'revolution' were incommensurable. Feyerabend went further and claimed that science really had no method and there were no rules that were not at some time violated. His anarchic slogan that 'anything goes' might be seen as a subsequent anti-methodological rule. Though, in fairness to Kuhn and Feyerabend, neither drew the relativistic conclusions that their followers, particularly in social science, later embraced.

WHAT ARE THE CHARACTERISTICS OF POSTMODERNISM?

One of the ironies of postmodernism is that to describe what it is, is to describe a unified system of thought, or movement – what postmodernists call a 'meta-narrative'. Postmodernists deny the possibility of universal explanation; it has an 'incredulity toward meta-narratives', which would include the philosophical positions (the 'isms' described in this book), but also economic theories such as Keynsianism, Marxism and so on (Lyotard 1984).

A number of other things lead too, or follow on, from this. It is relativistic toward truth because it sees all realities as socially constructed, as are the interpretations of those constructions. This rejection of truth extends to all spheres, including scientific truths and, crucially, moral truths. Thus, postmodernism is morally and culturally relativist, which means that postmodernists not only reject the idea that there is some objective, a-historical framework to which we can appeal in matters of knowledge or rationality, but also in terms of what is morally right or good. Whilst the latter leads to a doctrine of tolerance of others' beliefs and customs, it also leads to a conservatism that is unable to challenge (what non-postmodernists) might see as injustice or oppression.

The work of the deconstructionist Jaques Derrida is an important influence, in that postmodernists prioritise the centrality of the 'text' (not just words, but visual images as well) over the author, which according to Derrida is now 'dead' (1978). Though texts may be interpreted, these interpretations are relative and tell us nothing about reality beyond the text itself, thus the role of interpretation becomes a rhetoric of persuasion. It follows from this that, rather like more radical forms of hermeneutics, historical interpretation is similarly simply one reading of a text or texts and there is no historical truth to grasp. In the writings of Jean Baudrillard (1983), this takes an ontological dimension (if indeed the concept of ontology can mean anything in postmodernism) in which he maintains that we live in a world of simulacra nowadays. Whereas once, one could point to originals or copies (e.g. a master tape or photographic negative), the digital age has left us with an equivalence of image.

Finally, postmodernism is radically individualist (see **individualism and holism**), claiming that our identities are now fractured, we are unique, and what we call our 'identity' is subject to change or to disappear and reappear in different ways.

WHAT USE IS POSTMODERNISM?

Had I been writing this book fifteen, even ten years ago, I may not have thought to include an entry on 'postmodernism', regarding it as destructive, narcissistic, incoherent and far too influential in 'studies' of the social world. To paraphrase the late Margaret Thatcher, I would not have given it the oxygen of publicity (assuming the book would be read, of course). It is and remains all of those things in the above list, except influential, at least directly. Two decades after Rosenau's pronouncement we can perhaps take stock of the effect of postmodernism on social science and research.

The first thing to say is that many of what I would see as pernicious influences on social investigation – relativism, ontophobia (see **idealism**) – were already present and have their origins in hermeneutics, critical theory, ordinary language philosophy (see **language**) and the critiques of scientific reasoning and method in Hanson, Quine, Kuhn and Feyerabend

(Lakatos and Musgrave 1970). Certainly, to one extent or another, these influenced or were alongside postmodernism, but they did not constitute postmodernism.

What is perhaps moribund, at least in terms of social science, are the more radical forms of postmodernism associated with Lyotard or Baudrillard, but much remains and some of this has influenced social science positively.

First, there is postmodernism's first cousin, poststructuralism (some would say the family link is stronger than that), and particularly in the work of Michel Foucault. Although, like the postmodernists, he rejected Enlightenment values of truth and freedom, seeing them as leading to oppressive regimes of thought and action, his own work in areas of sexuality and punishment was a reflection upon the intersection of power and knowledge in our society (Foucault 1980). Whilst a 'modernist' need not abandon the concept of truth (see **logic and truth**), it remains possible to agree with Foucault that there are regimes of truth. If, for example, we take the morality or correctness of a situation as a given, certain truths will follow from that. Most of us work, or study, in organisations such as universities in which we are compelled to accept the ethos and rules, but these in turn produce other 'truths' because we initially accepted (or were constrained to accept) their foundations as givens. Such an approach can be refreshing in the study of power in organisations and more generally how social constructions come to exert power over us.

In Foucault and postmodernism, language is important (Foucault uses the term 'discourse', not just of language but to encompass thought and action) and whilst we may not want to buy into his (and Derrida's) assertion that the author is dead, it remains that language can, to a great extent, define reality by naming, but just as importantly, as Foucault claimed, by not naming. Absence can have as much power as presence, as for example in many of the practices of patriarchy (see **feminism**). Of course, the prioritisation of language can go too far (see **language**) and whilst it is a determinant of social life, it is not the only one. Even less is language, or discourse, a sole determinant of scientific or social scientific truth. Nevertheless, in social research, as Alan Bryman has argued (and Bryman is a long way from being a postmodernist), social research crucially depends on 'rhetorics of persuasion' (1998: 142). Topics of investigation, the way we investigate and finally how we present our investigations are very dependent upon rhetoric.

An area not often considered as being influenced by postmodernism is that of 'complexity'. Indeed Paul Cilliers has written a persuasive book (1998) in which he argues that many of the features of complexity revolve around analyses of the process of self-organisation and that a rejection of traditional notions of representation are consistent with postmodernism. Again, one can take this too far; stochastic systems are present in the social and physical world, but complexity (unlike post-modernism) wishes to account for the creation of order and stability. Postmodernism sees order as imposed social construction, and complexity is a rigorous science of non-linear systems.

As Kant once said of Hume, the latter's philosophy awoke him from his dogmatic slumbers. So it is with postmodernism for many of us. Yet, as Rorty, said it is parasitic, condemning everything, proposing nothing (cited in Blaikie 2007: 50). It has nevertheless made social scientists examine their beliefs and thought systems, because it has challenged them.

REFERENCES

Baudrillard, J (1983) *Simulations.* New York: Semiotext.

Blaikie, N (2007) *Approaches to Social Enquiry*, 2nd edn. Cambridge: Polity.

Bryman A (1998) 'Quantitative and qualitative research strategies', in May, T and Williams, M (eds), *Knowing the Social World*. Buckingham: Open University Press.

Cilliers, P (1998) *Complexity and Postmodernism: understanding complex systems*. London: Routledge.

Clifford, J and Marcus, G E (eds) (2010) *Writing Culture: the poetics and politics of ethnography* (25th Anniversary edn). Berkeley, CA: University of California Press.

Derrida, J (1978) *Writing and Difference.* London: Routledge.

Foucault, M (1980) *Power/Knowledge*. Brighton: Harvester.

Lakatos, I and Musgrave, A (eds) (1970) *Criticism and the Growth of Knowledge.* Cambridge: Cambridge University Press.

Lyotard, J (1984 [1979] *The Postmodern Condition: a report on knowledge*. Minneapolis, MN: Minnesota University Press.

Rosenau, P (1991) *Post-Modernism and the Social Sciences: insights, inroads and intrusions.* Princeton, NJ: Princeton University Press.

Williams, M (2000) *Science and Social Science: an introduction*. London: Routledge.

KEY READINGS

Alvesson, M (2002) *Postmodernism and Social Research*. Buckingham: Open University Press.

Rosenau, P (1991) *Post-Modernism and the Social Sciences: insights, inroads and intrusions.* Princeton, NJ: Princeton University Press.

Sayer, A (2000) *Realism and Social Science*. London: Sage. Chs 3 and 4.

KEY THINKERS

Jean Baudrillard; Jaques Derrida; Michel Foucault; Jean-Francois Lyotard

See also: *Complexity; Falsification; Feminism; Idealism; Individualism and Holism; Language; Relativism*

Pragmatism

Pragmatism is primarily associated with the US philosophers Charles Sanders Peirce, William James and John Dewey. Although a varied philosophy, it has at its core a theory of meaning and truth that places emphasis on the effects of these in the world. It is an important philosophical approach because of its effects on American thinking in social science (and beyond) since.

The section begins by briefly describing the origins of pragmatism in the US and its implicit influence on later US thinking, specifically symbolic interactionism, grounded theory and mixed methods. The theory of meaning and truth is central to pragmatism and this is critically discussed.

A VERY AMERICAN PHILOSOPHY

Pragmatism is a home-grown American philosophy that has some features of **empiricism**, but is quite variable in its emphases across the work of its founding fathers. In this short entry it is hard to do full justice to its nuances, but in practice its influence on American social research ranged from the fairly explicit, in the work of the Chicago School, to more implicit in symbolic interactionism, grounded theory and mixed methods. Indeed different commentators variously argue about its influence (see Hammersley 1989 and Manicas 2011 for quite different views). The influence of pragmatism on American public life and philosophy is not disputed, but in social research one often detects it in a almost anti-philosophical approach.

Like so many philosophies, pragmatism grew out of a particular historical culture (in this case that of 19th-century US) (Menard 2001). It was born of a problem-solving and practical culture and consequently its approach to philosophy emphasised the empirical over speculative metaphysics, indeed its original principles clearly have their roots in British empiricism (see **empiricism**). The seminal statement from Charles Sanders Peirce perhaps captures its spirit best, when he said that the sole object of inquiry is the settlement of opinion and not a search for truth (Peirce 1950). That opinion as an empirically knowable characteristic immediately sets pragmatism aside as less metaphysical in its ambitions and closer to 'common-sense' philosophy (Hammersley 1989: 48).

MEANING AND TRUTH

The core principle of pragmatism can be summed up as the 'meaning of a phenomenon derives from its effects on the world, rather than from any intrinsic properties it may have' (Dennis 2011: 464). The focus is on what practical difference an object, action, thought and so on makes in the world. William James maintained than in any matter of philosophical dispute, we should consider the practical difference it would make to one or other side being right (ibid.). This ontological principle is quite opposite to that of realism (see **realism**) because in pragmatism the reality of the world is constituted by our practical orientation to it. This was neatly summed up in the famous dictum of Thomas and Thomas: 'If men [sic] define situations as real, then they are real in their consequences' (1928: 571–2). Philosophically, pragmatism shares the characteristic of phenomenalism with empiricism; that is, we cannot claim to know anything outside of experience. A second characteristic of pragmatism is that of naturalism, the view that humans are all part of a natural order (see **ontology**): there is not separation between a 'human' and a 'natural' world.

The pragmatist theory of meaning is, in effect, a theory of truth (see **logic and truth**). James, true to the spirit of his time and location, refers to the 'cash value' of truth, that this has no meaning unless we can assimilate, corroborate and verify (1995: 430). He goes on to say that truth is what happens to us, what we verify through events.

Although pragmatism was first derived from the work of Peirce, his subsequent writings took him some way from the work of James and

Dewey and he developed a more phenomenological version (see **idealism**), which emphasised that the task of a pragmatist approach was to make ideas through delineating the properties of experience. In this way he prefigured much of later phenomenology (Crotty 1998:73), but also the idea of reflection so important to later interpretive approaches (see **interpretation and meaning**).

Though an historically important philosophy, particularly for American social science, it is not a clearly defined one and there are influences of empiricism, idealism and (in Peirce) a prefiguring of Popper's later critical rationalism (see **falsification**).

SYMBOLIC INTERACTIONISM AND GROUNDED THEORY

Though much of the philosophy of pragmatism, in symbolic interactionism, is implicit, it nevertheless adopts the pragmatist theory of meaning. Indeed it is precisely because in symbolic interactionism meaning is created through individual presentation and interaction, that it has been criticised for being 'anti sociological' (da Silva 2008) because it is unable to move beyond the subjectivity of the researcher and researched in order to theorise social structure and the role of agents within it.

It is not an exaggeration to say that symbolic interactionism is wary of theory, or at least working with prior theories. Rather, it aims to build theory, usually through the method of fieldwork exemplified by that of Goffman. The researcher enters the field without preconceived ideas and builds concepts through observation and comparison. Symbolic interactionism, in turn, has been critical of sociology for predefining its concepts as theories and then testing them, particularly through 'variable analysis' (Blumer 1969).

In terms of popularity, the variants of grounded theory have surpassed that of symbolic interactionism in recent years, but it shares the emphasis on developing post hoc theories and concepts from rigorous fieldwork. Theory is grounded in data (Glaser and Strauss 1967). What then counts as theory, developed in the field, is interrelated concepts that certainly function as explanations of the interlinking of social relations at a micro or meso level, but it is questioned as to whether the same empirical rigour might be maintained in developing these into testable macro-level theories. In fact, for most exponents of symbolic interactionism or grounded theory, there is no appetite to move to such explanation. Classic studies such as Becker's on the apprenticeship marijuana users undergo (1953) tells us much about micro-level socialisation and is testable in other similar situations (see **generalisation and laws**), but it is essentially social psychological in nature.

MIXED METHODS

Mixed methods research has been around a long time (see e.g. Campbell and Fiske 1959), but came into its own as a practical response to the antinomies of quantitative and qualitative approaches championed in the 'paradigm wars' of the 1970s and 1980s (Plano Clark and Creswell 2008: 5).

Within mixed methods there are a number of designs, but most involve the 'mixing' of qualitative and quantitative approaches at different stages. The claim frequently made is that this can achieve a triangulation of perspective on a research question (see e.g. Tashakkori and Teddlie 1998: ch. 3). There are numerous criticisms of this: whether it is epistemologically possible, or is really a 'category mistake', whether by identifying quantitative and qualitative methods, then mixing them, one actually ends up reifying what is often a false distinction, and whether one can adequately capture validity, particularly content validity.

Mixed method researchers, whilst acknowledging these kinds of antinomies, will often emphasise that the test of validity lies at a methodological, not abstract, philosophical level. Morgan (2007:52) refers to concepts in the work of William James, George Herbert Mead and John Dewey, such as 'lines of action', 'warranted assertions', 'workability' as guiding principles.

BACK TO MEANING AND TRUTH

Though pragmatism, in the work of Peirce, James and Dewey, was a nuanced and complex philosophy, a strength and a weakness in its subsequent adoption in social research was the relative simplicity of its theory of meaning. Peirce invites us to think of a concept and then consider its practical effects. It is only these that matter, so as Dennis points out the ontological effect is that the practical uses something is put to determine what it is, and consequently the central problem for sociology (and analogous disciplines) is an investigation of how things are defined and understood (Dennis 2011: 464). This is entirely congruent with the pragmatic theory of truth, is what is true is what practically matters. So, if a group of people have a set of beliefs, for them these beliefs are true and for the researcher it is true that they hold them. But does this exhaust what we can mean by 'truth'? If we abandon any attempt to assess whether those beliefs held are themselves true, in respect of some external criteria, then we can never make any sense of the social context in which those beliefs arose.

REFERENCES

Becker, H (1953) 'Becoming a marihuana user', *American Journal of Sociology*, LIX, 235–242.

Blumer, H (1969) *Symbolic Interactionism: perspective and method.* Eaglewood Cliffs, NJ: Prentice-Hall.

Campbell, D and Fiske, D (1959) 'Convergent and discriminant validation by the multitrait-multimethod matrix', *Psychological Bulletin*, 56: 81–105.

Crotty, M (1998) *The Foundations of Social Research: meaning and perspective in the research process*. London: Sage.

da Silva, C (2008) *Mead and Modernity: science, selfhood, and democratic politics.* Lanham, MD: Lexington Books.

Dennis, A (2011) 'Pragmatism and symbolic interactionism', in Jarvie, I and Zamora-Bonilla, J (eds), *The Sage Handbook of the Philosophy of the Social Sciences.* Thousand Oaks, CA: Sage.

Glaser, B and Strauss, A (1967) *The Discovery of Grounded Theory*. Chicago, IL: Aldine.

Hammersley, M (1989) *The Dilemma of Qualitative Method: Herbert Blumer and the Chicago tradition*. London: Routledge.

James, W (1995 [1907]) *Pragmatism: a new name for some old ways of thinking* (1907). New York: Dover.

Manicas, P (2011) 'American social science: the irrelevance of pragmatism', *European Journal of Pragmatism and American Philosophy*, III (2): 1–23.

Menard, L (2001) *The Metaphysical Club*. London: Flamingo.

Morgan, D (2007) 'Paradigms lost and paradigms regained: methodological implications of combining qualitative and quantitative methods', *Journal of Mixed Methods Research*, 1 (1): 48–76.

Peirce, C S (1950 [1878]) *Values in a Universe of Chance* (edited by P P Weiner). New York: Doubleday.

Plano Clark, V and Creswell, J (eds) (2008) *The Mixed Methods Reader*. Thousand Oaks, CA: Sage.

Tashakkori, A and Teddlie, C (1998) *Mixed Methodology: combining qualitative and quantitative approaches*. Thousand Oaks, CA: Sage.

Thomas, W and Thomas, D (1928) *The Child in America: behavior, problems and programs.* New York: Knopf.

KEY READINGS

Hammersley, M (1989) *The Dilemma of Qualitative Method: Herbert Blumer and the Chicago tradition*. London: Routledge.

Mounce, H (1997) *The Two Pragmatisms: from Peirce to Rorty*. London: Routledge.

KEY THINKERS

Herbert Blumer; William James; George Herbert Mead; Charles Sanders Peirce

See also: *Empiricism; Generalisation and Laws; Logic and Truth; Ontology*

Probability

(*Note*: this section should be read in conjunction with that on Statistics)

Probability is an important concept in philosophy and social research. The philosophical principles of probability underlie sampling, significance and statistical inference. It can be simply expressed as the ratio of a particular outcome to all possible outcomes, thus the possibility of a tossed coin coming up heads is 1 divided by 2. Philosophically probability is interesting because it can be about probabilistic knowledge claims, or the intrinsic properties of things themselves.

In this section a few simple principles of probability are first put into philosophical context. A key question is asked: what is the relationship of probability to certainty or necessity? The limits of probability and prediction are briefly described as are the important matters of populations and samples, bias and the 'gambler's fallacy'. Finally objective and subjective approaches, frequency and single case theories of probability are discussed.

In our universe some things are certain and some things are more probable than others. A useful way of thinking about this is to think of those things that cannot happen as zero and those things that must happen as one. Most events in the world and (it is my belief) all events in the social world have probabilities greater than zero, but less than one. Let me begin by suggesting some examples of 'ones' and 'zeros' and things between.

It is certain that you will die (1), that water must consist of hydrogen and oxygen atoms (1), that no human can fly unaided to the moon (0), energy in a system cannot be conserved indefinitely (0). Some things are very, very unlikely. There is the very faintest possibility that I could become the Prime Minister of the UK, but it is an infinitesimal possibility. It is much more likely that I will drink some wine tonight! One of the fascinating things about 'none zero' probabilities (i.e. between zero and one) is that they change over time. Think about your own life trajectory. Some things in it were fairly probable – that you would go to school, you would have friends, you would get a job. Other things are much less probable (and therefore less predictable). In fact our lives are so complex and so subject to change, that the probabilities (sometimes this is expressed as 'odds') of any particular event/characteristic would be very difficult to estimate when we were 10 years old. But being 10 years old in one set of circumstances can generate very different probabilities of outcomes than in others. I will say more about this below.

PROBABILITY AND PREDICTION

Foolish people who know nothing of probability will put probabilistic prediction on the same footing as astrology and say that it is impossible to predict the future. It is certainly impossible to predict the future with any specificity and the further the future is away, generally speaking, the less specific we can be. But it is a useful property of probability that knowledge of the past and present can help us to say something of the future. If we go back to those zeros and ones and the numbers between we can see that as time goes on everything becomes a zero or one. My favourite example (though a slightly macabre one) is the operation of the death penalty in the US. If you commit first-degree murder, what are your chances of being executed? Well, the starting probability will depend upon where the murder took place. The probability of execution increases massively if this happened in a state that operates the death penalty. Some states implement the death penalty more than others, so that changes things. How good is your lawyer? How rich are you? Are you Black, or do you have learning difficulties? All of these things increase/decrease your chances of execution. This carries right on until a) your sentence is commuted, or b) you are pronounced dead. Obviously, as time goes on and you have not won a reprieve, then your chances of execution get closer to one.

But everything in the end resolves into a one or zero. Either something has happened, or it can't happen. These ones and zeros then become the data for our predictions. The distribution of ones and zeros create particular patterns, such that future outcomes can be predicted. Let us imagine that you are an actuary who has to decide life insurance premiums. In one city, if we look at the age of death for its citizens, we find that they are a healthy lot and 70 per cent live into their seventies and eighties, but in the other city less than 10 per cent live this long. The actuary would have little trouble in deciding that the life insurance premium for a 50-year-old must be a lot higher in the second city than the first.

There are plenty of examples of such scenarios, and the early deaths of many citizens of the second city is explained by earlier events in their lives (the resolution into ones). They smoke more, they eat bad diets, they exercise less and consequently have more ill health events and so their chances of an early death are greater. Knowledge of these things changes our predictions. The social scientist might want to know why the citizens of the second city have such apparently dissolute lifestyles and get ill. The answers may be poverty, poor education, bad housing or a complex alignment of these. Statistical models can be built that both explain and predict high mortality or morbidity rates, and this is done so on the basis of our probabilistic knowledge of population characteristics.

BIAS AND THE GAMBLER'S FALLACY

The world consists of 'biased' probabilities. 'Bias', in this sense, has nothing to do with, say, political bias (see the section on **objectivity – subjectivity**). The bias arises from the distribution of different earlier chances of outcomes. Take two dice. The first of these is a 'weighted' dice an important tool for the street-corner huckster of old. A weighted dice does not give equal chance to each of its sides landing upwards. It might favour (say) a six, or a three. The huckster knows which one! An unweighted, or fair dice, has the same chances of each side landing upwards. A 1 in 6 chance of a 6, or 3 and so on. The same principal is true of a coin (1 in 2) or a roulette wheel (1 in 32). These are unbiased systems.

Such systems have two important properties. First, that in a long run frequency of throws/spins each side/number has exactly the same chance of coming up as any other. Second, each throw/spin is independent of every other one. The 'gamblers fallacy' arises when the first is understood, but the second isn't. Gamblers on roulette wheels, or lotteries, do so on the basis of them not being biased. The fallacy arises when a gambler believes that because particular numbers (which she or he has not bet on) have come up, perhaps several times, then the numbers they have bet on are more likely to come up soon. But this is a fallacy because the odds are 'reset' every time; however, in the 'long run' a fair dice/coin/wheel will yield exactly the same number of outcomes for each possibility.

POPULATIONS AND SAMPLES

This sounds rather abstract, but the idea of an unbiased system underlies a lot of our social science (even though we know that such a system is an ideal state). Epidemiologists often extrapolate from population characteristics to suggest the probability of a characteristic in a member of that population. Conversely, a random sample is a random assignment of a sample from a population that aims to represent the population characteristics in the sample.

Let us say that in a given population of the first city the chances of a 50-year-old male having a heart attack were 1 in 200, but in the second city they were 1 in 50. Do these odds apply to every male who is 50? Of course not, and even lay persons can reason this. The first city will contain some men who smoke, drink too much, eat badly and don't exercise. Genetic factors aside, they are more likely to have a heart attack. Conversely, in the second city there will be men with healthy lifestyles. The 1 in 200 or 1 in 50 is arrived at after 'averaging', and the averaging will be across a number of variables that can be 'measured' (such as morbidity, education, class etc.) and many that cannot. So in principle we can narrow the reference category. Despite the way the media often presents these things, scientific reports will alert the reader to these caveats. In social research the practice of reasoning unproblematically from populations to groups, or from samples to subsamples, is known as the 'ecological fallacy'.

Reasoning (with those caveats) from population to individual, or from sample to population, requires us to hold in our minds the notion of unbiased probability, but also an awareness that it is not achievable. This kind of reasoning between samples and populations is inductive in character (see **induction**) and can be thought of as epistemological probability.

In the dice example we know that in a long run frequency for throws of an unbiased dice a 6 will come up 1 in 6 times, with all of the previous caveats. But consider this simple experiment (due to Karl Popper 1995), which you can actually try out and record the observations. Take two dice, one biased (if you can find one!), one unbiased. Shake each for, say, 20 times. It is very unlikely that in those few shakes you will be able to tell the difference between the dice. Which is biased, which is unbiased? Eventually you should be able to tell – but only eventually! However, whether or not the dice is biased, the physical conditions of each throw will vary slightly and there are likely to be imperfections in the dice.

If this was the case, how could a statistician prove that long run frequencies will produce stable outcomes – how we can show that an unbiased dice will throw a 6, 1 in 6 times? If we take several dice and repeat the experiment, then over the total number of throws of each dice an outcome of 1 in 6 will come about. 'Several' dice is the number of dice we need to produce this outcome. This result is due to the 'law of large numbers', identified by the French philosopher Poisson in the 18th century (Hacking 1990: ch. 12). If a number of events is large enough, then regular patterns can be seen. If you are thinking that the roulette player maybe should just hang on in there, the illusive numbers will come up, this would only work in 'the long run' and very likely the croupier will have gone home for her breakfast, or the player will have run out of money.

This finding was crucial to the use of statistics to describe populations and the bigger the population, the more accurate the derived probabilities (see **statistics**). However, many social populations are very heterogeneous, or relatively small. To continue the dice analogy, it is as if we only have either two or three dice to test our conjecture, or that the imperfections in the dice, or its throwing, are not compensated by the number of dice available.

We can learn two things from this: first, the imperfections of our probabilistic knowledge of frequencies (for 'dice' also read 'population characteristics'); and second, that every throw of the dice has its own probability. Probability, then, is not just a calculating or predicting system (with its imperfections), but it is in the very character of the world itself.

In statistics there has been a long tradition of recognising 'frequency-based' approaches, such as those I described in the sample – population examples above, but also 'single case probabilities', where reasoning begins from the known properties of a single case (see Gillies 2000).

However, this approach has been much less used, yet is nevertheless both philosophically interesting and also potentially empirically valuable (see Williams and Dyer 2009).

The social world is much more complex than a dice. The odds of a particular thing happening are nested in earlier outcomes and these change constantly. The social world is possibly the most complex of all (see **complexity**), and we can only discern trends or patterns (though we can do it quite well). This complexity also means the social world does not possess 'natural necessity', that is, characteristics or outcomes that must be the case (Williams 2011). In the natural world probability is always grounded in the laws of nature, but if there are 'laws' in the social world they are probabilistic (see **generalisation and laws**). Indeed in classical physics, probabilities are much less used because non-quantum physical behaviour is governed by a handful of fundamental laws.

When you were 10 years old your life trajectory was very much more open than it is today (I am of course assuming you are somewhat older than 10!). But even at 10 years, your trajectory will be different to other 10-year-olds and will be shaped (but not wholly determined) by the circumstances you were born into. For most 10-year-olds in Western countries the prediction of a job in later life is a fairly safe one, but there are some communities where unemployment and poverty is so great that some families have not had a person in full-time work for three generations. If you are 10 in such a community we can predict that the odds of your getting a job are somewhat lower than in most other communities. But of course the actual probability resides in your own circumstances and we can only predict from aggregate data.

OBJECTIVE AND SUBJECTIVE PROBABILITY

There is another way to think about probability, that of 'degrees of belief', or subjective probability. The objective probability of something happening might be called 'chance' and our attempts to measure it (through primarily frequentist approaches) the 'taming of chance'. Indeed this is the title of an excellent book by Ian Hacking (1990) on the history and philosophy of probability and statistics. Hacking describes probability as 'Janus faced' (1990: 96). By this he means that probability has meant both objective (chance) and subjective (degrees of belief. Indeed even today there remains a dispute amongst statisticians about which approach is more useful, or mathematically consistent (Lindley 2000).

Above, I distinguished between epistemological and ontological aspects of probability. 'Chances' are seen to be objective properties and statistical strategies, ways of measuring them. But how do we assign probabilities when we have no numerical data based on sample frequencies or actual cases?

We may do this through logical reasoning where we have qualitative evidence to suggest one outcome is more likely than another. For example, if the gross domestic product of Ruritania is considerably lower than that of its neighbours, then we should be able to predict that measurements will indicate higher levels of poverty relative to the neighbouring countries. If we have measured poverty levels in these we should even be able to predict some data for Ruritania. The actual numbers predicted may be subject to error, but something of magnitude may be known.

However, sometimes we just don't know what to decide or predict. Two possible, but equally likely outcomes would be assigned 0.5 (or it could be four outcomes at 0.25). This is called the 'principle of insufficient reason'. One solution to this is to assign a probability to an outcome purely subjectively and is referred to as 'subjective' or 'personalist' probability. As we gain new evidence we increase or decrease our probability estimate. A way of doing this is through 'Bayesian reasoning', based on the theorem of Thomas Bayes. This is described a little more in the section on **statistics**.

Informally we make such calculations in our everyday lives, making decisions on weighing up the informal odds of X or Y happening. We may not assign actual probabilities to these decisions, but they seem fundamental to our everyday reasoning or decision making. What is fascinating, philosophically, is that by weighing up the odds of X or Y and acting upon them, we change the actual probabilities of the occurrence of real events!

REFERENCES

Gillies, D (2000) *Philosophical Theories of Probability*. London: Routledge.

Hacking, I (1990) *The Taming of Chance*. Cambridge: Cambridge University Press.

Lindley, D (2000) 'The philosophy of statistics', *Journal of the Royal Statistical Society. Series D* (The Statistician), 49: 293–337.

Popper, K R (1995) *A World of Propensities*. Bristol: Thoemmes.

Williams, M (2011) 'Contingent realism – abandoning necessity', *Social Epistemology*, 25 (1): 37–56.

Williams, M and Dyer, W (2009) 'Single case probabilities', in Ragin, C and Byrne, D (eds), *Case-Based Methods*. London: Sage.

KEY READINGS

Gillies, D (2000) *Philosophical Theories of Probability*. London: Routledge.
Hacking, I (1998) *The Taming of Chance*. Cambridge: Cambridge University Press.
Hacking, I (2001) *An Introduction to Probability and Inductive Logic*. Cambridge: Cambridge University Press.
Popper, K R (1995) *A World of Propensities*. Bristol: Thoemmes.

KEY THINKERS

Thomas Bayes; John Maynard Keynes; Pierre-Simon Laplace; Siméon-Denis Poisson; Karl Popper; Charles Sanders Peirce

See also: *Complexity; Generalisation and Laws; Hypothesis(es); Induction; Logic and Truth; Objectivity – Subjectivity; Realism; Statistics*

Rationality

Rationality is the actions, thoughts or organisational patterns that accrue the maximum benefit for the minimum expenditure of resources. Yet what counts as benefit or expenditure is socially situated. For example capitalist societies privilege economic rationality and this may serve as a pattern for all decision making. In other kinds of societies rationality may be expressed through other domains, such as ritual or religion. A major question is, therefore, is rationality universal or societally specific?

I begin by asking the question, what does it mean to act rationally within our everyday lives? Weber's forms of rationality are then examined. I then go on to discuss the issue of beliefs and desires and the attempt to produce a definition of rationality that unites actions, beliefs and desires. There follows a critical discussion of rational action theory. A key question is whether rationality is culturally specific and the attendant problem of relativism. The section concludes with a consideration of rationality and social research, specifically the reliance on a particular form of rationality to conduct research.

THE PROBLEM OF RATIONALITY IN EVERYDAY LIFE

It might be said that the social world depends on people within it acting rationally, yet we know that there are plenty of people who act irrationally. A car journey will usually provide examples of irrationality! At this everyday level, our judgement of rational and irrational action is dichotomous, yet look a little deeper and there are puzzles. First, what counts as rational? To continue the driving example, for most of us overtaking on the inside lane on a dual carriageway is irrational (and in most countries illegal), yet undoubtedly the person overtaking on the inside could give good reasons for doing so. Second, rationality and rule-following are not the same thing. Most of the time to follow a rule is to be rational and that social life seems to operate with rules, it follows that rules and rationality go together. But sometimes not to follow the rule is rational for the individual (if not the society), as in overtaking on the inside. Third, there is not always a dichotomy between rational behaviour and irrational behaviour. A massive amount of behaviour in the social world can be described as 'non-rational'; that is, behaviour that once might have been the outcome of a rational decision is now simply automatic, or – and this is where it gets really complicated – impulsive action that has a superficial rational basis to it but might offend a deeper rationality would be beneficial to an individual, or group. For example, the panic that can arise in a disaster, such as fire in a building, may suggest a quick and safe exit for an individual but actually jeopardises his or her chances of reaching safety.

Rationality is not just a problem for philosophers. How we define it, come to know it and employ it methodologically is also a key issue for social research.

WEBER AND RATIONALITY

Our starting point for the consideration of rationality is the work of Weber (1978). In fact rationality is at the heart of his work, including his approach to method. In particular an understanding of rationality is, for him, key to understanding the grand themes of his era, the development of capitalism. This, in his view, is an example of the outcome of the rational action of individuals acting together. Weber, as I discuss elsewhere (see **interpretation and meaning**), was primarily concerned with meaningful action. This leads him to a framework which captures actions, both rational and non-rational. He identifies four types of meaningful action.

First, there is *traditional* action, things we do habitually because we always have, but we do not reflect upon them. Such action, although present, is less common in modern society than traditional societies. Second, there is *affectual* action, which is primarily emotional (perhaps captured by the rush to escape the building fire), but this is not sharply distinguished from the next kind of action because some rational consideration may enter into the calculation of action. You may have knowledge of an exit door that may be opened to better allow people to escape.

The third kind of action (which Weber calls *Wertrational*) arises from possibly unreflective beliefs, say religion, but once those beliefs are considered as a motivation for action they become *rational*. Fourth, there is *practical* action (*Zweckrational*), in which an agent sets out to achieve something based on calculations of success and benefits related to other agents and things in the environment.

Weber's approach is not just to consider rationality as exemplified by that found in the society of his era, but a more generalised approach that can capture rationality across societies and time. Because historical change is at the heart of his work, this universalised rationality is necessary to explain change.

BELIEFS AND DESIRES

Weber's formulation initially seems to capture what we might mean by 'rational' action and 'non-rational' action. For Weber, *Zweckrational* is the basis of what it is to be truly rational, meaningful social action intended to bring about a purpose in the world – what we term 'instrumental rationality'. Although the description is convincing, it is also questionning about beliefs and desires. In order to act rationally, in this way, an agent must have a desire of an outcome and to hold beliefs about its possibility.

We might express it thus:

> Given any person X, if X wants D and X believes that A is a means to attain D, under the circumstances, then X does A.

However, as Alexander Rosenberg (1988: 25–26) points out, this formulation works only on the basis of 'other things being equal' (*ceteris paribus*) and it is easy enough to think of exceptions; for example, there may be other means than A to secure D and the agent must decide which is best; X may not know how to do A; D may be of several goals and a choice must be made. Further, as John Searle (2003) has noted, rationality presupposes free will. Free will goes beyond the constraint in wanting and doing, but rather the ability to 'will' freely in the first place.

RATIONAL ACTION THEORY

For some social scientists, rational action is the principle tool with which to explain both individual and collective action. This approach is especially prevalent in economics. In this approach a person is seen as always wishing to maximise utility in their actions, and to do this is to act rationally. It is, then, a more sophisticated version of the formulation above. A person will have preferences and is able to rank them. Economists have used this assumption of the maximisation of utility in an individual to explain pricing and the allocation of resources.

Now, of course, having preferences does not mean that these are available through action, or indeed desirable. For example, I would choose cherries over bananas, but cherries are only readily available at certain times of the year. I am very fond of eating certain rich desserts, but I know that in the long term they are not good for me. However, to continue that analogy, there are times when there is a perfect confluence of beliefs, desires and actions in the matter of desserts and I will eat one anyway!

The rational action theorist will say that my beliefs must be coherent (it's no good my desiring a £10 million pound house with a swimming pool) and that my choices must be informed by the best knowledge available to me. Now – note the best knowledge available, not the correct knowledge, so unknowing false beliefs are not a barrier to acting rationally. So, the rational action theorist will weigh up my beliefs and desires and the actions that ensue and declare whether or not my action was rational.

Now whilst an analysis of those things in me or you, rather like having one's fortune told, might be interesting and enjoyable, analyses only become interesting and useful when we consider the actions of many agents, because this is what makes social life. There are problems with individual-level analysis (which I will come too), but at the group level it gets difficult.

Humans are dependent on others to achieve their desires, but in acting individually we may not produce the best outcomes for the collective. Game theory (Elster 1986) sets up different kinds of scenarios to see what it might be rational for an individual to do and what outcomes this produces. In many of these the individual may maximise their utility at the expense of others, but different choices may maximise collective utility. Take my driving example above: the driver that 'undertakes' me may get to her or his destination more quickly, but their actions if repeated by many will cause accidents, or more mundanely, traffic jams. In this case maximum utility for all is achieved by following the driving rules.

Actions can imply moral dilemmas (see **ethics and morality**). Obviously, at an individual level, my desires (if actioned) may not be beneficial to others, but I can take a moral consideration into an ordering of my desires. I desire D, but to do A will harm another, so I may choose to do E instead. E becomes my preference. A campaigning organisation lobbies to get a larger proportion of health spending on D, but to spend more of a finite amount on D means that less or nothing will be spent on E, F, G and so on. An agent, in this case a collective one, such as a health authority, must then order its preferences, in a similar way to an individual.

One last caveat. Game theory would have us believe that individuals will often maximise individual utility at the expense of the collective. But an agent in possession of particular knowledge and/or holding particular moral views may well pursue actions that do not maximise his or her utility in any obvious way, but will contribute to a collective good, or the good of a different collective (e.g. charity giving to recipients in another country or continent). Rational action theorists would explain this through a different utility calculation, which satisfies an individual desire through sacrifice to a collective. The same reasoning can be used to explain heroism, sacrifice for another and so on.

IS RATIONALITY CULTURALLY SPECIFIC?

Nevertheless, in modern Western society the above may be a useful theoretical framework and has been extended beyond economics to explain human action and social structure more generally, for example, by the sociologist George Homans in the mid-20th century and more recently by the economist Gary Becker (Becker and Murphy 2001), but is it useful in explaining 'rationality' in other societies, or in history? Is the idea of rationality, as described above, culturally specific?

Charles Taylor (1982) reflects on the classic study of witchcraft in the Azande people (and Winch's writings on it). In Azande society witchcraft was said to be hereditary, yet the Azande would nevertheless examine a person's intestines for signs of 'witchcraft substance'. As Taylor notes, a few post-mortem examinations should settle the hereditary question once and for all, but the Azande continued to examine intestines for signs of witchcraft (1982: 88–89) and by Western standards this is irrational.

This example forces us to say that the Azande are irrational, or to consider their reasoning as a different expression of rationality. Winch (1990) thought of it in terms of them engaged in a different 'language game' (see **language**), incommensurate with the reasoning in our own 'language game'. Whilst not disagreeing with Winch, Taylor placed emphasis on a version of theoretical understanding that is at odds with our own. Sociologists and anthropologists have identified other forms of rationality that are more explicitly based on reciprocity, such as the exchange of gifts, the sharing of resources. These things are not necessarily (or indeed rarely) voluntary, but form social expectations in societies and are just as 'useful' in explaining such societies as rational choice theory might be in ours.

Does this lead to cultural or epistemological relativism (see **relativism**)? In the first case, almost certainly. As Weber himself noted, instrumental forms of rationality were a growing characteristic of capitalist societies. Indeed the individualist policies of the UK Thatcher government and the US Reagan government, in the 1980s, promoted the individual maximisation of utility as an economic and social good. It is perhaps not too big a gap from the explanation of action through utility behaviour, to it becoming normative.

Epistemological relativism is a harder case to make. The fact that anthropologists are able to identify and explain other forms of social reasoning and compare them to a Western model of rationality suggests that there is no necessary incommensurability of knowledge between 'knowers' in one society and another.

Furthermore it is the case, even if the specific reasoning can be shown to have flaws, that to some, possibly a great extent, people in Western (or Western-influenced) societies do attempt to maximise utility, and utility calculations by organisations and governments seem unavoidable, but it does not follow that a utility model of rationality exhausts social explanation in society, yet alone that it must be adopted as a normative model of behaviour.

RATIONALITY AND SOCIAL RESEARCH

Rationality is certainly a perennial philosophical problem, but the problem for the social researcher will depend enormously on the society she is researching. To use a utility-instrumental model of rationality may be useful in thinking about Western society, though with the inevitable issues of non-rational action, or rule exception, but it is possibly less useful in other societies, where it may be necessary to understand forms of reasoning (such as that of the Azande) that seem 'irrational' for us. However, since Evans Pritchard, Winch or even Charles Taylor were writing, globalization has changed most societies, with few untouched by Western mores. A different, possibly greater, challenge for the ethnographer is to understand how societies manage the contradictions of traditional and modern modes of reasoning.

Finally, in a much narrower sense, social research in developed societies relies on Western modes of rationality to be possible at all. It is an activity that is an extension of the kind of reasoning that Weber and later thinkers describe. Successfully administering a questionnaire, for example, requires a shared understanding of appropriate behaviour for both parties. An analysis of 'big data', such as Twitter feeds, requires an assumption of rational behaviour as a norm in order to explain group behaviour such as riots (see e.g. Guardian/LSE 2012).

REFERENCES

Becker, G and Murphy, K (2001) *Social Economics: market behavior in a social environment*. Cambridge, MA: Harvard University Press.

Elster, J (1986) *Rational Choice*. New York: New York University Press.

Guardian and London School of Economics and Political Science (LSE) (2012) *Reading the Riots: investigating England's summer of disorder*. London: Guardian.

Rosenberg, A (1988) *Philosophy of Social Science.* Oxford: Clarendon.

Searle, J (2003) *Rationality in Action*. Cambridge, MA: MIT Press.

Taylor, C (1982) 'Rationality', in Hollis, M and Lukes, S (eds), *Rationality and Relativism*. Cambridge, MA: MIT Press.

Weber, M (1978 [1925]) *Economy and Society: an outline of interpretive sociology*. New York: Bedminster.

Winch, P (1990 [1958]) *The Idea of a Social Science and its Relation to Philosophy.* London: Routledge.

KEY READINGS

Elster, J (1986) *Rational Choice*. New York: New York University Press.

Hollis, M and Lukes, S (eds) (1982) *Rationality and Relativism*. Cambridge, MA: MIT Press.

KEY THINKERS

Jon Elster; Steven Lukes; Charles Taylor; Max Weber; Peter Winch

See also: *Ethics and Morality; Interpretation and Meaning; Language; Relativism*

Realism

Realism has a long philosophical pedigree and can be contrasted with empiricism and idealism and in so far as it rejects strong forms of relativity about knowledge, is the opposite to relativism. It takes many forms, but each shares the view that physical or social phenomena exist independently of our perceptions of them.

The section begins by locating the key assumptions of realism in philosophy. Critical realism and the philosophy of Roy Bhaskar has been the most influential variant in social science and much of this entry is a critical engagement with this variant of realism. This brings us back to ontology and a consideration of objects and theories and finally the relationship of realism to mechanistic thinking and the issue of measurement in social research.

A PHILOSOPHICAL 'THIRD WAY'

Realism is sometimes described as a philosophical 'third way' between empiricism and idealism and although methodologically it borrows from both of these traditions, it is a distinct philosophy and especially philosophy of science, in its own right. There are many variants of scientific realism, but common key features are:

- That there is an actually existing world that is independent of our perceptions of it (see **idealism** for different perspective).
- That, although we cannot ever say we 'know' that world, our methods of investigation can provide knowledge of parts of that world

that we cannot necessarily observe and scientific explanation is therefore possible (see **empiricism** for a different perspective).

- That events are 'caused', but the causes may be complex (see **causality**).
- That properties (of things, or people) are dispositional (sometimes referred to as 'powers' or 'tendencies' and have the potential to 'cause' things, but these properties may not be actualised (see **contingency and necessity**).
- It is a naturalistic philosophy in that it sees no ontological disjuncture between the physical and social worlds and the ability of science to study them (see **idealism** for a different perspective).
- That change in complex systems is rarely linear and that the observed properties of those systems are often emergent (see **complexity**).

In the natural sciences realism has taken a number of forms and in many areas of science has become the dominant philosophical framework (see e.g. Harré 1986). In the social sciences its influence has been less and more recent. It remains that many accounts of the philosophical foundations of social research will simplistically pitch 'positivism' against 'interpretivism'.

In the social sciences realism emerged as a distinct philosophical position in the late 1970s, though some have argued that Marx and Durkheim were realists *avant la lettre*. Marx because of his argument that the material world and the economic arrangements that develop from it are the underlying determinants of social life, and Durkheim for his emphasis on the enabling and constraining nature of social facts.

One form of realism has become particularly influential, that of critical realism, but in more recent years other variants have arisen that draw more on the realism of natural science (see e.g. Pawson 2000).

CRITICAL REALISM

Critical realism has been associated with Roy Bhaskar (1998, 2008; Archer et al. 1998) and his followers.

Bhaskar's critical realism is indeed somewhat influenced by Marx, especially in its claim to emancipation through the critical evaluation of knowledge claims about the world and the elimination of false beliefs. In his latter years his work took a controversial, more metaphysical and quasi religious dimension, but the earlier key principles of critical realism remain important and have influenced a broader realist movement in social science.

Bhaskar's critical realism depends on what he terms a 'depth ontology'. In this the world is stratified into three levels: the domain of the empirical, which consists of our experiences of the world; the domain of the actual, those events in the world with causal efficacy; and the domain of the real, which are the underlying mechanisms that give rise to the events and our experiences of them. Science (including social science) aims to identify those real mechanisms, but it is accepted that this is an imperfect pursuit. The world does not obligingly reveal itself in a straightforward way to the investigator. According to Bhaskar, the world consists of the real entities, the intransitive objects, but the transitive objects are the theories, concepts and models the scientist uses to discover the real (Bhaskar 2008: 250).

Critical realism, and indeed other varieties of realism, depend on a particular kind of 'mechanistic' thinking. The term 'mechanism' evokes clockwork arrangements that work in precise and measurable ways, but the world and especially the social world does not behave with such regularity, though clearly there are regularities (i.e. patterns and events that are not random). Critical realism sees causal relations as existing as powers or tendencies, which interact with other tendencies to produce causes. Two simple examples illustrate this kind of mechanist thinking (see also **mechanisms and models**). The value of a currency will depend on a complex mechanism of its value in relation to other currencies, interest rates, inflationary or deflationary pressures and so on. Central banks have the power to devalue (or revalue) a currency, but that power exists within that mechanism. Thus, a currency devaluation will come about as a result of the 'firing' of that mechanism, such as an over-valued currency which deters international trade. The devaluation may be 'explained' by the mechanism in combination with a particular event, such as the over-valued currency. A police officer will have the power of arrest, but will exercise it only under particular circumstances and these circumstances will be embedded in particular mechanisms of the criminal justice system of a jurisdiction. The powers of arrest and the mechanisms underlying those powers are very different in, say, France than Saudi Arabia, but in both places an actual arrest will depend on a particular context.

However, whilst critical realism allows for a modulation in the exercise of powers (e.g. devaluation, arrest etc.), it also claims that there is natural necessity in the physical and social world; that is, when a certain effect cannot but happen, or cannot but fail to happen, such an effect or its absence is necessary (Harré and Madden 1975: 19).

CRITICAL REALISM EVALUATED

Bhaskar and other realists, such as Russell Keat and John Urry (1975), should take the credit for introducing realism to social science as a philosophical 'third way'. However, as I noted above, realism in natural science has a long history and in fact has continued to develop quite separately to critical realism, which is pretty much ignored in the philosophy of the natural sciences. Indeed its influence in social science has been more metaphysical than methodological, though in recent years an increasing number of social researchers, who hold to realist principles generally, have come to describe themselves as 'critical realists'.

In my view the methodological deficit is a result of the vagueness of the core principles of critical realism. It is true that realism must begin from certain metaphysical assumptions about the underlying existence of the real, though it is possible to make inductive assumptions that such an underlying reality does exist because it reveals itself to us historically (Williams 1998: 5–21). However, critical realism does not go much beyond asserting principles (such as its depth ontology, causal powers or natural necessity). There is a contradiction between the apparently contingent nature of causal powers and the claim to the natural necessity in their realisation (Williams 2011). Either there is an essential element in their realisation, in the way that a substance that has the disposition of being soluble in water must dissolve when placed in water, or the realisation of causal powers are the result of sufficient conditions and not necessary ones (see **contingency and necessity**).

A second problem for critical realism is that through its rejection of probabilistic causal inference derived from the observation of constant conjunctions, it either rejects, or is ambivalent about, the survey method (or indeed experiments) and by implication, probability itself. In practice this has left a methodological lacuna, in that whilst it is apparently a naturalistic philosophy, much of the research it has influenced has been interpretive. Without a theory of probability (see **probability**) critical realism is unable to measure the strength of the antecedents of an event. That is, all events that occur have a prior probability of occurrence, but this can vary enormously. Without the acknowledgement of the ontological probabilistic nature of social reality (see **complexity**) and a means of measuring this, then critical realism cannot move beyond statements of metaphysical principle.

A third problem, somewhat separate to the foregoing, is what has been described as the 'normative turn'; that is, the view that the methodology of critical realism permits discrimination between the many explanatory possibilities and can get closer to 'reality'. It is then said to follow that this confers a privileged epistemological position upon realists who should be 'critical' of uninformed lay positions. This blurs the 'is' of description and explanation with the 'ought' of moral or political action and has been criticised by Ray Pawson (2006: 18–20) and Martyn Hammersley (2002). Newer forms of realism are as much marked by the raising of one or more of these objections to critical realism as any distinct or unified doctrine. However, in recent years there has been something of a coalescence around what has been termed 'complex realism' (Byrne 2011) or 'contingent realism' (Williams 2011). These approaches emphasise the relationship of complexity to realism (see **complexity**).

REALISM ABOUT OBJECTS AND THEORIES

All forms of realism place emphasis on ontology. The ontology of natural science realism is less concerned with whether everyday physical objects are real and more concerned with the questions of whether an observation is of a real phenomena, or an artefact. This is frequently the case because phenomena are not directly observed, but through the proxy of instruments. No one has ever seen a photon, but only electronic signals that is evidence for its existence. Second, the scientist is concerned with the nature of reality (how and why it fits together in the way it does). Observations are prompted by a theory of how a particular part of reality works and how it relates to other parts of reality. Ideally, observations should confirm a theory and if they do they give credence both to the veracity of the observation and the theory. In practice it is much more messy, yet natural science realists place emphasis upon theory testing. A theory is a description and explanation of reality if it is empirically verified. It is possible, therefore, to be a realist about objects, but not about theories, which might be regarded as constructs. Alternatively one may say that if a theory is confirmed by rigorous observation, it is itself a real description and explanation of reality. The difference is subtle and not usually simply dichotomous.

Social science realism also emphasises theories, but is vaguer about how theories can be tested. The popularity of the ideas of complexity and chaos have made it popular to draw analogies between the indeterminism of many parts of the physical world and the social world. I do not want to push this too far, but suffice to say that physicists and biologists have long worked with statistical evidence to provide confirmation of theories; that is, theories are not categorically supported or refuted, but they are accepted, rejected or modified on the basis of a statistical judgement. This is because much of the world is ontologically probabilistic (see **probability**) and the social world is no different. Indeed the argument that critical realists make for natural necessity seems implausible in the social world (see **contingency and necessity**), where events are only ever locally (spatially or historically) determined (Little 2009).

MECHANISMS AND MEASUREMENT

The concept of the mechanism is common to critical realism and other forms of realism in social science. Ray Pawson has placed it at the centre of his thinking about policy interventions, which hitherto have employed a rather simplistic model of causality: that an intervention 'works' only if it makes a certain predetermined list of things happen. But social interventions (e.g. alcohol reduction, breakfast clubs for children etc.) and programmes do not happen in a vacuum, and what might work in Durham might not work in Devon. The important thing for the realist researcher is to identify the mechanism operating and differences in local contexts (Pawson 2006: 23). Indeed what counts as 'working' may itself be different in particular places and times, even if the identified mechanism is much the same.

Although the term 'mechanism' is used, it can be seen that what happens is not determined, but contingent upon other complex outcomes and properties. The challenge for realist research is to integrate a statistical theory of measurement with realism (see **statistics** and **probability**).

Measurement itself is not without its problems for realism because not only is the presence, absence or extent of the phenomena theorised, but also the measures themselves are theorised. Common sociological measures such as ethnicity or class are sociological constructs (unlike, say, age or biological sex). There is no one correct way of operationalising the theoretical construct of ethnicity with a variable that measures it. This, then, has important implications for whether social researchers can be realist about things and theories, or just things.

REFERENCES

Archer, M, Bhaskar, R, Collier, A, Lawson, T and Norrie, A (eds) (1998) *Critical Realism: essential readings.* London: Routledge.

Bhaskar, R (1998) *The Possibility of Naturalism*, 3rd edn. London: Routledge.

Bhaskar, R (2008) *A Realist Theory of Science*, 2nd edn. London: Routledge.
Byrne, D (2011) 'What is an effect? Coming at causality backwards', in Williams, M and Vogt, W P (eds), *The Sage Handbook of Innovation in Social Research Methods*. London: Sage. pp. 81–91.
Hammersley, M (2002) 'Research as emancipatory: the case of Bhaskar's critical realism', *Journal of Critical Realism*, 1 (1): 33–48.
Harré, R (1986) *Varieties of Realism: a rationale for the natural sciences.* Oxford: Blackwell.
Harré, R and Madden, E (1975) *Causal Powers.* Oxford: Blackwell.
Keat, R and Urry, J (1975) *Social Theory as Science*. London: Routledge & Kegan Paul.
Little, D (2009) 'The heterogeneous social: new thinking about the foundation of the social sciences', in Mantazavinos, C (ed.), *Philosophy of the Social Sciences: philosophical theory and scientific practice*. Cambridge: Cambridge University Press.
Pawson, R (2000) 'Middle-range realism', *Archive Européenes de Sociologie*, XLI: 283–325.
Pawson, R (2006) *Evidence-Based Policy – A Realist Perspective*. London: Sage.
Williams, M (1998) 'The social world as knowable', in May, T and Williams, M (eds), *Knowing the Social World.* Buckingham: Open University Press.
Williams, M (2011) 'Contingent realism – abandoning necessity', *Social Epistemology*, 25 (1): 37–56.

KEY READINGS

Bhaskar, R (2008) *A Realist Theory of Science*, 2nd edn. London: Routledge.
Hacking, I (1983) *Representing and Intervening: introductory topics in the philosophy of natural science.* Cambridge: Cambridge University Press.
Pawson, R (2006) *Evidence-Based Policy – A Realist Perspective*. London: Sage.

KEY THINKERS

Roy Bhaskar; David Byrne; Andrew Collier; Ian Hacking; Rom Harré; Ray Pawson

See also: *Causality; Complexity; Contingency and Necessity; Empiricism; Idealism; Mechanisms and Models; Probability; Statistics*

Relativism

Relativism is the view that the social environment is the principle, or only determinant of knowledge, beliefs or morality.

The section begins with the problems for investigation posed by epistemological relativism. Relativists cite the incommensurability of concepts and language as intractable, but the question is asked: can there be any commensurability of concepts and language? The particular features of epistemological relativism in the social world are considered and asked whether there can be facts of the matter in the social world? Finally moral and cultural relativism and the connectedness of morality, culture and knowledge are discussed.

To some extent all social scientists must embrace the view that the social world influences ideas of truth, beliefs or morality, but the challenge for most is to ground these things in either universals (conditions or characteristics that apply under all circumstances) or regularities (conditions or characteristics that apply under named bounded circumstances). Thus, various facets of relativism can be seen as opposed to rationality, realism and truth (see **rationality**, **realism**, **logic and truth**).

Relativism, like so many philosophical concepts, can be traced to Ancient Greece. Aristotle was reputed to have said 'Fires burn in both Hellas and Persia, but men's ideas of right and wrong vary from place to place'. Social 'science' relativism has, however, grown in popularity since the 1960s. I place science in scare quotes to indicate that if the more radical forms of relativism are adopted, such as those embraced by postmodernists, then a science of the social becomes impossible or irrelevant.

At the heart of such radical relativism is a rejection of truth as correspondence with reality, a cornerstone of science. Instead the truth of the matter is said to be a social construct that holds only in the social circumstances in which it is held. The anti-relativist can make the, perhaps trivial, logical point that to claim this is to maintain that one truth does indeed hold, that there are no truths. Such a logical stand-off does not take us much further in an evaluation of the claims of relativism.

Most relativists and 'anti-relativists' embrace much more sophisticated positions than these opposites. Space does not permit a detailed consideration of these, but a good starting point is to examine two main manifestations of relativism: epistemological and moral relativism.

EPISTEMOLOGICAL RELATIVISM

Epistemological relativism is the view that what we know, or how we know, is shaped by social context. This is put into sharp relief when the social contexts are very different. Benjamin Whorf, a linguistic ethnographer, studied the language of the Hopi Indians (Whorf 1956). He discovered that their whole metaphysical conceptual schema was completely different to our own and this was encapsulated in their language, which had no expressions for past, present and future (Little 1991: 204). In Western philosophy and science a concept of time is indispensible, not just for social organisation but for our beliefs about **causality**, in which if A causes B, then A must be prior in time to B. Are time and causality simply social constructs particular to Western society?

Ironically there is some support for this view from Western science. As I said earlier, Bertrand Russell noted in the early 20th century that physics has ceased to look for causes as a necessary connection between events (see **causality**). Moreover, modern physics, since the discovery of the expanding universe, does not distinguish between the concepts of space and time (but rather they are thought of as space-time). Without time there are no causes.

That Western science has come to occupy an apparently similar metaphysical position to societies, such as the Hopi, might be considered an argument for the privileged position of science (that it is conceptually capable of transcendence), but this is insufficient grounds for such a claim because it indicates no more than the possibility of metaphysical commensurability between two forms of society. The more moderate commensurability argument is actually quite a promising one, but first, what is the thesis of *incommensurability*?

Incommensurability is the claim that there can be no translation or cross-cultural understanding of the concepts of one society by another. A radical form of this was proposed by Thomas Kuhn (1970), a historian and philosopher of science who held that science is practised within 'paradigms'. Paradigms are self-contained explanatory, methodological and conceptual networks. A concept or explanation from one paradigm makes no sense in another. Kuhn's paradigms were largely coterminous with historic periods in science and, as many of his critics noted, failed to explain the transitions between paradigms, which inevitably required some form of translation mechanism (Trigg 1993: 139–140). The translation mechanisms are linguistic and the incommensurability thesis only holds if there can be no linguistic translation of concepts between cultures. But, of course, there are.

At the simplest of levels there are characteristics common to all humans that transcend our biology (though this is itself a characteristic we can *knowingly* share) and uncontroversially that humans have the capacity to communicate through language. We cannot know whether Whorf was indeed right about his characterisation of Hopi cosmology, but we must assume that he did not make it up and that in the course of his anthropological investigations there were means by which he could confirm his descriptions. Thus, the fact that Whorf was able to understand the Hopi language and the concepts it conveyed refutes any empirical argument of incommensurability. Commensurability is possible.

Of course it is possible to adopt an a priori argument for incommensurability, which is that we cannot ever know if the translation mechanism has produced commensurability, even though it appears to have done so. This argument takes on a radical linguistic form in the work of Peter Winch (1990) (see **language**). Winch maintained (and I radically paraphrase here) that to know a society (or religion etc.) you must be a member of that society and speak its language, that its concepts are embodied in and only known through its language. The empirical argument, of course, still holds but such an a priori one begs questions of what it means to 'know' and what it is to be 'social'.

Whilst it is difficult to make a meta argument for a privileged position for science, this does not rule out a realist argument for a reality which transcends language. Many of the things that Western technology or medicine can achieve were also claimed by societies which practice magic. Yet, for example, the ability of magic or penicillin to heal an infected wound can be empirically tested whether or not linguistic commensurability can be achieved. One can concede that knowledge is social, indeed that science itself is a social product, but it does not follow that all epistemic schema are equal when tested against physical reality.

Few relativists in the social sciences would support a radical relativism about the physical world, but would nevertheless maintain that there is no social equivalent of a physical reality against which competing knowledge claims can be tested. Moreover, many would also concede that empirically some form of linguistic commensurability can be achieved, but would nevertheless hold the view that knowledge of the social world is culturally specific and that there can be no cross-cultural universals in respect of social knowledge.

One version of epistemological relativism in respect of the social world has been strongly articulated by some feminists. This takes different forms (see **feminism**), but the core argument is that the organisation of most societies is androcentric. This goes beyond the argument that institutions and practices operate to favour men, but is rather the argument that our whole mode of thinking and conceptualising is masculine. This particularly applies to science where it is maintained, its purpose, problems and ethos begin from a masculine conception of the world (Harding 1986). This and similar arguments in post-colonial theory (Prasad 2008) are not anti-realist in respect of the natural world (though they may be silent on this on the grounds that a successor 'science' may lead us to different perspectives on and problematic about physical reality), but such views do render a social *science* difficult. This is because some of the core methodological principles of social science, such as explanation, prediction, or generalisation, are features of the andocentric or colonial science that is held to be relative to a particular form of social organisation. In particular it is held that there cannot be any truth of the matter about a particular thing and that there are many truths about the world that are socially or individually held (see **logic and truth**). That we act successfully upon them is simply a matter of social agreement as to what counts as true.

This is a powerful argument, but is one which begs a question. What will be our philosophical tools to transcend androcentrism or colonialism if there are no truths that transcend the groups that hold them? The consistent relativist will say that there are no such transcending truths. This is a version of the incommensurability argument. In this view even the idea that we can, or should, advance knowledge is a social belief particular to time and place. Whilst we might respect the philosophical purity of this argument, like the logical argument against epistemological relativism above, it does not advance our knowledge much.

If there is to be any form of knowledge accretion (whether or not we call it science) about the social world, then radical relativism must be abandoned. First, there is a moral argument for its abandonment, that whatever our views of what shall count as the 'good life', most societies have and continue to pursue it (I will say more about this below). Second, there is much we can know and compare across societies: demographic data, employment, education, gender attitudes, housing and shelter and so on. Our knowledge of these can help us produce the social technologies that are the equivalent of penicillin. For example, knowledge of agricultural practices can reduce food poverty, which in turn may reduce infant mortality and associated high birth rates. Third, in our 'global society', for better or worse, the empirical argument for incommensurability no longer holds. Fourth (and this is at the core of the realist argument about the social world – see **realism**), there are facts about the social world that transcend the knowledge of many of its members and moreover these facts enable or constrain individuals or groups in their actions. For example, I may hold the belief that Roman Catholic priests can marry and you hold the opposite belief, but however strongly I hold this belief, at the time of writing, I am wrong and it is a fact of the matter that such priests cannot marry. Beliefs about what is true in the social world, just like those about the physical world, do not always (or even usually) have epistemic equivalence.

Does this mean there is nothing to concede to epistemological relativism about the social world? No, because a great deal of the knowledge content of social science depends on one's starting theoretical stance. If I make the claim that after a rigorous measurement process I have counted 426 people who are homeless in a given city, technical and methodological issues aside, the initial definition of what counts as 'homeless' is subject to an ideological construction that will vary between times and places (Williams 2005). Similarly our definitions of employment, ethnicity, class and so on are subject to the same epistemic relativity that has its origins in an ideological or moral definition. But, just as relativity in relation to time-space locatedness of moving objects does not preclude cosmology or astronomy, social relativity need not preclude social science. It might even be said that even when there is no 'fact of the matter', but competing 'standpoints', then a comparison of these standpoints can itself advance knowledge (Scott 2012: 33–58).

MORAL RELATIVISM

It can perhaps already be seen that separating knowledge of what is from knowledge of what is thought should be the case, in the social world, is difficult because people's views of what ought becomes a matter of fact for others. The Holocaust resulted from a moral imperative amongst Nazi ideologues, but it became a terrible social and indeed physical fact for millions.

The term 'moral relativism', is often expressed as cultural relativism, and indeed the latter can be seen as a subset of the former, with no sharp divide between. A working definition might be seen as moral relativism describes the relativity of moral imperatives. Compare, for example, the moral imperative in some Muslim societies concerning adultery, which does not apply in Western secular society, or the Western moral taboo against sex between adults and children. Many past societies held no such taboos. Cultural relativism, however, describes cultural differences between societies. Violations of cultural norms may invoke sanction and their observance may be simply habit or conformity, but they will differ from society to society and indeed within particular societies. Moral and cultural relativism shade into each other and there is no logical distinction, but for the empirical social scientist it is important to entertain the difference.

In one sense it is impossible for a social scientist to be anything other than a moral or cultural relativist, in the sense of recognising morality and culture (as captured in the quote attributed to Aristotle above) is different between times or places, but how far can that extend to the position we take in relation to what or who we study?

Moral relativism refuses to privilege any moral position over any other and must equally sanction liberal moral values as those of totalitarianism. The same logical difficulty besets such a person as that noted above about epistemic relativism. Such a person who argues this position must do so from the moral position of anything goes. Ironically, this position has historically been held by those who would impose authoritarian values and controls on the basis of a Nietzchean argument of the primacy of the will (see McIntyre 1997). Few of us in our everyday lives are moral, or indeed cultural, relativists and the moral and cultural positions we hold are a complex interplay between social mores and our individual thinking about them. Our social position is one that we bring individually and collectively to our social science. Social science is not just a science of the social, but a science that takes place in the social, particularly in respect of its problematics and priorities (see **objectivity – subjectivity**).

REFERENCES

Harding, S (1986) *The Science Question in Feminism*. Milton Keynes: Open University Press.

Kuhn, T (1970) *The Structure of Scientific Revolutions*, 2nd edn. Chicago, IL: Chicago University Press.

Little, D (1991) *Varieties of Social Explanation*. Boulder, CO: Westview.

McIntyre, A (1997) *The Sovereignty of Joy: Nietzsche's vision of grand politics*. Toronto: University of Toronto Press.

Prasad, A (2008) 'Science in motion: what postcolonial science studies can offer', *International Journal of Communication Information and Innovation in Health*, 2 (2): 35–47.
Scott, J (2012) 'Relationism and dynamic synthesis', in Letherby, G, Scott, J and Williams, M (eds), *Objectivity and Subjectivity in Social Research*. London: Sage. pp. 33–58.
Trigg, R (1993) *Rationality and Science: can science explain everything?* Oxford: Blackwell.
Whorf, B (1956) *Language, Thought and Reality* (edited by J. Carroll). New York: Wiley.
Williams, M (2005) 'Definition, measurement and legitimacy in studies of homelessness', in Romero, M and Margolis, E (eds), *Social Inequalities* (Blackwell Companion to Sociology Series). Malden, MA: Blackwell. pp. 190–210.
Winch, P (1990 [1958]) *The Idea of a Social Science and its Relation to Philosophy.* London: Routledge.

KEY READINGS

Harré, R and Krausz, M (1996) *Varieties of Relativism.* Oxford: Blackwell.
Hollis, M and Lukes, S (1982) *Rationality and Relativism.* Oxford: Oxford University Press.

KEY THINKERS

Jean Baudrillard; Rom Harré; Peter Winch

See also: *Causality; Language; Logic and Truth; Objectivity – Subjectivity; Rationality; Realism*

Social Constructionism

Social constructionism is a development of idealism in the philosophy of science and social science and methodology which holds that all knowledge and that which experience as reality is created through human interaction with other people and the natural world.

The philosophical origins of social constructionism in idealism and its relationship to other philosophical and methodological positions are described. Meaning, intentionality and consciousness in social constructionism are then discussed. There follows a critical examination of the social constructionist critique of science and social science and the methodological consequences of this. Finally the work of Ian Hacking in dissecting the meaning of a social construction is introduced and the case is briefly made for the compatibility of social constructionism and realism.

Social constructionism has its origins in **idealism**. It is held that the only world we can know is that of ideas, or 'mind', and this can be contrasted with **realism** which maintains there is a mind-independent reality. Yet, like so many things in philosophy and social science, this simple dichotomy ends up being more complicated in practice, and at the end of this entry I have suggested that a moderate social constructionism is actually compatible with realism. The term itself widely entered the social science lexicon with the publication, in 1967, of Berger and Luckmann's *The Social Construction of Reality*. From the 1970s onwards it described a range of views in the social sciences and crucially the sociology of science (sometimes referred to as 'social studies of science'), that prioritised social construction as a primary explanatory concept.

Social constructionism, in its various forms, has come to dominate interpretive social science (see **interpretation and meaning**) and has become associated with both subjectivity and epistemological relativism (see **objectivity – subjectivity, relativism**). Yet, its formulation in Berger and Luckman's work emphasised both the social and construction. This subtle but important point, often ignored in more subjective and relativist approaches, is that whilst social constructs are the creations of human consciousness, these do not simply arise in individual consciousness, but are constructed from the raw material of the social world that the individual inhabits. To put it another way, whilst an explanation of the social might well be grounded in individual subjective understandings, those subjective understandings can only be understood in their social context.

MEANING AND INTENTIONALITY

For social constructionists, the world is meaning. Before there were humans to make sense of it, there may well have been a world, but the world we know is what it is because we give it meaning. Intentionality is important here. Philosophers use the word 'intentional' in a special way, not as we commonly do to denote purpose, but to mean directedness toward something. When we are conscious, we must be conscious of something. Non-intentional consciousness is, in effect, an oxymoron. So, it follows that we give things, we are directed toward, meaning and although you and I may be conscious of the same thing, it does not follow that we each give it the same meaning. Though it must be the case, for social life to be possible, to share meanings and act upon them. The French anthropologist Claude Lévi-Strauss (1966) used the helpful term '*bricoleur*' to describe how people make something new from the materials at hand. Indeed the French word '*bricolage*' translates, in contemporary English, as 'do it yourself' (DIY). An activity which some of us are better at than others, and all of us are better at some than other kinds of DIY. But to extend the analogy, not all things we make are as good as others; some things last for years whilst other things fail altogether, resulting in blown fuses, collapsing shelves and mess. So it is with the social world we construct.

Keeping this in mind, we might say that there is no DIY project that is the authentic or real one, there are just projects that are better, worse, fit or not fit for purpose. The social world version of this is that there is no authentic external reality we can measure our social constructions against and so no truth of the matter to act as a template or yardstick. It does not absolutely follow that this leads to epistemological relativism because (it is argued) that truth does not have to be correspondence with an external reality, but may be a matter of coherence, through social agreement or pragmatic understanding (see **logic and truth**).

Social constructionism, of different flavours, underpins a great deal of philosophy and social science, of phenomenology (Brentano, Schutz), **pragmatism** (James, Dewey), symbolic interactionism (Mead, Goffman) and in radical form in **postmodernism** and poststructuralism. One particular 'turn' is that of social knowledge, initially associated with Karl Mannheim (1936) and the aforementioned Berger and Luckmann. Whilst previous philosophers and social scientists had been concerned with social meaning in a general or everyday sense, the sociologists of knowledge specifically saw bodies of public knowledge as socially constructed, which is not especially controversial in art or literature, but to regard scientific knowledge as socially constructed was a radical departure and in due course was to radically challenge the epistemological foundations of science and to become a very bad tempered debate, sometimes characterised as 'the Science Wars'.

DE-BUNKING SCIENCE AND SOCIAL SCIENCE – THE BRIEFEST OF HISTORIES

To say the social world is socially constructed (mostly, it is said, through **language**) is not particularly controversial, but to claim that the physical world is socially constructed is radical and, on the face of it, quite mad. There was an historical precedent in the solipsism of 18th-century philosopher George Berkeley, who maintained that there are no material things in the world, merely ideas (see **idealism**). It is said that Samuel Johnson, on kicking a stone, declared to James Boswell (of Berkeley's solipsistic contention) 'I refute it thus'. The radical social constructionists do not go as far as Berkeley because they say that we simply can't know whether there is a reality beyond our social constructs as they are all we can know.

The sociologists of knowledge actually, at least initially, had little impact on the philosophy of science; the challenge actually came from within and most dramatically from Thomas Kuhn's (1962) reading of the history of science and his claim that scientific knowledge was not cumulative, but rather subject to revision through revolutions which challenged theories, findings and even the way in which scientists worked and thought. So, every time a Copernicus, a Newton or an Einstein came along, everything that we previously knew was thrown out in a dramatic revolution. This, at least, was the reading of Kuhn (see the essays in Lakatos and Musgrave 1970 for some initial key ideas in this debate), both by many of his followers and opponents. But what mattered was that this particular social construction of Kuhn's work was a very successful piece of *bricolage*! To spell this out, maybe a little simplistically, scientific theories are the social constructions of science, so it must follow that so also are the predictions of those theories and the subsequent findings. The first wave of the social studies of science, influenced by those such as Kuhn, Polanyi and Feyerabend and the sociologists of knowledge, held a dramatic and controversial view of scientific knowledge, namely that the physical world has a small or non-existent role in the construction of scientific knowledge (see e.g. Barnes and Edge 1982). This counter-intuitive claim about the physical world (so was the atomic bomb a social construction?) may leave most lay people shaking their heads in incredulity (it certainly had this effect on more traditional philosophers of science), yet if we go back to what is meant by social construction, is entirely consistent: that only the world we know, or can know, is socially constructed by us!

Though fascinating, the debate about science is tangential to our concern with the social world (I discuss this in much more detail in Williams 2000). However, it was important because it was seized upon by many in the social sciences as an epistemological model for the latter. They took the view that if natural science theories and findings are social constructions, then it must follow that those of the social scientist are likewise. The ill-tempered debate divided the social sciences into those who believed that at least some form of successful description and **explanation** were possible, using a battery of methods both quantitative and qualitative, against those who saw knowledge claims by the former as 'objectivist' or 'essentialist' (i.e. that there are 'objects' or things have indispensable, or fundamental characteristics. This was more than just an intellectual argument, because this was also a period of political radicalisation in social science that questioned normative characterisations. So it followed that if things like 'gender' or 'race' were socially constructed, so too were any 'scientific' claims about their characteristics.

This became important in respect of method and what could be claimed for methods. First, social constructionism rejected explanatory methods in favour of those which attempted to understand agent perspectives from a more participatory position, thus exclusively qualitative methods. Epistemologically, researcher accounts could not be privileged over lay accounts, and neither could one researcher account be privileged over another (see Jones 1998 for a critical account). These last few sentences cannot do justice to a very large body of writing and research that has embraced many other influences and methods, such as **feminism**, 'queer theory', ethnomethodology, autoethnography, **postmodernism**, poststructuralism, actor-network theory and so on. What is important is that the philosophical assumptions of social constructionism hugely influenced a large body of social research, both methodologically and epistemologically, that rejected and opposed the more traditional scientific approaches.

Some of the fire has gone out of these debates nowadays and it is possible to more calmly stand back and assess the epistemological claims of social constructionism and indeed incorporate some of the ideas into what would have been, hitherto, oppositional positions.

SOCIAL CONSTRUCTION OF WHAT?

This was the title of a book by Ian Hacking (2000) and is an in-depth exploration of what we might mean when we claim something is socially constructed. Hacking, in this book and elsewhere, does this through the illustrative device of the naming of phenomena, such as madness or child abuse. Are such categories socially constructed, or are they the naming of pre-existing phenomena? There is a lot at stake. Is mental illness real, or a construct of psychiatrists? As Hacking notes (2000: 100), many mental illnesses are transient: hysteria in late 19th-century France, multiple personality disorder in late 20th-century America, or the naming of schizophrenia in 1908. These are socio-medical categories, but it is easy to see how such naming might extend to forms of social deficit, such as education, social capital, integration and so on, and the implications of this for measurement and representation.

Hacking uses the device of 'kinds' to tease out what is socially constructed. Natural kinds are those things which we may name or classify, but the naming or classifying makes no difference to the kind itself. We may call a creature a horse or pony, but the distinction is irrelevant to the creature itself. Then there are indifferent kinds, things which may interact with us but are unaware of that interaction. Our world is full of technology that does just this. Finally, there are interactive kinds and to the social scientist these are the most interesting. People become classified as (say) disabled and this becomes a description that those so classified use. Indeed it is sometimes hard to avoid because such classifications will enable or constrain behaviour; for example, criminality may be denied by the bearer, but the classification will have effects on that person.

This is not to say that there is no mixing of kinds: I am partially sighted and that is a physical characteristic, but it is also a social category. Hacking's position is more nuanced than I can recount here, but in my view he helps us to arrive at a valuable position of compatibility between social constructions and reality. Social constructions involve naming, even inventing 'kinds', but once constructed or invented have real consequences, in the enabling and constraining of behaviour, for those so named.

It follows from this, and I have argued elsewhere (Williams 2009), that there is an accommodation to be had between a moderate realism and a moderate social constructionism. Take, for example, science itself (and for the purposes of current illustration we might include social science). Science is a social construction that emerged in particular societies in the late Middle Ages and early modern period (Williams 2000). It did not emerge in all societies and in some it began and floundered, but in many European countries scientific thinking and practice emerged through a symbiosis of technical, social and epistemological developments. Crucially, it grew through its success in explaining, predicting and technological achievement. Along the way it embraced certain values, such as truth, parsimony, accuracy and so on, social values that defined scientific practice. Prior to 'science' in European society was the practice of alchemy, which promised to turn base metals into gold. It too had rules and procedures that were social constructions, but no one ever turned lead into gold and alchemy faded away. But alchemy and science were both social constructions. The difference was that the former was able to demonstrably manipulate the world, to change objects and to show why things were like they are and on the basis of that make new things like optics, engines and finally aeroplanes and space probes. Social science has had less dramatic success than natural science, but it too is able to transcend common sense and produce testable explanations and predictions.

Why? Because although the world is social constructed, those social constructions are made from real things and some of those real things are and were social constructions themselves. Different practices and approaches to gender, in different societies, are indeed socially constructed, but they have real consequences for female and male life chances. Moreover, we can measure and explain those life chances. In my view understanding their context and the experiences of agents is not mutually exclusive of measuring and explaining what happens to them.

REFERENCES

Barnes, B and Edge, D (eds) (1982) *Science in Context: readings in the sociology of science.* Buckingham: Open University Press.

Berger, P and Luckmann, T (1967) *The Social Construction of Reality*. Harmondsworth: Penguin.

Hacking, I (2000) *The Social Construction of What?* Harvard: Harvard University Press.

Jones, T (1998) 'Interpretive social science and the "native's" point of view', *Philosophy of the Social Sciences*, 28 (1): 32–68.

Kuhn,T S (1962) *The Structure of Scientific Revolutions.* Chicago, IL: Chicago University Press.

Lakatos, I and Musgrave, A (eds) (1970) *Criticism and the Growth of Knowledge.* Cambridge: Cambridge University Press.

Lévi-Strauss, C (1966) *The Savage Mind*. Chicago, IL: Chicago University Press.
Mannheim, K (1936) *Ideology and Utopia*. New York: Harcourt Brace.
Williams, M (2000) *Science and Social Science: an introduction*. London: Routledge.
Williams, M (2009) 'Social objects, causality and contingent realism', *Journal for the Theory of Social Behaviour*, 39 (1): 1–18.

KEY READINGS

Hacking, I (2000) *The Social Construction of What?* Harvard: Harvard University Press.

KEY THINKERS

Peter Berger; Kenneth Gergen; Ian Hacking

See also: *Explanation; Feminism; Idealism; Interpretation and Meaning; Logic and Truth; Objectivity – Subjectivity; Postmodernism; Pragmatism; Realism; Relativism; Time*

Statistics

(*Note*: this section should be read in conjunction with that of Probability)

Statistics refers to the collection, analysis and interpretation of numeric data.

This section briefly traces the emergence of statistics and statistical reasoning. It demonstrates that statistics, though based on sound mathematical principles, is nevertheless an historical and social product, which has philosophical implications for its usage. Examples of this are illustrated through significance testing and objective and subjective approaches to statistical reasoning. The conclusion is that though statistics are socially constructed, they play a valuable role in practical social research.

Statistics is the study of uncertainty and was a relative latecomer in the history of science. Ian Hacking (1998: 6) notes that what we now call 'probability' dates to no earlier than 1660 and right up until the beginning of the 19th century, the idea that the world might be ruled by chance was seen as superstitious, or at best an indication of our ignorance. Early modern science had no need for statistics, and again as Hacking also notes, was not even particularly given to measurement until the 1840s. Necessity, as a doctrine, underpinned science and its discovery was the goal of the enterprise. The French philosopher Pierre-Simon Laplace famously believed that given a sufficient intelligence and available data, it would be possible to be certain of all things in the universe (Williams 2000: 17). By the mid-19th century, statistics were increasingly used by the state and had come to play a role in natural science and would begin to be important in the emerging social sciences. Nevertheless descriptive statistics, used to summarise data and fit models, dominated it. Descriptive statistics, used to describe populations, are statistics without probability and probability, as uncertainty, was something to be eliminated. The role of statistics was to eliminate error, and even the social sciences sought deterministic laws. Though there was a growing recognition of indeterminacy of social life, it took key developments in statistics, such as the sampling distribution (Fisher 1935), to provide the tools and the basis for a philosophy of statistics to underwrite social science methodology.

Statistical reasoning is both an empirical tool and an epistemology tool, because it is a belief that if we use those tools appropriately, then we are able to explain and predict things in the world that we would otherwise be unable to explain, or predict. In the rest of this section I concentrate on the philosophical aspect of statistics rather than its technical or mathematical properties, though with one caveat in respect of the second of these: that it is the mathematical property of the law of large numbers (described under **probability**) that makes statistics possible.

PHILOSOPHY HISTORY AND STATISTICS

The development of statistical methods has greatly influenced philosophy. For example, whilst the problem of **induction** is attributable to Hume, its practical (if not philosophical solution) came through statistical reasoning, which could give us some degree of knowledge of how uniform, or stochastic, the world might be. In the social sciences it is hard to conceive of measurement without statistics, and our use of statistics has changed our empirical and philosophical understanding of the social world.

Statistics increasingly influenced positivism in social science toward the mid-20th century, but positivists (if they are true to their Humean empiricist traditions) will deny whether we can ever know if the world is deterministic or probabilistic, though they do follow a reductionist programme that aims to reduce a hierarchy of statistical explanations to a smaller set of statements or laws (see e.g. Homans 1964) and in this sense they are epistemological, if not the ontological heirs of Laplace. Whilst the use of statistics in the social sciences is not wholly the preserve of positivism, historically it was positivist social scientists such as Lazarsfeld (see Lazarsfeld and Rosenberg 1955) who promoted the use of statistics in analysis, but also developed sophisticated causal models, particularly those based on regression. Thus, the development of statistics shifted the philosophical centre of gravity from causes as determined to causes as probabilistic (Tooley 2004) (see **causality**).

The utility of statistics to social science lies in their predictive and explanatory value, but statistics are a social product, not just in what they are used for but also statistical techniques themselves.

The roots of the social construction of statistics lie in their use by the early modern state. Audits of populations go back to the Roman period, but as the power and liabilities of the state grew in development of capitalism there was a growing need to count people and categorise people, for purposes of taxation, but more generally to know the power and potential productivity of the state. Data on births, marriages and deaths were needed, and later data on production, habitations, occupations and habitations. Urbanisation too was a driver of the need for statistical data, particularly in the sphere of public health because urbanisation brought with it the perils of tuberculosis and typhoid. By the end of the 19th century, data gathering in Western Europe and North America had become sophisticated, and this was partially due to the experience of the state in gathering statistics, but also in the development of statistics as a science.

The 'normal distribution' or the 'bell curve' is at the heart of statistics. It can be thought of in two ways, simply of a binomial distribution of two possible values, exemplified by a coin toss. A few tosses of a coin will produce an uneven distribution of heads and tails, but as the number of tosses of coin grows then a normal distribution, or curve, will result. A more sophisticated version was introduced via astronomy (Hacking 1998: 106) that provided for the idea of a mean and a dispersion of values, which came to be measured through the standard deviation. The closer the clustering of values to the mean, the more reliable the average is seen to be.

These are mathematical properties and in themselves devoid of social meaning. Coins, like dice (see **probability**), have objective physical properties and whilst these will, with the circumstances of their tossing, produce initially uneven results (and only in the long run produce a normal distribution), they do not attach to any meaningful social characteristics that we might want to measure. The early Belgian statistician and philosopher Adolphe Quetelet is credited as applying the notion of the mean to biological and social phenomena (Hacking 1998: 107). Put somewhat crudely, the mathematically neutral concept of 'normal', as in a 'normal distribution', was applied to the biological and social world and then, as now, those two realms are hugely intertwined, particularly around health and illness. One can see how some measures attach to relatively uncontroversial categories, for example mortality rates, but extend this to causes of death and issues of judgement and normative social values will contribute to the creation of the data, as Durkheim discovered (1952). The confluence of biology and social values was no more apparent than in the eugenics movement, social Darwinism and the 'discovery' of mental illness (Hacking 2002). It is possible to look back at the crude categorisations of the 19th and early 20th centuries and see them as the normative manifestations of a particular society, but that normativity is still with us in what we measure and how we measure it. Take, for example, the distribution of wealth. Often this is measured through earnings, but 'earnings' can be measured in different ways that may or may not include other monetary or non-monetary assets. Furthermore, it may make a difference as to whether, in a given society, we measure the mean or the median earnings. The former is almost certainly to be non-normally distributed and may hide huge inequalities of earnings.

THE INVENTION OF TECHNIQUE

I mentioned positivism above, because although with historical hindsight we can see that categorisation and measurement were social products, positivist statisticians believed that they were producing value-free techniques. Though now we can see that they were working in an environment where normative considerations shaped what they did (they still do, but we are more aware of it now). Sometimes spoken of as the 'father of modern statistics', Karl Pearson was an enthusiastic eugenicist, yet many of the techniques he invented (and those of his contemporaries) – chi square, Pearson's R tests and so on – can be used more universally and are not tainted by the context of their invention. But they were invented nevertheless and could have been different, or even born of different statistical assumptions.

Two examples suffice: significance and error, and probability, each discussed below.

Significance and Error

Along with the discovery of the law of large numbers and the normal curve came the idea of 'error'. The concept of error was conceived as a number of small and random mistakes which combine to produce an overall error. The amount of error in a measurement, if known, can tell us how close we might be to the 'truth of the matter'. Measurement of error became embodied in tests of significance on sample data. They are, then, at the core of modern statistics. The idea being that one's test of significance is able to indicate how reliable our results are and whether we are able to generalise these to our population.

Mostly researchers present significance as 'P values'. The P value is the probability of obtaining a statistical finding with as great a value as the one that was actually observed. This is done by setting up a null hypothesis, that chance alone accounts for the result obtained. The aim of the subsequent test is to falsify the null hypothesis, thereby accepting the alternative hypothesis, that the test has produced significant results (see **experiments**). There are at least three problems with this. First, the 'significance level', is a convention. In social research this is commonly $p = 0.01$ or even $p = 0.05$, though there is no good mathematical or philosophical reason for this. The second problem is that it is not sensitive to small effects in most samples. For example, we know that in every population rare diseases exist, but they may afflict less than 0.01 of the population. Highly sensitive measures may detect the disease, but a statistical test on sample data would almost certainly point to the acceptance of the null hypothesis, that the finding was a chance one (Gigerenzer 2008).

The third problem is that statistical significance is interpreted as having substantive significance. Of course this claim is rarely actually made, but there is hardly a social researcher who, having obtained statistically significant results, will not present these as a finding that confirms a research hypothesis (and conversely, will dismiss other results as 'not significant' and not worthy of discussion). Indeed it would be a rare social science journal that would publish results argued on the basis of substantive significance when in fact they were not statistically significant (Cohen 1994) (see also **hypothesis**).

Quite apart from the issues of measurement and definitions of what shall be measured, the specification of the population or sample, there is an absolutely fundamental issue at the heart of significance and it is that significance will increase as the size of the sample increases. In a smallish sample, finding significance of $p = 0.05$ is hard, but in very large samples one can find significance levels of $p = 0.001$, though the actual presence of the phenomenon in the population may be exactly the same. In research practice, the kind of consequences that flow from this are that, in relatively small samples, the analyst will resort to recoding of variables producing fewer categories and thus increasing significance, or using alternative tests that will show greater significance (e.g. commonly in nominal level data, using Fisher's exact test instead of chi square).

However sophisticated is the presentation of significance is a sleight of hand, though perhaps a necessary one, without a statistical escape clause, unless one adopts a Baysian approach (which I'll come too).

Probability

The second example relates to what we mean by probability (see **probability**). We can talk of two kinds of probability, commonly referred to as 'objective' and 'subjective' probability. The first assumes that probability is inherent in the world itself and the role of statistics is to make inferences about the distribution of characteristics in the world, whilst the second is concerned with our degrees of belief in a matter.

Objective probability divides into frequency interpretations and propensity interpretations, and the statistical procedures associated with each are quite different. The frequency interpretations derive their probabilities from the relative frequency of an event in a known sequence and is the 'standard approach', whereas the propensity interpretation is based on the measurement of dispositions or tendencies of a particular situation (Gillies 2000: 113–136). There are no good mathematical reasons why we should prefer one over the other, but in actuality the frequency approach has dominated and it is it that has produced virtually all of our statistical insights and techniques (and the limitations that go with them, such as significance). There is a wide philosophical literature on propensity approaches and there are advocates of this approach (I am one of them! See Williams 1999; Williams and Dyer 2009), but the absence of developed techniques severely limits its practical application.

Subjectivist approaches, usually termed 'Bayesian' (and derived from the theorem of Thomas Bayes, an 18th-century English cleric), have begun to attract adherents, particularly in epidemiology, in the last few decades (Howson and Urbach 1989). A Bayesian approach depends on the weightings of the relative plausibility of different hypotheses that can be quantified as probabilities and are then revised as new empirical data becomes available, or is further analysed. It is derived from Bayes theorem, which is an expression of the probability h if evidence e is added to the prior knowledge, a. Thus the probability h, relative to e and a, is equal to the probability of h relative to a multiplied by the probability of e relative to h and a and divided by the probability of e relative to a.

One may begin with assigning an equal probability both H1 and H2, but in due course this might be amended to 0.25 for H1 and 0.75 for H2 and so on. The idea is that the scientist 'closes in' on the truth of the matter until a hypothesis is confirmed or falsified. There is a fundamental objection to this approach that is aired far more often than the problem of significance in frequentist approaches to statistics and it is the issue of how one assigns probabilities to the initial 'priors': that is, how did the scientist come to decide on 0.25 for H1 and 0.75 for H2? Bayesians do not deny the plausibility of this criticism, but their responses usually will emphasise the self-correcting nature of the subsequent derived probabilities.

Frequentist, propensity or Bayesian approaches are not neutral in either a statistical or philosophical sense. One's starting assumptions about what probability is (or how it should be approached) lead to the adoption of techniques that underlie epistemological claims about the world.

LIES, DAMMED LIES AND STATISTICS?

The claim that the latter has less veracity than either of the former is attributed to Benjamin Disraeli and has remained the mantra of cynicism about statistics ever since. In one sense, the reason for this is that statistics developed as an instrumental of particular state of ideologies and scientific orthodoxies during a particular period. These things shaped not just what was measured, but also how it was measured and even the epistemological reasoning that underlay the way measurement was derived. One might say that statistics was grounded in politics, ethics and mathematics and remains so now.

But as Winston Churchill said of democracy, it is less bad than the alternatives. There is chicanery in statistics as any discipline, but more importantly there is error not born of ill intention, but often because, like every science, it is fallible. For example, the problems of significance outlined above do not go away, but rarely do social researchers make grandiose claims on the basis of one result. Moreover, the 'null hypothesis' approach to testing is not the only one. One can set up alternative statistical models, derived from theoretical ones, and then use model selection to decide between them (Williams 2013) (which model produces the best 'fit' – see **mechanisms and models**).

Critics of Bayesian statistics sometimes assume a democracy of ignorance amongst Bayesian statisticians in the selection of priors, as if the researcher had just plucked these out of the air. In practice (certainly in social science), the fixing of priors will be based upon at least a reasonable amount of evidence from earlier or related tests and may use informal reasoning and 'infer to the best explanation' (see **hypotheses**).

Like so many things social researchers do, statistical reasoning carries philosophical baggage. Though possibly mathematically sound, much of statistics is socially constructed, yet it is one set of tools amongst many that can lead us to good enough knowledge of the social world in order to act upon it.

REFERENCES

Cohen, J (1994) 'The Earth is round p < .05', *American Psychologist*, 49: 997–1001.
Durkheim, E (1952 [1896]) *Suicide*. London: Routledge and Kegan Paul.
Fisher, R (1935) *The Design of Experiments*. Edinburgh: Oliver and Boyd.
Gigerenzer, G (2008) *Rationality for Mortals: how humans cope with uncertainty*. Oxford: Oxford University Press.
Gillies, D (2000) *Philosophical Theories of Probability*. London: Routledge.
Hacking, I (1998) *The Taming of Chance*. Cambridge: Cambridge University Press.
Hacking, I (2002 [1983]) 'Making up people', in Hacking, I (ed.), *Historical Ontology*. Cambridge, MA: Harvard University Press.
Homans, G (1964) 'Bringing men back in', *American Sociological Review*, 29: 5.

Howson, C and Urbach, P (1989) *Scientific Reasoning: the Bayesian approach*. La Salle, IL: Open Court.
Lazarsfeld, P and Rosenberg, M (eds) (1955) *The Language of Social Research*. Glencoe, IL: Free Press.
Tooley, M (2004) 'Probability and causation', in Dowe, P and Noordhof, P (eds), *Cause and Chance: causation in an indeterministic world*. London: Routledge.
Williams, M (1999) 'Single case probabilities and the social world: the application of Popper's propensity interpretation', *Journal for the Theory of Social Behavior*, 29 (2): 187–201.
Williams, M (2000) *Science and Social Science: an introduction*. London: Routledge. pp. i –iii; 1–173.
Williams, M (2013) 'Probability and models', in Edwards, P, O'Mahoney, J and Vincent, S (eds), *Studying Organisations Using Critical Realism*. Oxford: Oxford University Press.
Williams, M and Dyer, W (2009) 'Single case probabilities', in Ragin, C and Byrne, D (eds), *Case-Based Methods*. London: Sage.

KEY READINGS

Childers, T (2013) *Philosophy and Probability*. Oxford: Oxford University Press.
Gillies, D (2000) *Philosophical Theories of Probability*. London: Routledge.
Hacking, I (1965) *Logic of Statistical Inference*. Cambridge: Cambridge University Press.
Hacking, I (1990) *The Taming of Chance*. Cambridge: Cambridge University Press.
Porter, T (1995) *Trust in Numbers*. Princeton, NJ. Princeton University Press.

KEY THINKERS

Thomas Bayes; Ronald Fisher; Francis Galton; Colin Howson; Kurt Gigerenzer; John Maynard Keynes; Blaise Pascal; Karl Pearson; Karl Popper; Peter Urbach

See also: *Causality; Experiments; Hypothesis(es); Induction; Mechanisms and Models; Positivism; Probability*

Theory

Theories are all propositional statements of the form 'if P then Q'. Logically they are equivalent to hypotheses, but theories are of quite different kinds. They may be informal 'folk theories', which differ little from everyday beliefs; they may be (in social science) 'grand theories', which offer an explanatory schema for a wide range of social phenomena; and 'middle range theory' (again in social science), which are close to those used by natural scientists and are testable statements which will explain a limited range of social phenomena, often within a particular socio-historical/cultural context.

Theory is a broad term. In this section I begin with a definition and go on to firstly discuss 'grand theories' and their limitation. These are contrasted with the 'middle range' theories of Robert Merton. Middle range theories may be applied and tested in social research. Finally I discuss the relationship of theories to scientific progress.

The word 'theory' comes from the Greek word *theoria*, which means 'looking at'. In everyday use, in natural and social science, it has come to mean a propositional statement. In everyday language we will say 'I have a theory that ...' or 'In theory X should be the case ...' simply to mean an understanding of how something works. In natural science, despite the influence of logical positivism (see **positivism, empiricism**), theory has always played a central role in reasoning about phenomena and providing a structure for investigation. Science is about producing and testing theories, propositional statements or networks of statements that will explain and predict. Logically theories, hypotheses, models and laws (see **hypothesis**, **mechanisms and models**, **generalisation and laws**) have the same structure, but differ in complexity and in their role in science. The terms 'law' or 'theory' are often used to describe similar classes of phenomena, thus we have Newton's *laws* but Einstein's *theories*, each of which has similar status in explaining the class of phenomena they intend to explain.

Social scientists do use theories in much the same way as natural scientists and I will return to this below, however, 'theory' has too other roles or usages. The first is that 'folk theories' can themselves be the subject of social science investigation, particularly in anthropology. Indeed some anthropologists and sociologists of science, in the tradition of Peter Winch (1990), or postmodernism, have claimed that social scientists should accord the same epistemological status to folk theories as scientific ones (see **relativism**, **rationality**).

GRAND THEORY

A second use of the term is in social theory. Social theory is almost a branch of social science in itself and has its origins in the social philosophy of Hobbes, Locke and Rousseau. These thinkers practised in an age when empirical social science, as we understand it, was yet to be born. In the 19th century their work inspired the first of the 'grand' or 'classical' theorists, in particular Marx and later Weber and Durkheim. Each of these did use empirical data (Marx, economic data, Weber, historical data, Durkheim, official statistics), but in the main it was used to reinforce or illustrate the arguments they made. The tradition of 'grand theory' (a term rarely used by its exponents) continued through the 20th century. The key feature of grand theory is the ambition of its explanation. In the case of Talcott Parsons (Parsons and Shils 1951) and his general systems theory is a claim that all systems from unicellular organisms to industrial society could be understood by using the same theories and methodologies. Indeed Marx, Weber and Durkheim claimed to explain the historical development of different kinds of society, often teleologically (e.g. Marx, communism, Durkheim, 'organic solidarity') (Durkheim 1961). This kind of theorising has continued to the present. Some theorists, such as Niklas Luhmann, have attempted to develop explanatory concepts (systems theory), which have gone on to inform more theoretical work (Luhmann 1995). Others, such as Anthony Giddens or Zygmunt Bauman, have developed conceptual frameworks that claim to explain how contemporary society came to be the way it is. Their work has more broadly influenced sociologists and historians (indeed Giddens talks of 'sensitizing' concepts). Indeed some of this work, in particular that of Foucault, Bhaskar and Giddens, might be described as 'meta-theory', 'insofar as theirs are philosophical theories about the nature and domain of a human science and how this is to be studied' (Manicas 2007: 21).

Whilst undoubtedly a source of interesting and productive ideas, grand theory is nonetheless fairly self-contained. Its propositions are rarely expressed in testable form and are of such a large explanatory sweep that logically quite opposite testable propositions may be developed from each. More critically, one might say that such theories are so broad as to explain everything and nothing. Indeed when practising social scientists claim their work is 'Foucauldian' (after Michel Foucault), Marxist, or Weberian, they usually mean that these thinkers have informed the conceptual schema of their work, much as a writer of literature, or an artist, influences or informs rather than to provide a testable conceptual framework.

MIDDLE RANGE THEORY

Middle range theory is usually associated with the sociologist Robert Merton (1968), but variations of it are widespread in social science and, for the most part, not necessarily acknowledged as such.

Merton described middle range theories as those

> that lie between the minor but necessary working hypotheses that evolve in abundance during day-to-day research and the all inclusive systematic efforts to develop a unified theory that will explain all the observed uniformities of social behaviour, social organization and social change. (1967: 39)

Merton's approach allows the testing of 'minor theories', through research, as a way of building knowledge of the social world. They are abstract enough to allow testable generalisations from one context to another. As in natural science, social scientists need to be able to abstract from one manifestation of a phenomenon to other phenomena and say that if P holds under circumstances S, then it can also explain Q.

As a practical solution, middle range approaches to theorising are widely used in social science, though unlike the natural sciences there is rarely a co-ordinated attempt to build them into bodies of coherent theory (which was Merton's ultimate goal) and indeed as I have noted, there is a virtual disconnect with grand theory.

APPLYING AND TESTING THEORIES

Although grand theory rarely translates into empirically testable theories, it very often sets the terms for the specifying of a problem and the theories which may explain it. For example Keynesian economists will see large-scale unemployment as economically dysfunctional, whilst neo-liberal economists have generally seen it as an unfortunate, but inevitable symptom of market adaptation. Thus any middle range theory to explain instances of unemployment in particular economies will have quite different initial assumptions built into them.

So, whilst middle range theories may be useful methodological tools, they are not ideologically neutral in their initial composition, and indeed probably could not be ideologically neutral. This is a big difference between theorising in the natural and social sciences. In the former, though local variations (say pressure, temperature, humidity etc.) may interfere with the operation of a law, ultimately nature will prevail. In the social world our actions and beliefs constantly change the social world (though that does not mean that such flux prevents measurement and explanation). Even without a broad ideological explanatory framework (which indeed the natural sciences have their equivalents), change between cultures and over time means that virtually any social theory will have a limit to its generalisability from one place or time to another.

Realists, such as Ray Pawson (2000), whilst welcoming middle range theory, have integrated this into the broader ontological setting of a mechanism (see **mechanisms and models**). Though there are different ontological and epistemological specifications of mechanisms, they nevertheless provide a broader explanatory framework within which to test particular theories. Unlike (say) broader specifications of ideological positions, such as Marxism, elements of mechanisms can be themselves tested.

Karl Popper was of the view that it did not matter where a theory came from, the important thing was whether it was falsifiable (see **falsification**). Well of course it does matter, not just because what you choose to try to falsify will be a matter of a prior set of decisions, but also because what does it mean to 'test a theory', particularly in social science?

First, as Popper himself acknowledged, it is easy enough to specify a theory such that it is easily falsified, or impossible to falsify. In the second case, Popper did not see these theories as 'scientific', but why would anyone want to try to falsify a theory? In the social world this is done often and usually very crudely in order to discredit and opposite ideological view. The Internet provides an excellent vehicle with which to sample selectively on a contentious issue and produce a result that will 'falsify' an oppositional position (see Popper 1959, 1989).

Second, there is the problem of theory choice, of how we choose between two rival (middle range) theories, which may explain the same empirical result but through different theoretical lenses, perhaps shaped by initial higher-level theoretical positions, such as functionalism or conflict theory.

Third, many, if not most, social scientific theories are tested through statistical evidence, often from sample surveys or administrative data sets. The operationalisation of variables, sampling and analysis may be technically first-rate, but rarely is the finding equivocal (yet alone a falsification). My colleagues and I have conducted research on student attitudes toward learning quantitative methods. A simple, but consistent finding is that (when measured through items on a Lickert Scale) around 60 per cent will say they are confident in using statistics and 40 per cent not so (Williams et al. 2008). Now, this result has to be 'interpreted', as must most survey findings, along with other items in the scale and in fact what is understood by 'confident' or 'not confident'. Claims of falsification, or confirmation of such simple statements, are rarely possible and hardly ever methodologically honest.

Finally, theory choice and theory testing are closely related to the issue of objectivity (see **objectivity – subjectivity**), particularly in the social sciences. As I have noted in the section on objectivity, what counts as 'objective' will be situated in context, though mediated by scientific values (such as truth seeking) which transcend particular contexts.

THEORY AND SCIENTIFIC PROGRESS

The question of whether there is 'progress' in science has long been controversial amongst philosophers and sociologists of science, though most of those who question the term 'progress' and its applicability in natural science will nevertheless concede that over time there has been an accretion of knowledge, that is, we know more now than we once did. Nevertheless natural scientists would mostly hold that there is progress in science, that certain theories are falsified (or discredited) and other theories are able to explain all that an older theory explained and more as well (Newton-Smith 1981). For example, in cosmology, the 'steady state' theory of the expansion of the universe, once energetically advanced by Fred Hoyle, has been wholly superseded by the 'big bang' theory and over time more and more empirical results support the latter. This might be seen as an example of a Lakatos 'research programme' that is presently successful but may eventually be superseded by a different theory.

Nevertheless, however one interprets theory development in natural science, there is an implicit teleological goal of scientists toward explaining more and more of the natural world. Whether such a goal is either possible, or desirable, in social science remains an open question. Technically we do know 'more'. In survey analysis we have come a long way from pen, paper and punch card computers to the ubiquitous use of SPSS (and now commonly STATA, R, MLwiN etc.). More fundamentally, the ability of social and computer scientists to analyse millions of Twitter feeds or transactional data quickly and efficiently will transform social science, though whether this will constitute theoretical progress in explaining the social world is, as yet, not known. Possibly the best social scientists can expect are historically and societally specific explanations, which of course may well be more successful as a result of technical progress.

REFERENCES

Durkheim, E (1961 [1912]) *The Elementary Forms of Religious Life.* London: Allen & Unwin.

Luhmann, N (1995) *Social Systems.* Stanford: Stanford University Press.

Manicas, P (2007) 'The social sciences since World War II: the rise and fall of scientism', in Outhwaite, W and Turner, S (eds), *The Sage Handbook of Social Science Methodology*. London: Sage.

Merton, R (1967) *On Theoretical Sociology.* New York: Free Press.

Merton, R (1968) *Social Theory and Social Structure.* New York: Free Press.

Newton-Smith, W (1981) *The Rationality of Science*. London: Routledge and Kegan Paul.

Parsons, T and Shils, E A (eds) (1951) *Toward a General Theory of Action*. New York: Harper & Row.

Pawson, R (2000) 'Middle-range realism', *Archive Européenes de Sociologie,* XLI: 283–325.

Popper, K R (1959) *The Logic of Scientific Discovery*. London: Routledge.

Popper, K R (1989) *Conjectures and Refutations*. London: Routledge.

Williams, M, Payne, G and Hodgkinson, L (2008) 'Does sociology count? Student attitudes to the teaching of quantitative methods', *Sociology*, 42 (5): 1003–1022.

Winch, P (1990 [1958]) *The Idea of a Social Science and its Relation to Philosophy.* London: Routledge.

KEY READINGS

Layder, D (1993) *New Strategies in Social Research: an introduction and guide*. Oxford: Polity.

Merton, R (1968) *Social Theory and Social Structure.* New York: Free Press.

Stinchcombe, A (1968) *Constructing Social Theories.* New York: Harcourt, Brace and World.

KEY THINKERS

Emile Durkheim; Karl Marx; Robert Merton; Ray Pawson; Arthur Stinchcombe; Max Weber

See also: *Empiricism; Generalisation and Laws; Hypothesis(es); Mechanisms and Models; Objectivity – Subjectivity; Positivism; Rationality; Relativism*

Time

Time is both an objective measure of the relationship between speed and distance, but also structures social relations both in the way it sets ontological limits and in the way it is subjectively experienced.

> *Idealist and realist approaches to time in philosophy are firstly considered and how the latter relates to conceptions of time in Newtonian and Einsteinian physics. Cultural conceptions of time in archaic and contemporary society are important to the social scientist, because they must take into account the ontological necessity of time in social relations. Finally time is considered as a social category investigated by researchers.*

Time is one of the most important philosophical concepts and the way it has been thought about and viewed has influenced literature and science. In turn the empirical findings of the latter have come to influence philosophical thinking. Philosophical and scientific understandings of time have direct implications for our methodological thinking, particularly that of causality (see **causality**). But also the ways in which time is conceived socially has been an object of study for social researchers.

TIME IN PHILOSOPHY AND SCIENCE

The physicist John Wheeler gave us a wonderfully succinct definition of time as 'what keeps everything from happening at once' (Buchanan 2003: 22), but it brought us no closer to an understanding of what time is.

There are two major views that have been held by philosophers. The first is that time is a fundamental feature of the universe, that it is a 'real' quality, and the second is that it, along with space and number, is an intellectual schema, within which humans sequence and order the universe they experience. This latter view is associated with Immanuel Kant (see **idealism**) who maintained that time and space were a priori concepts, necessary to structure our sense experience of the world. In other words, we cannot imagine anything existing outside of time or space. Nevertheless, he denies that they are 'real things' in themselves, that we can comprehend through experience (Körner 1955). Kant was undoubtedly right in his assertion of the necessity of time and space *to* experience, but was he right about our inability to know what it is?

Natural science has been more 'realist' about time (and space). The Newtonian concept of time was that it was a part of the fundamental structure of the universe, that it was invariant and measurable, and indeed this remains our practical and normative conception of time in post-Enlightenment societies. Clock time is an absolute for us, and we have ordered and agreed time zones across the world, within which social life is structured.

In much of modern science Newtonian time is also operationally retained in causal reasoning (i.e. in a causal sequence an effect must follow its cause), but Einstein's theories of relativity and their subsequent empirical verification has fundamentally changed what we know of time. Einstein unified the concepts of space and time into space-time in which motion becomes relative to the observer. The only constant is that of the speed of light. No object can attain the speed of light, though time and speed are linked such that we can define speed as distance divided by time. Einstein demonstrated that speed and therefore time are relative to that of the observer. A popular illustration of this is when two trains are moving, the person on the slower train only experiences the movement of the faster train in relation to their own speed. The faster train may be moving at 70 kph and the slower one 60 kph, but only the excess of 10 kph is noticed. The formula of distance divided by time could apply either to the frame of reference provided by the movement of one train relative to the other, or alternatively to that of an observer viewing both trains.

Time, then, is relative in an objective sense, though on Earth we have frames of reference within which our subjective experience of time (or speed) can be located. We know these things now, but we have not always known them, and a pre-scientific intuition of the relativity of time was common to many pre-Enlightenment and non-Western societies.

CULTURAL UNDERSTANDINGS OF TIME

Barbara Adam, in her definitive book on time (2004), discusses the issue of 'time transcendence' – making time stand still, a cultural practice widespread through 'archaic' societies, yet in different forms is common to humanity generally. Our evidence comes from archaeologists, historians and anthropologists, who have described the use of and rituals to make time stand still. Indeed in many archaic societies the linear notion of time moving forward and an infinitely long past just did not exist. The repetition of myth and ritual provided a framework of reality that required no notion of time as we understand it in Western society. Furthermore, our world changes rapidly and that change has accelerated as a result of an exponential growth in technology and the speed of the communication of knowledge. In archaic societies such change was absent and the only kinds of changes were cyclical through seasons and lifetimes.

In Western societies we have inherited some of these myths and rituals that live, sometimes uncomfortably, alongside our scientific insights. We continue to observe rituals of death, or rites of passage such as baptism or marriage, that mark time as stages in our lives. For theists time as experienced is that which is experienced by the body, with the 'soul' existing outside of our notion of time.

The role time plays in social life of archaic and modern societies has been an important object of investigation for anthropologists and sociologists. Emile Durkheim's *The Elementary Forms of Religious Life* (1961) was an important conceptual statement. Somewhat like Kant, he saw time as a category that frames experienced, but cannot be experienced. However, he provides a social dimension to time as an organising principle, which though it may differ from society to society is a necessary a priori condition for social life to be possible. Yet, whilst Durkheim maintained that understandings of time and cultural practices around time may differ between societies, he did not claim that social practices were independent of nature (and therefore time), but that society makes relations between things more explicit, though has no monopoly upon them (Adam 2004: 48). This view of time (and the relationship between society and nature more generally) prefigures modern realism (see **realism**), in which concepts of time may be socially constructed, but there remains a reality of time which is not necessarily accessible to us.

TIME AND NECESSITY

One ontological feature that is apparent is that of distance. In contemporary society this has been partially transcended through the increasing speed of electronic and digital communication, but the limit of time and distance is nevertheless more apparent to us now than it would have been in the distant past, ironically somewhat less so than in the fairly recent historical past. In archaic societies all of those people that one needed to communicate with were more or less co-present, though in many societies there was also a belief in communication with the dead. However, as societies utilised means of transport or began to migrate, issues of distance impacted on the time it took to communicate with others not co-present. Gradually, as a result of faster transport and eventually electronic communication, these things changed, but always they set limits to the extent and nature of social interaction. Even now, it is impossible for me to have anything other than electronic/digital communication with those at a distance. These things are perhaps trivially true, but they impose a physical grounding on the contingency of social relations (see **contingency and necessity**).

TIME IN SOCIAL RESEARCH

Time is important to social research in two fundamental ways.

First, how people experience and understand time and how they express this is fundamental to our understanding of society(s). We can view this in two ways: 1) that the expression of the experience of time by respondents is authentic, that is, what they tell us of a recollection of the past or a wish or fear for the future is how they construct their social reality; and 2) interviews or the examination of personal diaries do not seek to establish the 'truth', but rather the truth as the respondent, or writer, sees it. For social constructionists (see **social constructionism**) we need not go further than to uncover the stories that are told. However, for realists, such subjective insights can be triangulated to provide insights (say in a historic period) of a deeper social reality. This may not always be the case, because separate accounts may simply reproduce the myths or rumours of that society, rather than reveal underlying societal or historical truths.

The second way in which time is important to social researchers is through measurement. The most reliable recording of events, attitudes or beliefs is through longitudinal research. For example, the UK censuses have, for some time, carried a question concerning whether persons in the household suffered from any limiting long-term illness. Data on this measure at one census can tell us how much limiting long-term illness is experienced and this can be comparative with data at a further census, but if the records of the individuals are linked longitudinally, we can know which persons experience this over ten years (Ware et al. 2007). The temporal ordering of actual events in longitudinal research is one of the better ways researchers can get at causal sequence.

Researchers use other means to measure experiences over time. Respondents may be asked to recall events, during interviews. Often what is of interest here is not how accurately they do this, but rather how they prioritise what they remember, because individual recall of the past is notoriously inaccurate, or respondents will reconstruct the ordering or prioritisation of events to accord with the 'story' they wish to tell. However, to some extent, recall can be improved through the way things are asked. A question (in a questionnaire) might ask 'Have you visited the doctor's recently', but 'recently may' be conceived differently by respondents, so often a timeframe is specified.

One of the more recent challenges for social researchers is how we can capture the increasingly fast pace of social relations acted out through digital communication. New forms of social media analysis can capture large amounts of data, through Twitter feeds, in real time. Though these do not provide deep insights of the beliefs and attitudes of their authors, they nevertheless can provide large-scale aggregate data that can link expressed beliefs and attitudes to actions (see **complexity**).

REFERENCES

Adam, B (2004) *Time*. Cambridge: Polity.

Buchanan, M (2003) 'What is time – introduction', in Swain, H (ed.), *Big Questions in Science*. London: Vintage.

Durkheim, E (1961 [1912]) *The Elementary Forms of Religious Life*. London: Allen & Unwin.

Körner, S (1955) *Kant*. Harmondsworth: Penguin.

Ware, L, Maconachie, M, Williams, M, Chandler, J and Dodgeon, B (2007) 'Gender life course transitions from the nuclear family in England and Wales 1981–2001', *Sociological Research Online*, 12: 4.

KEY READINGS

Adam, B (2004) *Time.* Cambridge: Polity.
Barrow, J (2003) 'What is time?', in Swain, H (ed.), *Big Questions in Science*. London: Vintage.
Elias, N (1992) *Time: an essay*. Oxford: Blackwell.

KEY THINKERS

Barbara Adam; Emile Durkheim; Albert Einstein; Norbert Elias; John Wheeler

See also: *Causality; Complexity; Contingency and Necessity; Idealism; Social Constructionism*